RORY GALLAGHER
THE MAN BEHIND THE GUITAR

Julian Vignoles

Gill Books

Julian Vignoles, from County Wicklow and living in Dublin, was educated at University College Dublin. He worked for *Hot Press* in the late 1970s before joining RTÉ, where for over thirty years he produced music, factual and entertainment programmes on both radio and television. This is his third book.

For my family, Carol, Eoghan and Rory,
and for Rory Gallagher fans everywhere

Gill Books
Hume Avenue
Park West
Dublin 12
www.gillbooks.ie

Gill Books is an imprint of M.H. Gill & Co.

First published by The Collins Press in 2018
This paperback edition published by Gill Books in 2021

978 0 7171 8957 1

Printed by ScandBook in Lithuania

The paper used in this book comes from the wood pulp of managed forests. For every tree felled, at least one tree is planted, thereby renewing natural resources.

A CIP catalogue record for this book is available from the British Library.

5 4 3 2 1

CONTENTS

RORY GALLAGHER TIMELINE

1948   Born 2 March, in Ballyshannon, County Donegal.

1949   Moves to Derry (Londonderry) with his parents; his brother, Dónal, born.

1958   Moves to Cork with his mother and brother, enrolled in the North Monastery primary school, Cork.

1963   Joins the Fontana Showband, buys his famous Fender Stratocaster.

1965   Completes his Leaving Certificate at St Kieran's School; Fontana becomes Impact and travels to Spain for six-week residency.

1966   Impact disbands; Gallagher plays gigs with The Axills; in August, forms Taste (The Taste), with Eric Kitteringham (bass) and Norman Damery (drums).

1967   January–March: Taste play in UK and Germany. The band moves base to Belfast.

1968   Re-forms Taste (known as Taste Mark 2), with John Wilson (drums) and Richard McCracken (bass). November: the band plays support at Cream's farewell concert.

1969   *Taste* released.

1970   August: Taste play the Isle of Wight Festival. *On the Boards* released. December: the band plays its last gig.

1971   January: the first Rory Gallagher Band line-up, with Gerry McAvoy on bass and Wilgar Campbell on drums; his brother, Dónal, becomes his manager; first solo album,

Rory Gallagher, released. *Deuce* follws later in the year. The Rory Gallagher Band begins twenty years of prolific touring.

1972   Wilgar Campbell is replaced by Rod de'Ath, Lou Martin (keyboards) joins the band. *Live in Europe* released. Gallagher voted best guitarist by *Melody Maker* readers; contributes to *London Muddy Waters Sessions*.

1973   Releases two studio albums, *Blueprint* and *Tattoo*. His touring schedule peaks with 160 gigs.

1974   Completes Polydor contract with double album *Irish Tour '74*.

1975   Signs with Chrysalis Records and releases *Against the Grain*.

1977   Headlines the Macroom Mountain Dew Festival (the first of two years).

1978   Abandons an album recorded in San Francisco, reverts to a three-piece band, replacing Rod de'Ath with Ted McKenna, and later releases *Photo-Finish*.

1981   Ted McKenna is replaced by Brendan O'Neill.

1982   Chrysalis contract ends with *Jinx*.

1985   Starts his own record label, Capo.

1987   After a gap of five years, *Defender* is released.

1990   Releases his last album, *Fresh Evidence*.

1992   August: his final Dublin performance, at the Temple Bar Music Festival. Forms the last Rory Gallagher Band line-up, the first without Gerry McAvoy.

1993   November: plays for the last time in Cork.

1995   January: plays at Nighttown, Rotterdam, and collapses.

March: admitted to hospital.

April: receives a liver transplant at King's College Hospital, London.

14 June: dies from an infection.

19 June: funeral and burial in Cork.

MONTREUX, SWITZERLAND, 18 JULY 1979

They've been playing it for eight minutes, but Gallagher and the band keep pounding out the 'Shadow Play' riff. It is nearly time to end it. But instead, this time he spurs on the band and increases the pace. He pulls down two drum microphone stands. With the guitar at fever pitch and feeding back, he whips it off and places it on the stage. He begins a kind of primitive ritual as the instrument howls and the band keeps playing. Gallagher is paying homage to his guitar. He skips across the stage, gestures to the crowd, animatedly pointing back at the stricken instrument, appearing to accuse it of something, perhaps of dominating his life? He walks towards it in mock military step, and talks to it, this thing that he had mastered, and which had brought him so much fame. He grabs a white towel and fans the air around the Fender, adding to the electronics' distress, before waving the fabric at Gerry McAvoy and Ted McKenna – the bass and drums men – as if to cool them down from the fever pitch he has just engineered. Bouncing out front again, he drags his precious Stratocaster across the stage, by its cable. The strings screech, as if in protest. Ten minutes have passed, and the ritual is complete. He picks it up deftly and returns to the riff with an air of triumph, before the trademark, multi-crescendo ending, and the words, 'Thank you, thank you. Goodnight!'

INTRODUCTION

'There are certain nights that we all have, where you think, "God, these hands will do anything tonight!" You know, and you take yourself right to the edge, the limit.'

– RORY GALLAGHER[1]

He bounded across countless stages in a red check shirt. His compulsion was to entertain. The tones he could conjure from six strings made him a revered virtuoso. He was an unassuming star, courteous and polite. He was Rory Gallagher.

Blues, boogie, folk and rock 'n' roll fuelled the songs. In each, the guitar took its anticipated excursion – the famous Gallagher solo. For his fans, this is where he could make it talk – both to them, and to *him*, it seemed. 'Night after night, gig after gig, he's still thrilled by the sounds he can coax from it', a reviewer, Mick Rock, wrote in *Rolling Stone* in 1972.

Gallagher modestly described the power that flowed from head and heart to his fingers: 'What I try to do is split the difference between having enough technique to go into tight corners musically and having enough primal madness to keep it gritty. I'd like to be known for playing somewhere in between, as a guy who can keep primitive and physical at the guitar, but by the same token, not be just an aggressive player from the start.'[2]

Passion, both his and his fans', was never in short supply. It's what marked him out most, perhaps.

Rory Gallagher was just 47 years old when he died, and during his short life he experienced stardom, jubilation and loneliness. Unlike most of his rock peers, there were no wild parties, no expensive entertaining, no marriages or divorces. He was dedicated almost exclusively to music, particularly to the guitar and its possibilities. It was his life's purpose. His brother, Dónal, once described it as a 'vocation'.[3] The rock 'n' roll lifestyle wasn't for him. He disliked the mansions and cars associated with rock music fame, further endearing him to many, of course. When he eventually bought his own home in London, it was a modest apartment.

Gallagher's personal life, or his life outside music, is a puzzle. He avoided discussion of the subject and, though he gave many interviews, most of these were promoting tours or records, and give only occasional insights into Rory Gallagher. This guarded aspect of his persona makes the rare occasions when he was revealing more noteworthy. And there's another feature of Gallagher, one that is perhaps unique in the rock world: it is difficult

to find a negative word written about him anywhere. Yet
Gerry McAvoy, Gallagher's bass player for twenty years,
spoke from experience in the introduction to his book,
Riding Shotgun, published in 2005, describing his friend
as 'a mystery wrapped up in an enigma'. He says there
were people that would place Rory on a pedestal with
some of the most venerable Irish saints, but, 'I'm here to
tell you that he could be one of the most exasperating,
frustrating and infuriating people you could ever meet.
But also, without doubt, one of the nicest.'

There were two very different, distinct sides to Rory
Gallagher. He was the artist, the extrovert, the musician
who gave his all and more when on a stage, but offstage,
there was the shy, polite and gentle individual. And
even his confident onstage swagger was tempered with
vulnerability; he would often introduce a song with
the self-deprecating line, 'This is one from a few years
back – I hope you like it.' In a life of both success and
struggle, Gallagher experienced the paradox of adulation
and solitude side by side. Perilously for his personal
life, he admitted living for the time he spent onstage.
Performance was almost an addiction, and maybe even
an escape. Avril MacRory, a TV producer who got to
know him, says. 'There were always people there for him
– if he wanted them. But one of the reasons he was such a
great musician was because that's where it all came out.
That's where he expressed everything.' His songs are key
to understanding Gallagher. Often seen as vehicles for
his guitar playing, much of his lyric writing reveals the
mind and soul of its author. He was 21 when he wrote

lines for Taste's album *On the Boards* that contained a plea, one that in many ways amounted to an imperative for his life: 'Well if I can't sing, I'll cry / If I can't sing, I'll die.'

Many will be surprised that the great showman and rocker was a devout Catholic all his life. He also had a steely determination from childhood to become a guitar-playing performer. Contrary to belief, he was more a willing than reluctant member of an Irish showband. Most significantly – and ironically – Gallagher's gifts as a guitar player have tended to overshadow the subtlety and grace in much of his songwriting. Some of this writing is confessional, even revelatory. Gallagher, despite his gentle demeanour, had a tough side too, and could hire and fire to realise his musical vision. That vision was both principled and uncompromising. Though fans revere his memory, Rory Gallagher was strong-willed and focused on success. But the fame he achieved brought challenges for him. After his career peaked, he was a troubled person for much of his later life. He became increasingly subject to superstitious beliefs, and more and more drawn in his songwriting to the world conjured up in crime-fiction novels. His relatively short life ended in disillusion. When interviewed for a Dutch newspaper five months before he died, Gallagher was living alone in a London hotel. Weary and unwell, he had more than a hint of resignation about how things had unfolded for him. Yet there was still fire in his soul as he looked back on his early days with a Biblical image: 'As soon as I got one [a guitar] in my hands, I was raising

Cain. I was already touring before I knew what it was. Ireland is so small that you can always end up sleeping in your own bed, no matter where you played. That's if you wanted to, of course. And I did not want to. I still don't. Rock-and-roll was my religion, call and conviction.'4

His followers knew this well. They pounded their feet for him. They played air guitar. They chanted themselves hoarse.

Nice one, Rory,
Nice one, son,
Nice one, Rory,
Let's have another one!

Gallagher was a musical giant. For those who knew him, he was also a great human being. Christy Moore, Ireland's great folksinger and songwriter, is a huge admirer: 'We still love his sound, his rock 'n' roll, his folk 'n' trad, his blues roots, shapes, chords, licks, shirts, hands in pockets, collar turned up, his shy smile. He was a beautiful man who, I think, died real lonely.' His performances have become mythic for some: 'A Rory Gallagher gig was an amazing thing, celebratory, visceral, heart-stopping, brilliant – he brought to everyone's home town the blues, electric and magnificent and shot through with a wild Irish sensibility.'5

It was that brilliance and sensibility, along with his deep love of music, that brought Rory Gallagher both his great triumphs – and his trials. This is his story.

Chapter 1

NORTHERN ROOTS

'I remember hearing "Rock Around the Clock", and
I was only five or six years of age, honestly. I think
it's due to my relations and their musical souls.
They sort of stuffed music down my throat. They
let me listen; they liked it as well, and it worked out.'

– RORY GALLAGHER[1]

Twenty years after his death, the Shandon Bells of Cork paid their tribute, in June 2015. Notes from his song 'Tattoo'd Lady' rang out across the city. A song of fairground life, restlessness is one of its themes. The child narrator 'roams from town to town'. In some ways, it's Gallagher's life story.

He effectively became a Cork person by the age of ten. He forged his art on the banks of the River Lee. He never lost his city accent. But his roots were at the other end of

Ireland. County Donegal was his birthplace; he spent his early childhood in Derry and influential teenage years in Belfast. His adult life was spent in exile in London. Through lifestyle choice, he was a resident of countless hotel rooms around the world.

The story begins, symbolically, with a large engineering project in the 1940s to supply much needed electric power in Ireland. Rory Gallagher was in his mother's womb as his father, Danny, worked on the Erne Hydroelectric Scheme in Ballyshannon, County Donegal. His brother, Dónal, would say later about their father: 'It's ironic that he was part of what delivered electricity to Ireland, as his son ended up playing electric guitar. If my father hadn't done that, there would have been no electricity for Rory's amps.'[2]

Danny Gallagher was born in Derry on 17 April 1919. At 21, he enlisted in the Irish Army in Raphoe, County Donegal, and served in the intelligence section of the 20th Infantry Battalion. The Irish Army, despite Ireland's policy of neutrality, was expanded during the Second World War, the period referred to by the Irish government as 'The Emergency'. Gallagher's battalion had its headquarters in Athlone, but he was moved to various posts in Western Command, including Finner Camp, close to Ballyshannon, a town he later became familiar with. In 1944, he was commissioned as a temporary officer, at the rank of 2nd lieutenant, in Southern Command in Cork. He trained recruits in Collins Barracks and the Maritime Inscription. While in Cork, he met Margaret Monica (Mona) Roche, a native of the city. They were married in St Patrick's Church on 5 August 1947. After being discharged from the army, though he remained in the reserve, Danny took up employment with the Erne Hydroelectric Scheme, so the young couple moved north to base themselves in Ballyshannon, County Donegal.

Danny Gallagher's ancestors can be traced to a small townland, Ballyholey, near Raphoe, in east Donegal. The family later moved to Derry (or Londonderry as it is also known), and is recorded as living in Donegal Place on the 1901 census. Danny's father, William, worked as a messenger boy, and later as a docker on Derry Quay. On 25 December 1916, he married Mary (known as Minnie) Feeney in the Long Tower Catholic Church. William and Minnie lived at 31 Orchard Row, close to the banks of the Foyle. A son, Charles, was born on 25 November 1917, and two years later on 17 April, Daniel, known as Danny.

The political backdrop of this time was the Irish independence movement, the upheaval that began with the campaign for Home Rule, and the opposition to it in the northern part of Ireland, followed by the 1916 Rising, the War of Independence, the Anglo-Irish Treaty, and the partition of the island. The city of Derry is close to what became the border, so during this time of change, the city was separated from its County Donegal hinterland to the west. Its population was, of course, mainly nationalist, pro Free State, but political destiny had it remain in the United Kingdom as part of Northern Ireland.[3]

Danny Gallagher played the piano accordion and became well known in Ulster music circles. He was a member of Charlie Kelly's Céilí Band, a well-known Derry group in the 1940s.[4] Rory Gallagher made a reference to the traditional music in his background in a BBC radio interview in 1987. 'It affects me with my chords and certain ideas for songs, but generally I start with blues roots and work from there. You can't keep a strong tradition like Irish music out of what you're doing.'[5]

Ballyshannon, County Donegal, became home for Danny and Monica Gallagher in 1947. This is how William Allingham, the poet born in Ballyshannon in 1824, described his town in *The Winding Banks of Erne*:

Adieu to Ballyshanny!
Where I was bred and born;
Go where I may, I'll think of you,
As sure as night and morn …

The mother of former British prime minister Tony Blair, Hazel (née Corscadden) was born in Ballyshannon in 1923.[6] By coincidence, Rory Gallagher's nephews attended the same secondary school, the London Oratory, as the Blair children. There's a folk legend in this part of Donegal that might have interested Rory Gallagher, given the fondness he developed for mystery stories. A local woman gave an account of a happening at Wardtown Castle near the estuary of the River Erne, west of the town: 'One night three girls who were attending a party in the castle went outside for a "breath of air", as the story goes. They were never seen again and it was believed that they fell into a small lough nearby and were drowned. Locals in the past claimed to have frequently seen three ladies in the bottom of the lough, combing their hair. The water is since called Loch na mBan Fionn – the lake of the fair women.'[7]

* * *

The Erne Hydroelectric Scheme, where Danny Gallagher worked as a 'schemer', as the workers were known, was one of the new Irish state's bold engineering projects. The Electricity Supply Board (ESB) had decided to harness the Erne River's 40-metre drop in level between Belleek and its estuary at Ballyshannon. As well as the engineering challenges, there was a geopolitical complication to overcome: since 1922, 1,900 of the 4,000 square kilometres of the river's catchment were in Northern Ireland. To proceed, the ESB had to get permission to undertake extensive dredging and civil engineering works across the border. The plan involved building two power stations, the second at Cathleen's Fall, just east of the town. A 6km channel had to be excavated, involving the removal of 600,000 cubic metres of earth and rock from the riverbed. The bulk of the work involved hard and dangerous manual labour. There were casualties, with twelve fatalities.[8] Danny Gallagher was employed between 1947 and 1949 in a clerical/technical position with the main contractor, a British firm called Cementation, doing quality checks on the concrete used to build the dam. Tom Gallagher (not a relative), who also worked on the scheme and played music with

Danny Gallagher, and who still lives in the town, recalls that such were the work shifts that 'the beds in the lodging houses never cooled'. The cross-border cooperative nature of the project has an echo in Rory Gallagher's career, because even at the height of 'the Troubles' in Northern Ireland, he was – and is still – admired for always returning to play in the city, and for appreciating his cross-community support base.

At that time, Ballyshannon had a local hospital in the area south of the town known as the Rock. The building, beside the old workhouse, now has a plaque recording the fact that in a room on the second floor, on Tuesday 2 March 1948, Monica Gallagher gave birth to her first son. He was baptised in St Joseph's Church nearby. In accordance with the long-standing Gallagher family tradition of naming the eldest son after his grandfather, he was registered as William Rory Gallagher. Just a month previously, Ireland's first coalition government had been formed. In autumn that year, that government, in a historic step, declared the country the Republic of Ireland. As for entertainment, the Abbey cinema was running a show from Dublin's Olympia Theatre, called 'Funzapoppin', starring Danny Cummins. The Rock Hall near the hospital had its weekly dance, with music by the eponymous 'Rock' orchestra, a decade before the global musical use of that word arrived. In New York in June, Columbia Records unveiled what became an enduring piece of technology, the long-playing record.

After Rory's birth, the family moved from their rented house on the Bundoran Road, to another at East Port in the town. Their landlord was a publican, Frank O'Neill, whose licensed premises was just down the street. His son Owen Roe, now proprietor of the bar Owen Roe's, remembers locals who knew Danny and Monica Gallagher. P.J. Drummond, a drinking companion of Danny's, also performed babysitting duties on occasions: 'He always maintained that his great claim to fame was that Rory Gallagher pissed on his knee.'

Danny Gallagher was a member of a local dance band, the Modernaires. Tom Gallagher was, too, and is now the last link with that musical era in the town. He remembers a day in the spring of 1948 when he called to pick up Danny Gallagher at the house the family was renting, to be greeted by Monica with a baby in her arms – the infant Rory Gallagher. Danny Gallagher also played with Joe McBride, who ran the Marine Ballroom in Bundoran, the seaside resort nearby. Danny was something of a local star. An advertisement appeared in the *Donegal Democrat* during 1948 for a Friday and Sunday night dance, with Joe McBride's Ballroom Orchestra, 'featuring Danny Gallagher, the Wizard Accordeonist'. Danny Gallagher wrote at least one song, 'Harty's Ragtime Band', which P.J. Drummond was known to recite on occasions down through the years. Monica Gallagher was also drawn to performance, and was involved with the Premier Players, an amateur drama group in the town. They made local headlines in 1948 when they came third in the Bundoran Drama Festival with *The Righteous Are Bold* by the playwright Frank Carney, in which a young woman is possessed by evil spirits until an exorcism by an elderly priest. Danny Gallagher's conviviality had another, problematic side, an overfondness for drinking. Mick Butler, whose father, Bert, worked as a 'schemer' with Danny Gallagher, says that both men would head for a pub, given any opportunity.

The Gallagher family left Ballyshannon in 1949 and went to live in Derry, at 31 Orchard Row, with Danny's mother, Minnie, widowed since 1942. A new addition to the family came when Danny and Monica's second son, Dónal, was born in August 1949. (Dónal was later to become Rory's manager, and guardian of his estate after his death). The street was a two-up two-down terrace, with basic facilities, and has since been completely redeveloped. Myra Doherty, who lived nearby on Foyle Road, remembers being given the job as a ten-year-old of bringing Rory out in his pram. 'He was a lovely wee baby. I can still see his face,' she says.

Derry has always claimed to be a particularly musical city and America was a significant influence. As the North was part of the United Kingdom, US soldiers began arriving in the city in 1942. Famous entertainers followed. Bob Hope and Al Jolson were among those who made appearances during the war years. The toddler Rory apparently first heard blues music from an American army source. American Forces Network (AFN) began broadcasting in the UK on 4 July 1943, with the network including several transmitters in Northern Ireland. Though intended for US military personnel, AFN had unintended consequences and became an inspiration to many famous non-American musicians. Robert Plant of Led Zeppelin was one: 'We could turn our dial and get an absolutely amazing kaleidoscope of music.'[9] The Belfast-born singer and songwriter Van Morrison, one of rock music's greats, recalled this formative period of his life in a song co-written with the poet Paul Durcan, 'In the Days Before Rock 'n' Roll'.[10] The journalist and political activist Eamonn McCann, several years older than Gallagher, described an encounter with the station: 'Eventually, my father and Jim Sharkey [father of Feargal of The Undertones] from across the street, rigged me up a contraption from a gramophone speaker and a roll of wire so I could listen to the music in the attic, even though the radio downstairs in the kitchen was turned off. This was amazing. I was wired up to a secret world, the sound snaking its way silently up the stairs bringing the voices of black people roaring out about sex and announcing it was OK to feel free.'[11]

We can speculate on other intangible stirrings in the young Rory's imagination, perhaps prompted by sounds in his environment. A train on the rail line that passed close by, running along the banks of the Foyle, possibly. Referring to that period of his life, Gallagher said later: 'When you're that age you like songs about trains, motion.'[12] The poet Seamus Heaney, who grew up in rural County Derry, found a metaphor in a steam train that used to rumble by, just a field away, behind his family's farmhouse. 'We were as susceptible and impressionable as the drinking water that stood in a bucket in our scullery: every time a passing train made the earth shake, the surface of the water used to ripple delicately, concentrically, and in utter silence.'[13]

Music began making an impression on the young Gallagher, his brother told Mark McAvoy for his 2009 book *Cork Rock: From Rory Gallagher to the Sultans of Ping*. 'Rory had managed to get the family radio and would surf it. He knew the schedule, like the night Chris Barber had a programme.'[14] Gallagher himself recalled: 'I suppose I had the slight benefit of hearing it before I knew what it was. By the grace of God, because I didn't have a record player, I heard primal blues radio recordings of Lead Belly and Big Bill Broonzy. AFN was playing them on jazz programmes and, also, BBC.'[15]

But firstly, there was formal education. Rory attended the Christian Brothers primary school, known locally as the Brow of the Hill, not far from Orchard Row. Dermott Gallagher (no relation) has a clear memory of something from that time. He was attending the nearby school, St Columba's, known as the 'Wee Nuns' School'. As was the custom, the kids would walk home for their lunch. He'd often meet Rory and Dónal Gallagher. Corporal punishment for learning issues was then commonplace and Dermott had got a beating that morning from one of the teachers, Sister Agatha. He had accepted his fate, till Rory asked him what the mark on the side of his face was. This brought everything into the open. Dermott's elder brother, Peter, who also attended the Brow of the Hill, got involved and the upshot was that Sister Agatha never laid a hand on him again, apparently. He credits this to the vigilance of Rory, then only nine years old.

The writer Nell McCafferty, who grew up in Derry about this time, paints a picture of faith and frugality in the city. As teenagers, she and her friends would go to a local café to share a plate of chips just so they could play the jukebox. As for religious observance, she recalled: 'the Church gave you loads of paintings, stained-glass windows and statues to look at. And, through confession, it gave you a clean start and a sense of purpose every Saturday morning: three Hail Marys and your soul was pure again; one round of the Stations of the Cross and you had saved hundreds of dead people from hell.'[16] However, another world was breaking through. Dónal Gallagher remembered a regular stroll with his brother around 6 p.m. to the Diamond area of the city during the mid 1950s, to a shop with a demo version of an incredible new invention: television. They'd stare through the window at the BBC's very first pop show, *Six-Five Special*, he said. 'The fact that we couldn't hear the sound didn't matter to the young Rory,' he said. 'He already knew the lyrics to loads of the songs, so he'd unconsciously sing out loud as the bands were playing on screen, and provide great entertainment for the other people gathered there.'[17]

* * *

In these Derry years, Rory developed what seems like a fixation with the guitar, his brother recalled:

'My earliest memories of it was Rory trying to describe to his parents the instrument that he had in his head that he wanted. Rory started making it up with a round cheese box with a ruler and some elastic and saying – "it's like that but bigger". I remember then my father had a pal, a musician, Charlie McGee, and he had a guitar. I recall my father bringing him down to the house and saying to Rory – "is that what you're talking about?"[18]'

Rory's parents decided to source an instrument by mail order. It was William Doherty from Foyle Road, Myra Doherty's father, who was the agent for several catalogues. According to her brother, Ivor, Rory's parents paid for it in instalments with what was called a club card, at the rate of one shilling and threepence each week, the last payment being made in February 1958. This fairly basic instrument, a four-string ukulele type, was, arguably, where Rory Gallagher's career began. 'It was always a piece of family history that our Da sold Rory Gallagher his first guitar.'

They were a 'lovely family', Myra Doherty says, 'Monica was a stunning-looking woman.' However, by then, Danny had developed a serious alcohol problem, and the Gallagher marriage ended in separation. In 1958, apparently, or maybe earlier, Monica took her sons and moved back to her family in Cork. Though there were attempts at reconciliation, Danny Gallagher remained living in Derry until his death in June 1975, at the height of Rory's fame. Cathal Póirtéir, who grew up in Derry, says many people his age would remember Danny Gallagher: 'He was one of a group of middle-aged men who hung around the bottom of William Street, tapping passers-by for a few pence to help towards the next drink. He was the most likeable and well mannered of the men.' Póirtéir recalls another legend in the city; after Gallagher's gig in the Guildhall in 1971, the by now famous rock star took the time to seek out his father and help him financially. Danny Gallagher, or Dan as he was also known, used to frequent O'Hara's Bar on Bishop Street, close to his home. Antoin O'Hara's parents ran the pub. 'My father and mother had great time for him.' The view locally was that it was his drinking that caused the marriage break-up, O'Hara confirms. 'He was heartbroken and would talk about the boys a lot.'

Danny Gallagher must surely have felt joy, particularly as a musician himself, when his son became world-famous. According to Antoin O'Hara, 'he was aware of Rory's music, and very proud of him.' Rory rarely spoke about his father, and never referred to the marriage break-up, but his brother, Dónal, chose to continue the family naming tradition by christening one of his sons Daniel. Danny Gallagher may or may not have known that his elder son, in a gentle, indirect way, wrote about him. Few would have guessed that 'Sinner Boy', written during the Taste period, was personal. In its stomping blues rhythm, the song asks the listener to take pity on someone who has become an outcast, a street person, with 'hands on the bottle'.

'Take that sinner boy home / Wrap him up, keep him warm / He won't do you no harm.'

The Derry connection remained during Gallagher's later childhood. He and his brother were sent there on several occasions for holidays with their grandmother Minnie. Gerry McCartney's family lived in number 37 Orchard Row. He remembers music being a passion for young Rory. 'He tried to get a wee skiffle band going on the street.' Another childhood flashback comes from Dermott Gallagher, whose family's back yard was a great meeting place. 'It was all new to me, to see a large box with a broom handle stuck in the middle with a string tied from the top of the pole to the outside of the box.'

Gerry McCartney remembers Gallagher coming back many years later to give his former neighbours tickets for his gigs, both when he played at the Embassy venue in the city in 1968 (with Taste), and the Guildhall in 1971. Many years later, Gallagher became a Derry local again when he was asked about the city's band, The Undertones: 'I don't dare say anything bad because they're from Derry. I think they have charm and naivety.'[19] Proclaiming Gallagher's Derry roots, the Bogside Artists, well known for their work on gables in nationalist areas of that city, painted a Gallagher mural for the part of Ballyshannon named Rory Gallagher Place.

Acknowledging the town of his birth, Gallagher revisited it several times, accompanied by his mother at least once in the 1980s. The town's memory also includes a story that, on one occasion, while his mother went to meet Patsy Croal, an old friend and a central figure on the Ballyshannon drama scene in the 1940s, Rory went into one of the town's many pubs, Maggie's Bar. He then overheard some men playing darts say, 'that fella looks the image of Rory Gallagher'. The famous man couldn't resist turning to the men to say, 'I am Rory Gallagher.'

But with the move south in 1958, Rory Gallagher's close relationship with the city of Cork was about to begin.

Chapter 2

TO THE LEE DELTA

'It's the kind of place where everybody nearly knows everybody else. If you want to meet someone, you know where to find them. If you don't want to meet them, you can more or less go where you won't meet them, which is kind of nice.'

– RORY GALLAGHER ON HIS ADOPTED CITY, IN 1974.[1]

County Cork is known as the rebel county, a designation dating back to the Wars of the Roses in the fifteenth century, when the city took the Yorkist side in the English civil war. Cork people also refer to their city – and not always tongue-in-cheek – as 'the real capital'. This is partly a throwback to the city's role as the centre of the anti-Treaty forces during the 1922–1923 Irish Civil War, an insurgency by those opposed to the limited independence that the Treaty provided. The Cork person's traditional antipathy for Dublin is part of the city's pride – and its charm.

According to tradition, Saint Finbar founded the city in the seventh century. The name derives from the Irish, 'Corcach Mór Mumhan', the 'great marsh of Munster', because the city is built on islands on the River Lee, which were marshy and prone to flooding. The waterways between the islands were built over to form some of the main streets of present-day Cork. The channels re-converge at the eastern end before the Lee flows on to Lough Mahon and Cork Harbour. This estuary has imaginatively been referred to as the 'Lee Delta', the topography and the romance of the musical connotations inspiring at least one band name, the Lee Delta Blues Band.

Monica Gallagher returned to her native city to live with her sons at her parents' public house, The Modern Bar (later known as Roche's Bar) at 27 MacCurtain Street. She had two sisters, Noreen and Kathleen, and two brothers, John, who ran the pub, and James (Jim), who became a favourite uncle to Rory and also a musical influence. Dónal Gallagher later recalled his role in their lives: 'Jim was an inspirational figure for Rory. He was a terrific man. In '68 and '69, he'd come over and take courses in computers at IBM in Sandhurst. I'd take the Taste van and drop him off. I'd pick him up a week later, he'd come and crash on the floor at our bedsit.'[2]

Monica Gallagher's family had a passing connection with one of the great musical figures of the twentieth century in Ireland, Seán Ó Riada. Her family was de Róiste (the Irish-language version of Roche) from Cúil

Aodha in the West Cork Gaeltacht. Monica was born after the family moved to Cork city. Dónal Gallagher told Mark McAvoy that Ó Riada frequented the family bar on MacCurtain Street. Rory, in later life, must surely have been fascinated by Ó Riada's metamorphosis from jazz and pop musician John Reidy to Irish-speaking traditional ensemble leader and innovator, as well as authority on musical heritage, Seán Ó Riada. And, coincidentally or not, Rory would later develop a strong attachment to Ó Riada's setting of the Mass. When Ó Riada moved to Cúil Aodha with his family in 1963, the de Róistes were neighbours. A first cousin of Monica's, Johnny de Róiste, and his wife Siobhán, who live and work in the area as farmers, are aware of the family's connection with the rock music legend: 'We were never into the rock music', says Siobhán, 'but we have two granddaughters in Kenmare with lovely voices and we often wonder did they get this from Rory.'

MacCurtain Street has several well-known landmarks: the Everyman Theatre and the Metropole Hotel. The tower of St Anne's Anglican Church on the hilly neighbourhood of Shandon can be seen from this elevation, and the sound of its famous bells heard. The young Rory would surely have looked down from this height on the River Lee's two channels below, and might have thought of the Mississippi Delta and its sounds – the rich music he had become aware of and would later deeply explore. Close by is the steep rise of Saint Patrick's Hill, an elegant nineteenth-century street, where he was often photographed strolling confidently.

Looking south towards the city, St Patrick's Street is below. On it a statue looks north over the river towards St Patrick's Hill. It is a representation of Father Mathew, the nineteenth-century clergyman, known as the temperance priest because of his campaigning against the abuse of alcohol. Coincidentally, in 1993, Gallagher was asked by *Hot Press*, 'Who would be the last person you would invite to your birthday party?' He answered: 'Father Mathew'.[3]

Gallagher recalled being intrigued while in Derry by AFN radio. So what were the musical influences on him as the family settled in his mother's home city? He remembered experiencing music in 'the ether of his childhood', in 1977. 'Even as a toddler, I think I was very aware of hearing people like Guy Mitchell and Tennessee Ernie Ford on the radio, along with things like the "High Noon" theme, and all that. Apparently, I was always singing around the house, because most Irish families are interested in music in the first place – not necessarily pop music, but they were all singing around the house.'[4]

The young Gallagher had already become aware of the popular singer Lonnie Donegan through his 1955 hit, 'Rock Island Line'. The Glasgow-born performer's work was also a route to the blues for Gallagher. Another song Donegan recorded, 'Bring a Little Water, Sylvie', is an example of how blues art emerged. The holler, as it was known, had developed as a way of communication for people working in the fields, in this case to ask that water be brought to deal with the heat. Its latent musicality was revealed and became global after Lead

Belly added his guitar to turn the water-call into a song. According to Chicago-born Jack White, of the White Stripes: 'When you're digging deeper into rock 'n' roll, you're on a freight train headed straight for the blues.'[5] Paul Oliver, the famous blues historian, summarised the music that began to draw Rory Gallagher: 'Blues is the wail of the forsaken, the cry of independence, the passion of the lusty, the anger of the frustrated and the laughter of the fatalist. It's the agony of indecision, the despair of the jobless, the anguish of the bereaved and the dry wit of the cynic.'[6] Blues was also the popular music of the black community in the 1930s and '40s; performers from the American South became famous stars. But it wasn't all pain and woe; as one writer put it: 'It was the music's up-to-date power and promise, not its folkloric melancholy, that attracted black record buyers.'[7]

During 1958, Rory Gallagher became a pupil of the North Monastery primary school, just north of the city centre. Billy Barry, who sat next to him on his first day, remembers an extremely shy classmate, who, when he did speak, had a Northern lilt in his voice they weren't used to, one that he lost fairly quickly. He was enrolled through his Irish-language name, Ruadhrí Ó Gallchobhair, as was the custom then, but because he had gone to school in Derry, Irish would have been less familiar to him. As the boys grew older, Barry recalls that Rory did not share the majority's passion for hurling and football - he was to shine differently. 'If he had been good at hurling, well, the whole story would have been different', he says.

Gallagher recalled Cork as a 'guitar-free' place at that time. But he remembered two buskers, one blind, who entertained playing fiddle and banjo on football match days at their regular pitch at the Prince's Street entrance to the city's famous indoor emporium, the English Market. 'They were like the Mississippi Sheiks of Irish music', he said.[8] They were well-known local men, the Dunne brothers. Pete Brennan was a contemporary and can still picture the men's long gabardine coats and the Clarke's shoebox in which they used to collect coins. Gallagher's memory of these musicians may have partly inspired his 1978 song, 'Mississippi Sheiks', a celebration of humble music-making in the work of the 1930s American country blues group of the same name:[9] It felt like a dream, he says in the song, or time travel, as he imagines seeing the band on a street corner.

The eventual master of the guitar was still taking his fundamental steps. By the age of ten, he had graduated to an acoustic six-string guitar, one apparently bought in Crowley's, the shop in Cork that later became famous in the Gallagher story. A neighbour on MacCurtain Street, James O'Brien, who ran an ice-cream parlour, helped the young Rory. Gallagher later recalled: 'He used to tune my guitar for me, otherwise I'd never have been able to tune it myself! I worked out "It Takes a Worried Man" and "Freight Train" and all those folkie things, and then bit by bit I had a bash at Eddie Cochran songs and Buddy Holly ones, and the rhythm 'n' blues came later, once I'd learned there was more to rock 'n' roll than met the eye.'[10] In 1975, Gallagher gave another snapshot of the genesis of his career: 'I got photographs of Lonnie Donegan and people like that and tried to figure out what shape their hands were in on the photographs.'[11]

Gallagher regretted not being able to read music: 'I went into the library once and got *Teach Yourself How to Read Music* or something, and it said, "Sit down at your piano." We didn't have a piano, so that went down the chute. Then I worked out F, A, and C and gave up, because I was too impulsive, and I was already delighted that I could play "Lost John" and a couple of other songs. Then, next thing, I was playing blues and rock 'n' roll, which is fairly instinctive and primitive stuff anyway.'[12] In 1987, he returned to that theme, saying that the soul of his music was the blues. It brought him to Lead Belly: 'I wanted to check out the originals of "Rock Island Line" and "Bring a Little Water, Sylvie". It's not too far then to get to Big Bill Broonzy.'[13]

Rory Gallagher was beginning his lifelong engagement with this music. It was a commitment that would become total for him. However, it's difficult to know how he saw his own worth. He was certainly determined, but did he sense he had a superior talent? Some musicians are fortunate to have an early awareness of a special talent. For example, Mike Scott of The Waterboys tells of a key moment for him when he was on a bus one day, aged just nine. He was hearing sounds in his head, so began stamping his feet in response. The driver stopped the bus and remonstrated with the child. Scott thought that his banging was 'a sophisticated rhythm to a magnificent soundtrack'. So the driver's annoyance was for Scott 'a rude awakening'. He realised that the sounds were in his imagination and *only* in his imagination. He concluded: '... figuring out a way to let other people hear this music will become the object of my adult life'.[14]

In his last radio interview, in January 1995, for Radio Hengeland in Holland, Gallagher recalled something from his early years, the time he went to the Cork School of Music when he was about twelve: 'They would not allow a guitar. They said if you would like to learn to play like Segovia we will teach you. And I said: "No I want to learn to play like ..."' 'John Lee Hooker?' [the interviewer suggests]. 'Yes. Or whoever.' Later in the same interview, he remembered the time he came across a Lonnie Donegan songbook. 'It had quite an effect on me and I taught myself in, I won't say 24 hours, but in one day I could actually sing a song and play three chords. I mean since that I've learned a little bit more, I hope, I hope.'

Late in his life, Gallagher described the process – the difficulty – of moving on from just playing chords:

> Between the ages of twelve and fourteen, say, I was really struggling with it – in the sense that I'd come from the acoustic guitar, which was very much rhythm stuff. Then I started picking out the obvious Ventures and Shadows type things, and Buddy Holly solos. I wasn't that concerned with solos at the time, because there was no solid group, but by the time I did join the showband, I knew the 'Brown-Eyed Handsome Man' solo, and 'Wishing' and a couple of Chuck Berry solos.[15]

The great Irish footballer John Giles had a reflection on the subject of realising talent, which could be applied to the young Rory Gallagher. 'I knew early on I had a gift to play football, to control the ball and pass the ball. But I had a second gift – to realise I had the first gift. I knew a lot of players who were gifted but who never realised the gift they had, who didn't make the most of it. And it's making the most of it that's the important thing.'[16] With the young Rory, there was a certain single-mindedness, according to his brother. 'It was a strange experience having Rory as your older brother, because at a very early age he realized what he was destined for. He was a man with a mission, and either you supported him totally or he was not interested. There was no halfway house.'[17] In an interview for Mark McAvoy's book *Cork Rock*, Dónal Gallagher remembered his brother's thirst for performance: 'Rory would play at the drop of a hat anywhere. He would go and play what was the asylum up in Sunday's Well. He would play for patients when he was around twelve or thirteen.' His fellow primary school pupil Billy Barry remembers when Rory did his Gene Autry impersonations at school talent shows: 'We'd break our arses laughing at him with his cowboy hat'. But, he admits, the deriders ended up as passionate fans not long afterwards. Barry and a group of twenty friends hired a bus to travel to Belfast for a Taste gig on St Stephen's night, 26 December 1969, and then slept in the bus before travelling back to Cork the next day to see their hero play the City Hall.

By 1963, there was an important step for the elder Gallagher brother to take to realise his vision. He had by then graduated to playing a Rosetti Solid 7 electric guitar. Then he saw a picture of Buddy Holly[18] with an impressive-looking instrument in his hands. He wanted one of these.

Chapter 3

ENTER FENDER GUITAR
NO. 64351

'He seemed to live for playing the guitar, and to me he represented the idea that if you wanted you could live all your life in a room with your guitar and an amp and that could be your world forever.'

– JOHNNY MARR[1]

The most famous guitar in Irish music history rolled off the production line in Fender's Fullerton factory in California as the 1960s began. When it eventually reached Rory Gallagher's hands it was not only a well-crafted piece of wood, metal and electronics, but was destined to become something of a mythical instrument for his fans. It has often been recounted how the fifteen-year-old Rory came to buy it, but one admirer, Jean-Noël Coghe, in his 2009 book describes it as a sort of twentieth-century folk tale, one about a passionate young man and a musical instrument shop, set in Cork in 1963: 'Rory walked faster and faster till he caught sight of the shop sign. His quest for the Holy Grail was almost over. "I hope she's still there!" At the shop front, he stopped and looked in the window, holding his breath. His eyes swept from left to right, from right to left. Where was she? There! She was waiting for him.'[2]

The actual story is more prosaic. Crowley's Music Centre on Merchant's Quay in Cork was a shop run by Michael Crowley, a music enthusiast.[3] The guitar that became Gallagher's was once owned by a member of the Royal Showband, Jim Conlon. He had bought it new while in the US, as he bought a new guitar every second year the band toured there. 'I bought them in New York in Manny's Music Store. I believe they cost about $150 then in the early '60s. I think I bought the sunburst Strat in '61 or '62. When Manny, the owner, used see me come in there, he used say, "here comes the Irish guy!"'[4]

Jim Conlon disputes the commonly held belief that when the band changed their uniforms the sunburst-coloured Fender didn't fit their new pink attire and so they changed it for a red one. 'It's a fairy tale someone made up', he says. The Royal were based in Waterford and Conlon thinks he traded in the guitar to another shop, perhaps Cantwell's in the city, and it found its way then to Crowley's. He didn't follow the progress of the guitar. 'It was only many years later that I came to know about its fame in Rory's hands.' Conlon says his guitars took a lot of beating because his fingers used to sweat so much – 'from fear' – and he concludes modestly: 'I was not remotely in Rory's class, but I wasn't a dummy either. I never mastered the instrument, but I did my best with it.' Conlon emigrated to the US and returned to his accounting career, later getting a senior position in the finance division of worldwide music rights firm BMI, working in New York and Nashville. He died in New York in December 2018.

* * *

Crowley's Music Store was a Cork institution. It was on Merchant's Quay when Rory Gallagher was a teenager, but later relocated to MacCurtain Street.[5] When Crowley's was forced to close in the summer of 2013, Dónal Gallagher recalled in *Hot Press* what happened 50 years before.

> The guitar was sitting in the window; it had pride of place there. Rory brought me down and he explained to me that it was similar to Buddy Holly's guitar – it was his ambition at the time to have a guitar just like Buddy Holly. I think every guitarist wanted one. To me, the contours, the shape of the instrument … it's a classic shape, similar to something like a spaceship. It wasn't what I had imagined, we were so used to the round shape of a guitar and electronics were such a new thing. We couldn't understand how the sound could come from it. It was love at first sight. It was destiny.

Michael Crowley recalled it all in a matter-of-fact, folksy way for Mark McAvoy's book: 'I came up to his grandmother's pub and said, "Mrs Roche, will you tell Rory, when he comes home from school, that I've got a guitar in for him, if he's interested?" The shop closed for lunch, but when they re-opened at 2 p.m., Rory was waiting. I took the guitar out of the case and he just looked at the body and neck and said: "Yeah, that's it!"'

It has become a celebrated day for many in Cork rock music folklore, so perhaps the romantic account by Coghe in his book is appropriate, if fanciful: 'Invited by Michael [Crowley] to try out the guitar, Rory hesitated before lifting it off its stand. Surprised by how light it was, he held it in position against him and ran his fingers over the neck, teasing the strings. His head bent in concentration, everything around him faded into the background until he was alone with his guitar, Rory the kid and his mythical Fender Stratocaster '61.'

Coghe's depiction is borne out by what Gallagher himself recalled: 'I mean, for weeks, every morning I would wake up, I'd go over and look at the guitar in the case, and treat it like a living being or some kind of magical thing. Even the smell of the case – I mean, I was really standing on my head at that time.'[6] Rory's future bandmate Oliver Tobin later recalled the Stratocaster's arrival: 'After a few days with it, he was a different man.'[7] Other musicians have described their bond with their instruments. Robbie Robertson of The Band was fifteen years of age when he sold his Fender for the train fare from Toronto to Arkansas, to get a start in Ronnie Hawkins's band. 'I had to do whatever it took to get to Arkansas. I was on a mission, but leaving that beloved Strat behind cut deep.'[8] Bruce Springsteen described a similar feeling: 'I took it home. Opened its case. Smelled its wood (still one of the sweetest and most promising smells in the world), felt its magic, sensed its hidden power.'[9]

Fender can be forgiven for boasting about the instrument they invented after their success with the Telecaster and the Precision bass: 'Perennially sleek, stylish, smooth playing and tonally versatile, it has transcended its role as musical tool to become nothing short of a cultural icon.' The Fender Stratocaster was the first guitar to feature three pickups in what is called a 'spring tension tremolo system', as well as being the first Fender with a contoured body. It became a standard instrument for many genres, from country to punk. In the Beatles' two-guitar unison solo on 'Nowhere Man', Harrison and Lennon were playing their new Stratocasters. In a *Times* feature on the Strat in 2004, Keith Richards said, 'Leo [Fender] is an artist, an original. The Strat is as sturdy and strong as a mule, yet it has the elegance of a racehorse. It's got everything you need, and that's rare to find in anything. The man made a work of art here.' Mark Knopfler of Dire Straits has credited his 1961 Stratocaster for transforming one of his most famous songs, 'Sultans of Swing': 'I thought it was dull, but as soon as I bought my first Strat in 1977, the whole thing changed, though the lyrics remained the same. It just came alive as soon as I played it on that '61 Strat.'[10] Gallagher had more praise for the Fender. 'It's just such a resonant guitar. I love the three pickups, especially the middle one. I like the five-way selector and the way the volume and tones work – the guitar never gets "dead" if you take it below 7. And it's a good tough guitar – you never have to treat it like a baby. I like all sorts of things about it – it's good and clangy!'[11]

Gallagher made his own modifications to the instrument. The tuning pegs are replacements, and odd ones: five Sperzel pegs and one Gotoh. This is an insignificant detail except that in once referring to it, he revealed a primitive belief: 'The machine heads have been changed a million times, except this odd man out here, I left this sixth one out for the gypsies. It fell one night and the back came out of it, so I just left it there. It was a little bit spooky so I left it alone. It's a superstitious thing.'[12] The pick guard was changed during his time with Taste. Only the middle pickup is original. The final modification was that of the wiring: Gallagher disconnected the bottom tone pot and rewired it so he had just a master tone control along with the master volume control. He installed a five-way selector switch in place of the vintage three-way one. He wasn't afraid to get quite technical on occasions as he talked about the guitar. In 1977, he was asked about liking a high action on his Strat:

Yeah, it's not very low. It's similar to the action on an acoustic guitar. I've always had a high action. You bend a string and the pressure's against the finger and you can bend it up a tone or whatever a lot better. Considering I'm using light strings – by 'old' standards – it's better. If you hit a real power chord and you've got real thin, wispy strings on, you're gonna get a buzzy nothing. Even if you're using my strings with a low action, you're not gonna get a chord with real conviction.[13]

Gallagher rarely played a Gibson guitar. He was asked about this in New Zealand in 1975, and confirmed he was very much a Fender man:

You see, Gibsons are so easy to play that they tend to control the player. They literally only have about two tones. Plug them into any old amp and they still sound great, but plug a Strat into the wrong amp and it sounds like a tinny toy. With a Strat you really have to work on it to get the menace out of it and they give you the freak tones that Gibsons don't. Also, I think Fenders are more versatile. Their single pole pickups give you that strangled sound and you can get to the volume and tone controls quicker than you can on a Gibson. As for the harmonics, they're purely a Strat thing. I didn't know what they were at first, but now I can get three types of harmonics.[14]

People have speculated about the reason for the gradual loss of the sunburst paint, beginning in Gallagher's Taste days. Although the Strat was left abandoned in a rainy ditch for days after being stolen in Dublin, this is not believed to have caused any ill effect. Dónal Gallagher has said that his brother's sweat was particularly acidic and 'was literally like paint stripper'.[15] But paint loss on Fender guitars is not unheard of; for example, the Fender bass played by Sting for many years has similar paint loss. At any rate, many have concluded that the battered appearance of Gallagher's instrument was entirely in keeping with his public persona. He told Dan Hedges: 'I've got a lot of salt in my blood, and the sunburst finish never lasts anyway. I guess I don't feel like getting it repainted because I've grown so fond of it. But it's eventually going to crack up. If I walked out onstage with another one …? I mean, you get branded with a certain guitar. Have to keep up the image, you know!'

The guitar is only part of the sound, of course. Gallagher used various makes and models of amplifiers during his career. In general, however, he preferred smaller 'combo' amplifiers to the larger, more powerful stacks approach popular with rock and hard rock guitarists. To make up for the relative lack of power on stage, he would often link several different combo amps together.

In the Fontana and Taste, he used a single Vox AC 30 with a Dallas Rangemaster treble booster plugged into the 'normal' input. Examples of this sound can be heard on the Taste albums, as well as on *Live in Europe*. Regarding reverb and the use of effects, Gallagher believed in keeping it simple. He told Cameron Crowe, then a young journalist, that Taste avoided the trendiness of psychedelia: 'At the time everyone was using reverb echoes on their guitar, I just wanted to cut an album of hard rock that was raw and direct. None of *that* gimmicky guitars-in-the-wilderness [sound].'[16]

Brian May, Queen's guitarist, had this to say about Gallagher's sound: 'He was one of the very few people at that time who could make his guitar do anything, it seemed.'[17] May saw Taste at the Marquee Club on Wardour Street one night, observed Rory with the Stratocaster, and wondered, 'How does that [sound] come out of there?' He stayed on that night till the venue was being cleared, and got talking to the Cork man. Rory showed him the AC 30 amp and described how he used the control booster and the master treble control. 'So Rory gave me my sound. And that's the sound I still have.' The Edge of U2, in a mini-documentary set in a Fender plant, where he examines a Gallagher Stratocaster replica, recalled seeing Gallagher at the 1977 Macroom Mountain Dew Festival in west Cork. His immediate reaction was that he wanted to 'sound like that'. Of the Stratocaster he says: 'There's something amazing about the fact that this was designed in the Fifties and it's pretty much as it was day one'.[18]

Michael Crowley kept an interest in the fate of the sunburst Stratocaster and its owner. He recalled walking along Camden Quay on one occasion and, passing St Kieran's school (Gallagher's second secondary school), noticed Rory. It was after the lunch break when kids were going back in to class. 'I spoke to him for a while and you could see with Rory that his heart was elsewhere.' Not long after that, he heard him practising with the Fontana and was surprised by how far he'd progressed. 'Knowing how other people at the time might struggle with fairly simple tunes, he was obviously a unique talent.'[19]

The Strat's theft from Taste's van in Harcourt Street, Dublin, on 10 June 1967, and eventual safe return, also throws light on Gallagher's superstitious nature. 'It's a kind of good luck charm.'[20] In 1988, he used an Irish literary reference to describe the relationship: 'It's the *Third Policeman* syndrome – you become so attached to something it actually becomes part of you. Trying to replace that guitar would be like trying to replace a limb.'[21] (In Flann O'Brien's novel of that name, a policeman and his bike become one because of the 'interchange of molecules' between the two).

Gallagher's partnership with the Stratocaster became, arguably, the great musician–instrument relationship of Irish popular music. 'His improvisational journeys with the Stratocaster actually go somewhere without getting lost in transit', was the view of music writer Shiv Cariappa. 'On stage he coaxes a whirlwind of deft harmonies and feedbacks from his open-chorded guitar in a sweat-drenched workout.'[22] The musicologist and musician Mícheál Ó Súilleabháin recalled in *Hot Press* in June 1995 seeing Gallagher in the Cork Opera House when he himself was a student of music at University College Cork, and being struck particularly by that relationship with the guitar: 'His improvisations were constantly moving, reaching out, going somewhere, extending the potential of the instrument itself.'

This would all make Rory Gallagher very famous. But back in the summer of 1963, the fifteen-year-old had just found a stage to express himself with his new guitar.

Chapter 4

A SHOWBAND APPRENTICE

> 'It was often a case of arriving back in Cork with the
> Fontanas at 8 a.m., after playing the night before in
> Galway or somewhere, gulp down my cornflakes and
> heading off to school.'
>
> – RORY GALLAGHER[1]

A musical life had mystique. By 1963, England had produced the Beatles, the Rolling Stones and many more. Stardom seemed attainable. By the time Rory Gallagher was fifteen, a beat club scene was starting in Cork. But Gallagher instead chose another route, and joined a showband, a conventional dance band of the time. He was anxious to get playing, but it might also have been a strategic choice. He clearly saw his future as a professional musician, and beat groups were generally part-timers, incompatible for someone with an eye on the longer road. To suggest he stumbled into a showband, or joined for convenience doesn't give him enough credit for having a plan. He said years later, 'I was able to learn the whole professional band scene though I was still at school.'[2] 'Rory Gallagher had talent, but he also had vision' is how Dave McHugh puts it. McHugh, a guitarist himself, is a keen observer of Gallagher's career.

Rory used to keep an eye on advertisements in the *Evening Echo* and *Cork Examiner*, newspapers that could be found lying around his grandparents' bar. In the summer of 1963, brothers Oliver and Bernie Tobin from Drinagh in the south-west of County Cork, placed an advert seeking a lead guitar player. They were forming the Fontana showband. Bernie played trombone, Oliver, bass; they later added John Lehane on sax and Eamonn O'Sullivan on drums. The Tobins had a céilí dance band, before deciding that pop music was where they needed to go. Feeling their way, they added their first guitar player that summer, Jimmy Flynn. He remembers being offered £3 a week, whereas he had been getting £2 on the dole. Bernie Tobin then told him that he had got other replies to the advert, one from 'a young fella called Rory Gallagher'. He asked Flynn to sit in on the audition they were having for Rory and three other applicants. He remembers calling to the bar on MacCurtain Street to collect the aspiring lead guitarist. The fifteen-year-old Gallagher, of course, got the job.

The Fontana were playing their first gig together when, at the break, Flynn recalls Rory being asked if he wanted to try a solo spot. Gallagher launched into some Buddy Holly material, including 'That'll Be the Day'. At that time, Flynn, about four years older, had discovered how to play a major 9th chord. Gallagher 'watched him like a hawk' until he figured out how to do it. Flynn remembers a short time later being pleased with himself that he had mastered The Shadows' hit, 'Geronimo', before the kid Gallagher heard him play it and then had it learnt, 'in what seemed like a minute'. Jimmy says he then decided that his £3 a week was in serious danger, and left the band by mutual consent. For his bandmate from MacCurtain Street, there was no looking back. Gallagher later recalled in an interview with journalist John Spain the time he was doing his final school exams: 'I remember it was like that when I was doing the Leaving [Certificate]. The night before the first exam we played in Lixnaw in Kerry and there I was in the van on the way home to Cork trying to sleep on top of the speakers.'

The showbands were a force to be reckoned with in 1960s Ireland. 'The showbands burst onto the scene when there was no scene to burst onto', is how Derek Dean of The Freshmen summarised the era.[3] These ensembles, originating in the northern part of the island, were a slimmed-down version of the larger dance bands of the 1950s. Showbands are viewed nowadays with nostalgia by some and disdain by others, but in terms of musical history, they were innovators in their day. In discussing Gallagher and the rise of rock 'n' roll in Ireland, Bob Geldof, for one, castigated the showbands, saying they 'destroyed Irish musicians', referring once to 'the showband crap'.[4] The contrary view is that many members of the bands were highly competent players who successfully entertained many thousands of people. There were literally hundreds of showbands, and premier-league ones like the Capitol and Royal were hugely popular. The Royal had seven number 1s in Ireland between 1963 and 1965; the most enduring of these was 'The Hucklebuck', sung by their charismatic singer, Brendan Bowyer. Declan O'Keeffe of the Fontana makes a strident case for the bands: 'The Beatles couldn't do what the showbands did, but the showbands could do what the Beatles did.'

Joining a showband was a logical step for guitarist Arty McGlynn from Omagh, who died in 2019. His career began in the Plattermen, later he spent years in Van Morrison's band, and became an accompanist of choice for many traditional musicians. It wasn't just the allure of performing pop music that motivated him; there was the thrill of discovering and playing American jazz. He remembers the excitement of hearing something new on radio, then 'the chase', as he describes it, ordering it by mail and waiting excitedly for its arrival. He discovered Lionel Hampton and Arty Shaw this way. 'Swing era and diminished chords opened up a whole new world, and Dixieland bands excited me too.' His antennae were always up for talent closer to home, too. The Plattermen were playing the Arcadia Ballroom in Cork one night in 1963. The Fontana were supporting. 'There was a young fella of about fifteen playing the lead guitar with them that night, and you knew even then he was special.'

Gallagher made many references later to his showband years. 'You'd be playing for five hours at a time and never get a clap ... it was all dancing. I only joined a showband because there was no other place to go with an electric guitar. We'd have to play all the Top 20 stuff. You learn a lot of basic stuff. Mostly you learn what sort of music you don't want to play.'[5] He told *Hot Press* in 1980: 'I joined out of frustration. I was fifteen, which is pretty young even by contemporary standards. But I didn't realise I was that young, you know? I'd been playing since I was nine, so in my own eyes I was a bit of a trouper!'

Despite what he might have said about this period of his career in different interviews, he was usually speaking with the hindsight of his later success. The fact remains that he spent nearly three years in the Fontana and Impact.

There may be echoes in Gallagher's attitude of Shakespeare's famous passage in *Julius Caesar*:

> ... 'tis a common proof
> That lowliness is young ambition's ladder,
> Whereto the climber upward turns his face.
> But when he once attains the upmost round,
> He then unto the ladder turns his back,
> Looks in the clouds, scorning the base degrees
> By which he did ascend ...

Gallagher's alternately blowing hot and cold on his showband years is a curious, but very human, feature of his life. On RTÉ Radio in 1976, he was fairly upbeat about it: 'I enjoyed the first two years. It was a great experience, a great training ground. I don't regret it.'[6]

The journalist John Waters, in a tribute following the death of Billy Brown of The Freshmen in 1999, recalled Gallagher mentioning his reaction to seeing the Beach Boys when they played Belfast in May 1967. After The Freshmen, the support act, had done their Beach Boys medley, the 'real thing' later that night didn't sound nearly as good, Rory thought.[7] Taste played support to The Freshmen on several occasions and Derek Dean describes how Gallagher and Billy Brown, the band's musical axis, formed a 'mutual appreciation society'. Dean also describes how, as the band rehearsed their Beach Boys harmonies, even with five people singing, Brown's ears could easily detect someone bluffing their line. Dean recalled a gig in Crosshaven, County Cork, in 1966, when members of The Freshmen stood at the side of the stage watching Gallagher with the Fontana, who were, he says, 'wondering why such a talent should ever have to play support for anyone'.

Declan O'Keeffe joined the Fontana as rhythm guitarist a couple of months after Gallagher, replacing Jimmy Flynn, who had auditioned Rory. 'I was never going to challenge him as a player,' he admits. 'But he was so generous … you could ask him anything about music or the guitar.' Rory was 'always one step ahead'. When the Byrds' 'Mr Tambourine Man' came out, he recalls being amazed by the way Gallagher could somehow get the twelve-string sound of the intro on a six-string guitar. As further evidence that showbands were, in their own way, trailblazers, he recalls a gig in 1964 in Portmagee, County Kerry, where the Fontana played their 1960s pop set to an indifferent crowd, with nobody dancing, before a local traditional music act had everyone on the floor as the Fontana took a break.

The band played or rehearsed seven nights a week, though they were not a 'first-division' act on the scene. Bernie Tobin's day job was running a travelling grocery shop. Each night he had to take the stock out of the van, drive to various locations to pick up band members, go to the gig, then drive back to Drinagh, empty the gear and reload the van for the next day. O'Keeffe confirms what Oliver Tobin recalled in his memoir, that it was his brother, Bernie, who quietly paid for the famous Vox AC 30 amplifier for Gallagher.[8] Gallagher recalled that time for the RTÉ broadcaster Dave Fanning in 1980 when Fanning quizzed him about joining a showband, saying, 'It was a chance to play through an AC 30 box, which I thought was the biggest thing that could happen to you.'[9] Fanning's line of questioning was why did a person who 'was into blues, join a showband?' But then, as a fifteen-year-old, Gallagher had yet to seriously discover this music. Declan O'Keeffe bears this out, saying that he doesn't remember such an interest in blues from his bandmate at that stage.

Oliver Tobin recalled Gallagher's arrival in the Fontana line-up in the book *Cork Rock*: 'Rory came to play with us at fifteen years of age. What people don't know at all is that he was very introverted, shy, and he stood back in the corner [when on the stage]. At fifteen he could play the guitar as well as someone of twenty-five. He knew every Buddy Holly tune there was to know. He was an artist of unbelievable talent. On stage he was able to bring that something special out in people who had it in here [pointing to his heart].' He also suggested that it was his brother Bernie who helped Rory gain confidence on stage, revealing that Gallagher was not always the commanding showman he later became. 'Rory would be playing at the back of the stage and Bernie would go in behind him and grab the neck of the guitar and drag him out the front. He would say, "Go on, Rory, go on, Rory. It's like having a hard crap. You are consti-pated. Get them going!"' he told Mark McAvoy. Declan O'Keeffe recalls the performances as anything but sombre, once the band got into their stride. 'We would go mad onstage. Rory would be on Bernie's shoulders, but playing the guitar with it behind his back.' The band had a routine for 'Walking the Dog', where John Lehane would go down on 'all fours' with a guitar cable as a 'lead' while Rory played the number. Little did the shy Rory Gallagher know then that in 1979 he would be striding confidently, performing that song for a huge TV audience with the Scottish singer Frankie Miller as his guest, at Rockpalast in Wiesbaden in Germany. But on the other hand, maybe that is just where he expected to be. Declan O'Keeffe also recalls a steely side to Gallagher beginning to appear: Oliver Tobin wanted to buy himself a Fender Jazzmaster bass. Gallagher wasn't pleased, as he regarded himself as the Fender standard-bearer in the band and didn't want to be upstaged by a competing instrument. Gallagher got his way.

Rory was attending the North Monastery secondary school when he began playing with the Fontana. He apparently got a beating from one of the Brothers because it was discovered he was in a band, and had refused to cut his hair. In the Brothers' worldview, pop music – and particularly rock 'n' roll – was something to be frowned upon. The issue came to a head after a fight broke out at a Fontana gig in Coachford, County Cork, when some of the audience took the late arrival of the guest act, Bridie Gallagher, out on the Fontana members.[10] The incident was reported in the newspapers so came to the attention of the school, Dónal told the *Examiner* in 2011. 'That was how they found out Rory was in a showband. After the beating, he got a terrible flu, which was actually distress, so he couldn't go to school. And when he did go back, he had a note from my mother saying he'd had flu. But of course, it had been all over the *Examiner*, with all the band members' names. It was front page. You can imagine what it was like in school. "Where's Gallagher today?" "In the paper, Sir."'[11]

To substantiate this attitude by the Christian Brothers, Theo Dorgan, the Cork poet who attended the North Monastery a few years behind Gallagher, says he doesn't think he himself went a day without getting a belt of one kind or another. He testifies to how far the school's ethos was from the milieu its talented pupil was embracing: 'I remember a Brother seeing my brother looking at Rory on the cover of *Melody Maker*, remarking, "Ah, poor

Rory, we didn't hit him hard enough."' Dorgan also makes the point, which many who grew up in Ireland in the 1950s and 1960s would agree with, that it was not just the religious orders in schools like this who could be violent: the lay teachers could match them. In a sense, it was accepted as part of teaching then.

The North Monastery website asserts the following: 'Our ethos is one that values and prizes each student as an individual created and blessed by God.' The school's crest features an Irish wolfhound holding aloft the banner with the numerals 1811, the year the North Monastery 'arose to give battle for the cause of Irish Catholic Education'. It goes on to say past pupils have excelled in politics, science and the arts. It mentions Tomás MacCurtain, the former Mayor of Cork, and Jack Lynch, Ireland's Taoiseach during the 1960s and 1970s. Surprisingly, there's no mention of Rory Gallagher. However, the North Mon primary school has a picture of their famous pupil in the main corridor.

Whatever occurred in the North Monastery evidently did not diminish Rory's religious faith. Pete Brennan recalls that when he attended service at Trinity Presbyterian Church, just off MacCurtain Street, he would regularly meet Rory hurrying to Mass in St Patrick's Church on the Lower Glanmire Road. 'He always wore a white shirt and black jacket. I'd say he never missed Mass.' Art Lorigan, also from Cork, and a member of Sleepy Hollow, a band that played support to Gallagher several times in the 1970s, remembers that side of Rory. Unlike his peers, Gallagher would gladly offer to explain the importance of the sacrifice of the Mass, and willingly reveal his faith. 'I remember him once saying, "Do you know the way you have good days and bad days? Some days are three out of ten and another day might be eight or nine out of ten?" His belief was that this doesn't happen by accident, that there's a higher power involved for all of us, that there is divine intervention.' Lorigan also remembers that if a coarse joke was being told in company, Gallagher would be the one to demur politely.

At any rate, after his brush with 'official religion', Monica moved her son to St Kieran's school on Camden Quay, by all accounts a more liberal school, and more likely to tolerate a less-conventional teenager. The principal, Thomas Pearse Leahy, who was blind and a member of the Labour Party, became Lord Mayor of the city in 1969. St Kieran's ethos earned it the description 'Butlins by the Lee', after the famous holiday camp chain. Monica Gallagher told the school authorities that her son was going to be a musician and would be late some mornings. It seems the school tolerated this. Jack Lyons, known as 'Irish' Jack, was five years behind Rory in the school. His mother knitted the school scarves. In a talk he gave in 2005, he still remembered the classroom smell. 'The room always smelled of a particular floor polish. And to this day when I go to visit my company doctor, the rooms are the same and the scent of that polish is still there.'

Another St Kieran's pupil, Mick 'Tana' O'Brien, who later played with the Lee Valley String Band, and who was also a 'refugee' from the North Mon recalls that some of the Christian Brothers in that school were great, but others he describes as 'deranged'. St Kieran's was innovative, for its time. For one thing, it was co-educational. O'Brien remembers that he and Rory were part of a class of 21: six boys and fifteen girls. The boys stayed at the back of the class, he recalls. It must have been a tolerant school because in his Leaving Cert. year, the final year, Rory was allowed an absence of two weeks for the Fontana's visit to London. 'He still was able to pass his Leaving Cert. What I remember most about him was that he was very quiet and always polite. He was clever. I think he could have done anything – he was that kind of a fella.' He also recalls Rory taking to drawing during class. 'I remember they were really detailed drawings.' Actually, Gallagher at that time attended night classes in the School of Art in the city. Wednesday afternoons were always free and the six boys would head off on a good long walk, Mick remembers. They were all of like mind; they talked about music and girls, though none of them followed sport, strangely. Mick remembers the time The Searchers' song 'Needles and Pins' was popular. Rory brought a guitar in to school one day and astonished the others by showing them how the riff for the song was played. 'I had a few chords myself, but Rory was in a completely different league!'

The season of Lent, the 40 days preceding Easter, was taken very seriously in Ireland in the 1960s. A person always made a sacrifice for Lent (many still do), 'giving up' some pleasure as a penance. Dancehalls were closed, which gave musicians an inadvertent chance to travel.

The music scene in Hamburg, Germany, beckoned, just as it had once done for the Beatles. Gallagher recalled his time in the city for Bill Graham, using a religious metaphor. 'The first guy we met over there, he definitely wasn't a member of the Legion of Mary. But when you're 15 or 16 that little bit of greenness or naivety keeps you going. You think, "that poor man has to keep the club going, I suppose". Besides if you didn't do it, you'd be beaten up or something!'[12]

About this time, Gallagher adopted the hairstyle that he kept, unchanged, for the rest of his life. Mick 'Tana' recalls Rory returning from a Fontana trip to Germany with his hair slicked back with Brylcream. It was part of the Fontana image. Rory's classmates were not that impressed and, not long afterwards, the oily fashion statement was abandoned and their soon-to-be-famous friend started to let his hair grow. He was also being noticed in his home city. Mick Moriarty, from the Blackpool area, recalled: 'He was instantly recognisable, with his long flowing locks, walking across Patrick's Bridge with his guitar. At that time he was playing in the evenings after school.'[13]

What is not widely known is that the Tobin brothers' advertisement in 1963 was not the only one the young Gallagher answered. As further proof of his intent on a professional career, it has been revealed by Art Supple, leader of one of Cork's most successful showbands in the 1960s, the Victors, that Gallagher auditioned for them in 1965. The band was really impressed with his playing, but they had a non-musical issue with the teenager; long hair was not part of their style. '"Your hair is a bit long", we told him gently. It was short back and sides and a suit – that was the way things were, as far as we were concerned.' So that was that. However, Gallagher technically became a member of the band[14] when he agreed to fulfil a recording engagement for the Victors in a Dublin studio. They were cutting a parody of a popular TV programme of the time, *The School Around the Corner*, called 'Showbands Round the Corner'. Supple recalls an incident as they travelled to the capital. They had stopped for tea in Port Laoise when one of the band members, in a sleepy daze, accidentally closed the car door on Rory's hand. It was 'an ouch! moment', he says, though no real damage was done. But years later, Rory recalled the incident when they met: 'He said something like, "I've sometimes been playing a gig and if I'm suddenly conscious of my fingers, or they're cold, all I can think of is Art Supple and the Victors!"' Another side of Gallagher was evident on the occasion they recorded in the Eamonn Andrews Studios in Dublin; a session guitar player had been hired and Supple remembers he and Rory weren't hitting it off, musically. 'When some intervention was called for, Rory was asked what he thought the other guitar player should do to resolve the impasse, he just said, very gently, "He should switch off his amp".'

Art Supple says that Gallagher 'always seemed to have his own musical direction at the back of his mind. So he went his way and we went ours.' He concludes that Gallagher was 'a symbol of everything that was good about Cork'. His abiding memory of Rory's determination

is from when they met a few years later at a snowbound
Cork Airport. All flights had been cancelled, but Gallagher
just had to get to a gig in Germany that night. A little
while later Supple watched as a solitary Rory walked out
across the tarmac through the ice and snow towards a
private plane that had somehow been organised by 'the
most soft-spoken fella you could imagine'.

And there's more evidence of Gallagher's engagement
in the showband scene.

He applied to join the country-orientated
Hoedowners.[15] Tony Lynch, who played guitar in that
band, recalls being with the band's manager, Oliver
Barry,[16] as he sifted through applications he'd received
for a guitar player. Because Lynch was from Cork, he says
Barry asked him about Rory. Lynch is still aware of the
irony of his assessment then: 'I said he was a very good
guitar player, but not a great singer!' But when he added
that Gallagher had long hair and wouldn't get it cut, Lynch
says the manager immediately threw the Gallagher appli-
cation in the bin. It was the prevailing climate.[17]

Gallagher had been both school pupil and professional musician for nearly two years when, on 8 January
1965, the Rolling Stones visited Cork. Sixteen-year-old
Rory Gallagher was at the gig with Tom O'Driscoll,[18]
from west Cork, who became a roadie and lifelong friend.
Girls were screaming, particularly at the sight of Brian
Jones and his locks, but as the young Englishman and
his band replicated Chicago blues, Rory Gallagher was
also noting a particular detail, something he hadn't seen
before, the technique of slide guitar. (It was exactly ten

years later to the month that fortune found Gallagher jamming in a room in Rotterdam with Mick Jagger and Keith Richards, at their invitation.)

Gallagher indicated how formative this period of his development was in a *Sunday Independent* interview in 1976. He believed that 'the rawness of approach that you learn in the early days should stay with you'. The implication was that this time of his life was crucial musically: 'Keith Richards still has that Neanderthal rawness. Progression is something you stick on to that. But I wouldn't ever like to lose the rawness I picked up at the age of fourteen or fifteen.'[19]

The Fontana did not lack ambition and in February 1965, they went on a twelve-date tour of England. The *Evening Echo* on 24 February carried a story about their triumphant return. The Dixies showband even took out an advertisement congratulating their rivals. Gallagher was itching for new freedom, however. Later in that spring of 1965, the Fontana began using the name Impact, partly to change their image, partly because they discovered another Fontana in the north of Ireland. There was also a band, Wayne Fontana and the Mind Benders, in Liverpool and the Fontana record label. It has often been said that the name change was Rory's idea,[20] though Declan O'Keeffe remembers it as more of a collective decision. The two names became interchangeable for a period. There was quite a furore in 2012 when a reel-to-reel tape was unearthed, which contained five songs cut by the Fontana in February 1965, in Regent Studios in London during their English tour. It had always been believed that they had not ever recorded. Gallagher sings 'Slowdown' and 'My Bonnie Lies Over the Ocean'. The recordings and some photographs came to light when one Tim O'Leary, a friend of Sarah Prendergast, widow of the Fontana's manger Philip Prendergast, was listening to a radio programme where an appeal was made for Gallagher memorabilia. He remembered that, years previously, she had given him a plastic bag containing some material. Neither had realised the dust-covered items' value. When Tim O'Leary revealed the content's existence on radio, he was inundated with TV and radio requests and also significant money offers for the tapes. He was surprised when in the midst of all the publicity Sarah Prendergast demanded their return – the tapes she had given to him. She then went on to sell them to an unnamed US collector. There was an almost comic sequel to the story: Sarah gave O'Leary another bag of various LPs. Out of an album by the Stylistics fell two 45 rpm singles by the Fontana. Kevin Prendergast had had them pressed in order to qualify for the BBC programme *Pick of the Pops*. In the end, the Fontana did not make it onto the TV show. The songs on the two discs were 'Slow Down'/'My Bonnie Lies Over the Ocean' and 'Valley of Tears'/'I Want You to Be Happy'. O'Leary, though he sold the recordings to Dónal Gallagher, sums up the affair: 'What did I get out of the whole thing? Grief!'

In April 1965 there was an event that showed the shy Rory Gallagher having steely intent. He caused an upset on the Telefís Éireann programme *Pickin' the*

Pops, a Saturday evening review show, on 22 April. He and Impact/Fontana were due to perform the Buddy Holly number 'Valley of Tears', but Gallagher changed at the last minute to the Larry Williams R&B song, 'Slow Down'. Art Lorigan remembers the talk around Cork the next morning was, 'Did you see that fella on the telly last night?' The veteran RTÉ DJ Larry Gogan (1934–2020) was presenting the show: 'He caused a sensation when he played something that no one was expecting. But he drove the audience wild ... He was probably the greatest guitarist I've ever seen. I remember on a TV show many years later he gave me great praise for being one of the first DJs to play him.'[21]

Johnny Campbell, who played drums at one stage with Impact, reported on how driven Gallagher was as a teenager; that there was little other than music on his friend's horizon: 'Like we were all fairly football crazy and everything else, but there was no ... I mean he'd kick the ball around but not with the same zest. Most of us wanted to be Jimmy Greaves, but he simply wanted to play music. He'd have a bit of fun kicking the ball around, but it was only a diversion.'[22] Art Lorigan recalls Gallagher advising him to 'keep your mind on what you want to be doing and don't get diverted by other things'.

Impact went to Spain in June 1965 for a residency of several weeks in the American Air Force base outside Madrid, just after Rory, then seventeen, did his Leaving Certificate exam. Spain was still in the grip of Franco's regime and Rory had to have his hair cut to be allowed in. Whatever about fascism's evils in the background, which might not have been apparent to outsiders, what irked Rory was that his picture appeared in the *Cork Examiner* with that haircut. Publishing it, of course, was proof that what this particular school kid did was a story. Oliver Tobin recalled that Rory always said he got his strength from his long hair, and wrote in his book that Rory 'was like Samson in the Bible'.

Impact's manager, Philip Prendergast, was quoted in the same newspaper, saying that they hoped to record soon: 'Rory has written some really great original numbers.' For their time in Spain, the band was provided with a house in Alcalá de Heneres, about 30km east of Madrid, coincidentally the birthplace of Miguel de Cervantes, author of *Don Quixote*. Oliver Tobin recalled Declan O'Keeffe teaching them how to swim that summer; and the cruelty of a bullfight some of them attended, in the same arena where the Beatles played earlier that year.

He remembers how miffed Rory was when The Who's song 'My Generation' came out, but Bernie Tobin kept it for himself to sing, a kind of band-leader privilege. In his book, Oliver Tobin claims that Gallagher wouldn't speak to the others in the band for a week, after which, because Bernie Tobin's throat was sore, Rory got to sing the coveted song, and harmony was restored. On their return from Spain, *The Examiner* asked band members for their impressions of the country. Rory reported: 'The guitarists in Spain are fantastic … but the food is "cat"!'[23]

That same article also contained a musical straw in the wind: when Declan O'Keeffe was asked who his favourite composer was, he replied 'Rory'. His bandmate had given him, on the back of one of one of their flyers, the handwritten lyrics of what may be the very first Rory Gallagher composition, 'She Isn't Worth It'. It's a song of teenage angst, giving advice to someone to forget a particular girl; that someone else will come along. 'She isn't worth it, you know she's not / That kind of girl is better off forgot …' He must have had at least some idea of a melody, because he specifies the key of F.

On their return from Spain, the band played Bandon Carnival, on 12 September, before a three-week trip to Britain. Tobin's account also recalls a driven Rory Gallagher. They had a residency at the 32 Club on the Harrow Road, London, playing support to bands like The Kinks, The Hollies, The Yardbirds and even the Beach Boys. He says Gallagher would study what the lead guitarist in each band was doing and imitate it. 'This worked very well. Rory would practise and practise like crazy, trying to get the same sound off his own guitar. Every night he would take the guitar to his bedroom and play quietly, sleeping with the guitar under his bed.' Tobin describes a charismatic Gallagher, whether in England or on his home turf, and recalls his performance of the Fats Domino song made famous by Buddy Holly, 'Valley of Tears': 'Girls would come up and stand around the stage gazing up at him as he did his stuff.' A Cork native, Peter Harding, recalled the time the Spencer Davis Group came to the city in 1966 and Rory and Impact were supporting. The English band, with multi-instrumentalist and singer Steve Winwood, had reached the top of the UK charts with 'Keep on

Running'. 'I said to a friend of mine the next day, "Japers, that young fella from Cork blew him away, he was ten times better!" But my buddy just laughed, because he couldn't believe that a fella from Cork could be better than someone who was in the Top 10.'[24]

In Cork, Gallagher's reputation had been growing. Gill Eakins (later Gill Bond) was thirteen when, one day on MacCurtain Street, she saw a good-looking lad with long hair. She stopped him, saying, 'Your hair is great. You must be in a band.' She and her friends were immediately smitten by his quiet charm. It sounds romantic, but the relationship was absolutely innocent, she insists, not a boy/girl thing at all. She remembers Easter 1967, when she and her friends argued over which of them was to give Rory his Easter egg. She was aware that Rory lived with his mother and brother, and had a father living somewhere else, though she would never ask him about this. 'I wouldn't have wanted to embarrass him.' Eakins, a Protestant, went to Cork Grammar School, the same school that Gallagher's later Taste bandmates Norman Damery and Eric Kitteringham attended. She recalls a small cultural curiosity from the time: when there were dances in St Luke's Church of Ireland Hall in Montenotte, kids she knew who were Catholic were convinced that to get into the dance you had to show familiarity with tenets of the Protestant faith. She claims kids would even go to the extreme of learning the beliefs of the Church of Ireland in order to convince the door staff.

Eakins looks back wistfully now, having settled for many years in Nottingham, saying 'it was a great time to be young in Cork'. She and Noelle Corcoran were with the band the night the Stratocaster was stolen in June 1967. Noelle's family home was in Rathmines, where Taste often chilled out with tea (and her mother's apple pie – a favourite of Rory's) after a Dublin gig, before the return journey to Cork. However, that night after the gig in the Scene Club on Parnell Street, they went on to the Number Five Club on Harcourt Street, a venue run by Pat Egan, who later became a reporter for *Spotlight* magazine and, later still, a record retailer and promoter. While they were there, the van was broken into. Whatever about other missing items, the horror was that the Stratocaster was missing. 'I remember clearly a quietness just set in over all of us, but particularly over Rory,' she says. They attended Mass en route to Cork that Sunday morning, where prayers were offered in hope, according to Noelle Corcoran. The guitar was discovered sometime later in a ditch after an appeal on Teilifís Éireann's *Garda Patrol* (in which, in an attempt at being light-hearted, the officer presenter suggested that the thief in taking it had done the owner's neighbours a favour). Gallagher and the guitar were virtually inseparable for the next 28 years.

Gill Eakins was so sure of Rory's ability to make it big, she started a scrapbook of his career in 1965, which she still has to this day, with every photograph in it signed by him, along with postcards and Christmas cards he sent her.

Impact had disintegrated by early summer 1966. A three-piece band, consisting of Gallagher, Oliver Tobin and Johnny Campbell, decided to head again to Hamburg, to a club called The Big Apple. A technicality they had to overcome was that the venue wanted a four-piece only, so they sent a picture of a fourth member (a keyboard player) but on arrival, announced that he couldn't travel. They performed in Hamburg as The Fendermen, he later told Dave Fanning.[25] Oliver Tobin, in his book, recalled that the band members were watching TV in a bar as England were playing in a World Cup game. When England took the lead, a man started shouting at Gallagher in German, something along the lines of (after an audience member offered to translate), 'How come you English always have to win?' Tobin said Rory firstly agreed with the statement regarding England, before emphatically clarifying his nationality, after which he got a big hug from his translator. Most significantly, during the trip Rory told Tobin that he had come to what was a fateful conclusion, that 'he could make it, if he had a good three-piece' (the implication being that this three-piece wasn't the one).

The Fontana and Impact[26] had left a mark, but their lead guitarist was already planning the next move. This involved him fronting a band, and then challenging, rather than imitating, the likes of Eric Clapton.

Chapter 5

NEXT MOVE: TASTE

> *'I just try and break the rules, I never play lazy blues, I*
> *always try and keep it hard and edgy. I'm an Irishman*
> *– that puts me in a funny category. I think like a folk*
> *musician, while my soul is blues and my energy is*
> *rock.'*
>
> – Rory Gallagher[1]

The Long Valley is one of Cork's convivial pubs, where, as well as alcoholic beverages, they continue to serve their famous 'honest-to-God' sandwiches, on crusty two-centimetre-thick white bread. This food has nourished many a Cork musician and the bar was the scene of many a famous encounter in Cork's cultural life. But a momentous meeting for Rory Gallagher happened upstairs here in the late summer of 1966.

It is commonly believed that Gallagher was a member of three bands, Taste (or The Taste), the Fontana and Impact. However, technically he was briefly a member of another Cork band, The Axills (as well as the short sojourn with The Victors). The Axills were known as Cork's answer to the Beatles, because of their haircuts and the adulation they enjoyed from young Leeside women. They also had a grip on the Fab Four's music. Barry Johnson, who was at North Mon junior school with Gallagher, recalls: 'When *Rubber Soul* came out, they had it in a flash.' The band was Derek 'Doc' Green, Peter Sanquest (whose brother, Kevin, became Taste's first manager), with Norman Damery on drums and Eric Kitteringham on bass. Kitteringham once described the band as 'diabolical'.[2] But Peter Sanquest has fonder memories, and describes their *modus operandi*: 'We'd sit down with a record player and listen over and over again to the latest Beatles record, then we'd attack the numbers – tear them to shreds. Then we'd have it.' He recalls, with more than a hint of musical snobbery that prevailed at that time, that as far as he and his friends were concerned, Rory had 'sold out' by joining a showband. At this time, rock and pop were left-field challengers in the music world. In Cork, the Dixies showband was the mainstream, led by Joe McCarthy and Brendan O'Brien.[3] Norman Damery sums up the Dixies-versus-Axills rivalry: 'They looked down on us, and we looked down on them.'

When Green and Sanquest left The Axills in the summer of 1966, about the same time as Rory Gallagher parted company with Impact, Gallagher agreed to step in to fulfil some gig commitments they had. Peter recalls getting to know Rory Gallagher this way: 'I remember going up to his house. We'd fiddle around with guitars. He'd do his impression of Django Reinhardt, and I'd show him my attempts at Brazilian music.' The Sanquests' sister Roz[4] became something of a stylist to the band and others in Cork, through a little business started when she was only eleven years of age: 'When Rory saw the ties I knitted for The Axills as part of their formal uniform (Beatles-like jerkins, narrow trousers, white shirts), he ordered a slim black one. He was very definite about what he wanted.'

Damery describes the fateful Long Valley meeting in August that year, when Rory, he and Eric decided to form a three-piece unit. He says the band's name came from a beermat of the time, one that proclaimed the superior taste of the famous stout brewed in the city, Beamish. And so, probably Cork's greatest rock band was born. Rehearsing began on the upper floor of 5 Park View on Victoria Road, Eric Kitteringham's family home near the city centre. Eric began sharing vocal duties with Rory, before the guitarist took over 'doing 99.9 per cent'. Eric told Dan Muise that his younger brother, George, remembered the sheer excitement for him as a ten-year-old, this loud, daring-sounding music being made in an upstairs room of his house. He recalled a quiet, demure Rory, who always addressed him politely, despite the eight-year age gap. And he always addressed Eric and George's parents formally as 'Mr Kitteringham' and 'Mrs Kitteringham'.

Pete Brennan is another Cork person who recalls those days. He helped out as a roadie (and later played bass for many years in the Lee Valley String Band) and remembers one of Taste's first gigs, a school hop in the Imperial Hotel's ballroom, on Grand Parade in Cork city. He can recall much of the band's early numbers: As well as 'Carol' and 'Roll Over Beethoven', they performed 'All Your Lovin'' by Otis Rush and Mose Allison's 'Parchman Farm', both songs covered by John Mayall's Bluesbreakers on the famous *Beano* album, released that summer. The Yardbirds' psychedelic 'Over, Under, Sideways, Down' also featured, as did B.B. King's 'Rock Me, Baby'. To slow things down, Eric sang 'Here, There and Everywhere' and Rory took on Dylan's 'Don't Think Twice, It's All Right'. The Walker Brothers' song 'Everything Is Gonna Be All Right', a hit that year, might seem a strange choice, 'but Rory did it his way, as only he could', according to Brennan. Mick 'Tana' O'Brien described early gigs by Taste: 'Rory would sing "My Generation" by The Who. The place would go mad. The girls used to be screaming and going crazy.'[5]

Original songs were being 'pieced together', Brennan says, recalling 'Railway and Gun', destined to be one of the most famous Taste songs. He and Norman Damery remember an early incarnation in the Victoria Road house of 'Blister on the Moon', which became another of the band's big numbers. The eighteen-year-old Rory mixed surrealism with rebelliousness: 'Everybody's saying what to do and what to think / And when to ask permission when you feel you want to blink.' The song goes on to complain that 'rules are all pre-set', and unusually, the psychedelic-sounding title does not appear in the lyrics at all. The Major Minor label later released the song as a double-A side with 'Born on the Wrong Side of Time'.[6] *New Musical Express (NME)* said: 'This is a disc laden with interest – rippling guitars, a thundering beat, an intriguing lyric and a startling tempo change.' However, it concluded, 'not everybody's cup of tea'.

'He was different to everyone else,' Brennan says of Rory's playing. 'He heard the note in his head and it came out in his fingers, no matter what the speed.' As for dexterity, he says Rory even used his left-hand finger-nails for a slide technique. But again he remembers Rory as almost two different people in the same body, as many have testified. One a shy, quiet young man, who never got angry, never swore. When he got on a stage, however, 'one light went off and another came on', he says. Rory's new friends all concluded there was 'something special about this guy'. Paddy Kitteringham, Eric's cousin and sometime roadie for the band, remembers what he calls Rory's 'purity' as a person, and, as a performer, the way he could 'read the audience' like no one else: 'He just couldn't wait for the next chance to get in front of an audience.' Freddie White, a Cork native who later found fame as a song interpreter, was a member of a band called The Krux when he was a teenager and remembers opening for Taste at a number of school dances. 'I used Rory's amp more than once and was frustrated, of course, that my sound was pretty shitty compared to his. He was always very sweet and helpful on those occasions to this snotty-nosed kid.'

Whether they were The Taste or just Taste, they were cool. Syd Bluett, an artist, remembers being in Cork for a schools' football match in autumn 1966. The Taste van was parked near the ground and Rory was showing enthralled kids some guitar technique. Bluett thought he'd be brave and ask him something that had been plaguing his teenage mind: 'What's the best chord to get the girls?' Rory replied, flashing his bottleneck on the strings: 'This one – E major 9th.'

And what of Rory Gallagher the shy teenager, rather than the budding rock star? The Kitteringham brothers had an older sister, Patricia, or Trish, who was very fond of the dashing guitar player from MacCurtain Street. He later gave her a drawing he made of Bob Dylan, which she always treasured. But while she was interested in him, there is no evidence of any romantic feelings on his part, according to George. Pete Brennan thinks that this was the closest Rory got to a relationship with the opposite sex during this period of his life. Norman Damery's view on this aspect of Rory was that, since they knew each other well ('lived out of the same suitcase for two years', as he puts it), Rory wasn't interested in 'men, women, or drugs'. Art Lorigan recalls that after gigs in the 006 Club on Leitrim Street, many people would head for a coffee shop called Shambles, but Rory would more often choose the solitary option, to practise his playing, his vocation. Later in his life, Gallagher reflected on this formative period of a musician's life.

The trouble with a lot of rock players is all they listen to is rock. They should listen to a little jazz and folk music as well. Not that there's any rule, but it's fun to play a solo that's actually more like a jig or jazz phrasing. And no rock fan in the front row is going to say, 'What's this? Jazz?' Too many guys just play on the beat, on the bar, straight on the line – and that's all they do. You have to have a sense of rhythm – not rhythm as in bash, bash – but rhythm as in fooling around with it, playing against the time, in independent time, or in mandolin strokes.[7]

Taste's business model, if it could be called that, was to have three musicians, a Volkswagen van (painted with 'Taste' by Eric), some equipment, including a Ludwig drum kit, two 'crazy boxes' (a kind of improvised PA in the showband era), a Vox AC 30 amp for Rory's Strat and a Fender Bassman for Eric's Fender Precision or Burns Bison bass, and a willingness to play anywhere for very modest money. Their first manager was Kevin Sanquest, a brother of Peter Sanquest of The Axills. Among the issues that had to be dealt with was what now seems a quaint one: bands allowed on stage in mainstream venues had to supplement their line up with 'paper' musicians to meet Musicians' Union rules. A similar rule had applied in Hamburg, and caused Rory to resort to sending a picture of the band's 'keyboard player' but later tell the venue owner he got seasick on the journey, so they were there as a trio.

Taste was on the road by the autumn of 1966, but they were soon looking further afield than Cork and Dublin for gigs. By the end of that year, they had another option, north of the Irish border, in Belfast. Their connection with that city's thriving 1960s blues scene, partly came about by accident. The Belfast band, Just Five, came to Cork for a gig without one of their guitarists, Tiger Taylor. Gallagher stood in, so much to the band's satisfaction that he was asked to join it, according to Billy McCoy, who became a lifelong friend. A seed must have been planted, because a short while later, as McCoy recalled for the writer Trevor Hodgett in 2015, Rory arrived unannounced at McCoy's house in Belfast. Once again, the Gallagher charm was a hit. 'My mother and sisters wanted to throw me out and keep him because he didn't drink or smoke and he was really polite and well brought-up and a really nice guy.'[8] The Belfast guitarist Rab McCullough has a similar story, showing how rough and ready the scene was then. He and Gallagher had met up and because it was getting very late, he suggested to Rory that he stay at his place. The next morning Rab's mother came down the stairs and saw this body with long hair sprawled out on her sofa. She stormed into her son's bedroom shouting, 'I've told you before, you're not to bring back strange women into this house!' Rab apparently replied, 'Ma, that's Rory Gallagher.' Realising this was someone important, she made her way down the stairs to find the soon to be famous guitarist awake, before using her charm and a culinary institution: 'Ah, good morning, son. Would you like a wee Ulster fry for breakfast?'

Taste's first gig in Belfast was in Sammy Houston's Jazz Club, Great Victoria Street, on Saturday 17 December 1966. Bill Morrison, a member of The Group,[9] recalled a bandmate coming up to him to say, '"Come here quick, you gotta hear this!" On the stage was a really good, play-loud blues/rock group.'[10] For several weeks, Rory, Eric and Norman were just known in the city as 'the trio from Cork', he recalled in 2015. The Cork men made a big impression on Morrison and his bandmates when they played support to them at an afternoon gig in the famous venue, The Pound, several weeks later. 'Once they started up, no one in the room could take their eyes off Rory and his low-slung Strat. His voice was compelling and he sure could play that guitar.'[11] He also recalls the band's general appearance, looking 'like they'd been living rough for a week', and also Gallagher apparently spending much of his offstage time in Dougie Knight's record shop on Great Victoria Street. Later in his life, Gallagher made an unfavourable musical comparison between Cork and Belfast. 'There was no one in the city that I came from who knew anything about these sort of people [American bluesmen]. You could discuss the Ventures with them, or the Shadows, or Fats Domino, fair enough, but anything deeper was a bit of a closed shop. If I had lived in Belfast where Van [Morrison] and Them and all those people were playing it might have been different.'[12]

Blair Whyte is a Belfast native who remembers his first encounter with Gallagher. It was in an upstairs late club at Sammy Houston's. 'I had never heard anyone play guitar like him – and I'd seen Clapton at that stage. I decided I was going to have to say something to him, to thank him.' A friendship began, with meetings in coffee places rather than in pubs. The Belfast guitarist Eric Bell, a member of several bands, including Them, and later a founding member of Thin Lizzy, remembers Gallagher's arrival in the city. A friend, Billy Moore, was always asking him to come and see a new guitar player on the scene. When he mentioned Gallagher, Bell thought 'here we go again'. He was glad he went that time, however. 'He had such confidence on the stage, such conviction in his voice, and he was so musical.' Colin McClelland, also from Belfast, and who worked as a journalist for many years with the *Sunday World*, remembers this time in the city. It was 1967 and the 'Summer of Love' hippie ethos had even rubbed off a little on Belfast. The symbol of that was the Marquee Club in the Astor Ballroom off Royal Avenue. 'If the Troubles hadn't come about, Belfast could have been a different, non-sectarian model', McClelland says. 'In '67/'68 you stopped wondering what religion the person standing next to you was. By 1969, people had all scurried back to their ghettos. There were people you never saw again.' In his view, 'there were vested interests that didn't want this "new dawn" for the city to happen'. The poet Gerald Dawe described it this way: 'Before the curtain dropped in the late 1960s and the city, despite the best efforts of thousands of ordinary men and women who braved the terror, fell into a kind of fragmented darkness, Belfast's vibrant music scene was a liberation.'[13]

When Taste and Rory Gallagher, 'with his magnetic, electrifying stage presence', arrived, McClelland recalls, 'everyone knew from his accent he was from the South, but it didn't matter'. The journalist and broadcaster Sam Smyth, another Belfast native, remembers the city in the same way: 'like a window to what could have been. Community relations were the best they had ever been in the mid to late 1960s. It made you feel good.' Smyth ran Tiffany's, a rival to the Marquee Club, in the Astor. Taste was a regular booking. He remembers Gallagher's graciousness and wondered was it a Cork phenomenon. 'He had a level of politeness that was really refreshing.'

As an indication of a creative, if rough and ready, technical environment, Colin McClelland and Blair Whyte offered to see about stage lighting for the band. Whyte even managed to get to sit with Pink Floyd's lighting crew when they played in Belfast, to try and pick up some basics about lamps. Both Colin and he point to one result, a Belfast Marquee Club innovation: the idea to use lighter fuel on a projector slide, to create a primitive kaleidoscope effect on the stage. Coloured ink was put into the slide and the heat from the projector caused this to 'explode'. Combined with an ultraviolet spotlight, 'it felt like it was London', McClelland says. He also recalls that after closing time at the venue, on several occasions, Taste and the staff challenged each other in five-a-side soccer, on the ballroom's sprung floor.

Blair Whyte has his own lasting memento of that time. He once noticed that Rory's shoes were falling apart, so he gave him a pair of his. In later years, when

Gallagher was performing one of the crowd favourites, 'Going to My Hometown', he'd sometimes substitute the line 'The day I left, the rain was pouring down' with 'The day I left, I had shoes upon my feet'.[14] Any time Blair heard this, he liked to think that Rory was referring to that time he had helped the Cork man out with footwear, in those frugal Belfast days.

In January 1967, Taste left their Cork base to travel, via England, to Hamburg. Gallagher later detailed the work schedule at that time.

> We'd play 45 minutes in each hour, and we'd go on stage about four or five times a night – that's weekdays. On Saturdays we had to do seven sets. I was never there for months on end, like the Beatles, but it was good hard labour all the same. I wasn't complaining though, because in the showband it wasn't unusual to do five hours on your feet without a break … you'd get off the stage and your fingers would be mashed to pieces. I enjoyed every minute of Hamburg though. It was fun unlimited really, because you often shared the bill with another band, and we used to have a lot of good times.[15]

The three men discovered non-musical contrasts between Hamburg and Leeside, according to Norman Damery. 'We were three innocent young Paddies. We saw things you didn't see in Cork!'

For the trio's return in mid March, Gill Eakins and Noelle Corcoran were among a group of girls (including the Church of Ireland Bishop of Cork's daughter), who organised a huge banner made from bed sheets, with the slogan 'Welcome Home, Rory', to bring to the city quays very early one morning when the ferry *Innisfallen* was docking, carrying the returning Taste. George Kitteringham has another image from that time: seeing the band's van being hoisted from the hold of the ship (roll-on roll-off ferries had not arrived then), and watching the three men come down the gangplank, his brother sporting a huge mop. All he could think was, 'What are the folks going to say?' The *Evening Press* that week proclaimed that 'Cork's rave raisers, The Taste' were returning to play in Dublin. It added that they would be bringing 'some unique numbers which they discovered in Hamburg'. For Cork fans, their triumphant return gig was at the Cavern Club on Sunday 26 March 1967.[16] That early Taste time is still a vivid memory for Gill Bond: 'He really did generate an enormous amount of feverishness and exhilaration in many youngsters craving something different from the showband and traditional music scenes.'

Taste had made an impression in Cork, Belfast and Dublin, so London beckoned. They played their first London gig at the Marquee Club, 90 Wardour Street, on 1 July 1967. However, hand-to-mouth living was what awaited the Cork teenagers in the big city. Eric Kitteringham remembered how frugal things were. He told Dan Muise: 'We actually ended up sharing a basement flat with an old school chum of mine that he was renting in Belgravia. We had absolutely nothing.'

His friend knew someone who delivered vegetables to restaurants in the city. 'He'd siphon off about twenty mushrooms out of each basket ... not enough to be missed, but we used to have fried mushrooms for dinner. That was it.' A trumpet player from Cork, Tommy Rooney, who played in several dance bands and orchestras and had crossed paths with Gallagher in the Fontana, recalled for *The Archive* meeting Taste on their uppers in London: 'Him and the band, they were broke, they hadn't tuppence. So we put a couple of bob in the kitty and gave it to him.' Despite the living conditions, London in 1967 had its charm. For many who arrived there, the city's culture was seductive. Jack Lyons, a postman from Cork and a contemporary of the Taste members, had emigrated and 'gone native': he developed a cockney accent and became an associate of The Who. However, Art Lorigan distinctly remembers, in the summer of 1967, Gallagher disapproving when they met two sisters from Cork who had bought into the whole Swinging London idea. 'As one who had definitely "bought in" myself (what was not to like about '67 in London?), I was quite surprised.' This was the side of Rory Gallagher that believed in traditional things, Lorigan thinks. 'There was a sort of straight-laced, down-to-earthiness about him,' he concludes.

It was something of a musically turbulent time. Gallagher and his friends were not immune either, as a quaint struggle raged between the 'folkies' and the 'rockers', particularly when Dylan 'went electric' in 1966. Doe Hill, a friend of Rory's at the time, recalls an argument breaking out when Taste was playing in Tralee, County Kerry, during the Rose of Tralee Festival in August 1967. A folk player with a guitar was holding forth, denouncing rock music as vulgar and noisy. Hill remembers Gallagher didn't say a word as the discussion grew heated, only smiled politely. At the time, Davy Graham's tune 'Angie' was a rite-of-passage number for aspiring acoustic guitarists.[17] She remembers Gallagher quietly picking his moment before asking the folkie, '"Excuse me, but would you mind if I borrowed your guitar for a moment?" He then proceeded to silence the room – and end the discussion – by playing, "Angie". It was game, set and match,' she says. 'It showed not only his versatility, but his politeness – and his humour, too.' Doe Hill has another significant memory – how abstemious Rory Gallagher was then. 'We smoked and drank anything we could get our hands on. I only recall him with one beer. Tragic, in light of what happened later.'

Belfast was still Taste's base in the second half of 1967. In a 1985 interview, Gallagher fondly recalled his affinity with the city, referring to it as his 'second home'. Its musicians had 'a casual but serious way of playing and you get a bit of ESP going', he said. He particularly admired his native Belfast band members, Gerry McAvoy and, at that stage, Brendan O'Neill. 'There's a humour you can bounce off, and short cuts, mentally, which is great.'[18]

It was a nomadic existence in the city, with accommodation in McCoy's home, then The Seamen's Mission, and later in an Ormeau Road guesthouse. They lived briefly in Castlereagh, outside the city, before making the move further east to Ballyholme, a suburb of the seaside town of Bangor in County Down. According to Norman Damery, the houses were all owned by relations of Eddie Kennedy and were 'free'. Bangor has always been a 'good' address for Northern Irish people, with its elegant Victorian seafront. The sectarian divisions that would soon erupt into strife in other parts of the North were perhaps not apparent, or at least of no concern to the Cork men. The huge upheaval in that part of Ireland, commonly referred to as 'The Troubles', was then only a year away. Dónal described their arrival in the town:

> Rory told driver/roadie Tony Falkner to pull up – my brother being a true Piscean was soon down to the water's edge. 'I kinda like here', Rory said. 'Come on, let's check the house out.' Purely the fact that all five of us would each have their own bedroom won the day for the dwelling. To avoid alarm, the VW [the band's Southern-registered vehicle] was discreetly parked up and a scouting foot party was hastily arranged to source [scout] the locality. So Eric Kitteringham, in his red synthetic coat and matching frizzy 'Hendrix' hair-do, together with Tony and I, headed into town. We returned with the good news of a cinema, record store (part of a department store), train station and timetable.[19]

A music writer and native of County Down, Colin Harper, evokes an idyllic era of tranquil summers, musical innovation and general joy. John Mayall, Dusty Springfield and the Kinks were among the legendary visitors to the town. Some of the more mainstream pop acts of the time were also seen in north County Down: among them, Dave Dee, Dozy, Beaky, Mick and Tich, Freddie and the Dreamers and The Tremeloes. The Dubliners, led by Ronnie Drew (who later became a friend of Gallagher's), were an attraction during 1967, following their freak UK hit, 'Seven Drunken Nights' (though only five of the 'nights' were allowed airplay). The venues were Milanos and The Electric Honeypot. Advertisements for the Honeypot invited kids to 'Tune in – drop in – freak out – live and love – come colour your mind.' Taste played there on several occasions, but there was a view that they should be moving on, as they had already been to play gigs in London. A *Bangor Spectator* journalist reported an overheard remark to the effect that, 'If Taste are so good, what do they keep playing round here for?'[20]

The reality of mainstream life in Northern Ireland could be present as well; Blair Whyte was with Taste when they supported John Mayall's Bluesbreakers (a post-Eric Clapton line-up at that stage, with Mick Taylor on guitar[21]) in Portstewart, County Antrim, on 14 November 1967. When Mayall left the stage without playing the customary 'God Save the Queen', he was told in no uncertain terms, though he protested, to go back on and play it. Tommy Rooney recalled in *The Archive* in 1997 that when you played for the Protestant community, which he preferred, he says, because the hospitality was better, 'you couldn't play the Irish national anthem, and you were warned three or four times about this earlier in the night'.

In his foreword to *Seaside Rock*, Dónal Gallagher mentions his brother asking to be directed to the record shop that had been discovered in the town. There, Rory bought an album by Canned Heat, their first LP released that year. He was particularly taken with side 1, track 2, and the song soon went into the Gallagher creative vault. It was called 'Bullfrog Blues'.

Chapter 6

FROM BELFAST TO THE WORLD: TASTE MARK 2

> *'If music is manufactured, you can just reproduce it*
> *every night, for better or for worse. But the kind of*
> *thing I play, for me anyway, it doesn't end with those*
> *two hours. It's with you all the time.'*
>
> – RORY GALLAGHER, IN *Irish Tour '74*

By the middle of 1968, Taste's[1] spirit of adventure and relative innocence was coming to an end. The advantages and perils of professional management decisions were about to change dramatically the career of the three musicians, Rory, Norman and Eric. Eddie Kennedy, a ballroom dancer and music entrepreneur, had already become their manager after he travelled south in August 1966 to see them play at the Cavern Club in Cork (later named the 006 Club). Because it looked like Kennedy would bring them more success, given his connections, Kevin Sanquest relinquished his management role. His brother, Peter, though he does not recall the details, says of his late brother that he 'wouldn't have been the grabbing type'. The management change was the beginning of a fruitful, but chequered and ultimately negative relationship with Gallagher, and which later caused a lengthy legal wrangle. Eric Bell recalls Eddie Kennedy as a 'fly-by-night bloke', a 'Colonel Tom Parker type'. And he recalls Kennedy's sartorial style: 'He'd wear a yellow shirt with a red tie.' Kennedy saw the opportunity that rock and blues presented. He took over the Maritime, Bell recalls, then closed it to refurbish it, and changed the name to Club Rado. 'It had been a dive, but we preferred that,' he says. He remembers Kennedy appearing on the Club Rado stage with a blackboard and easel on which he wrote the names of about a dozen bands of the day. Bell says it was bizarre, but canny. 'He said, "Well, boys and girls, who are the best bands?"' He then went through each of the names, to gauge the temperature. When it came to Taste, the cheer was particularly loud. It was confirmation for Kennedy, Bell says, that he was right in attaching himself to the trio.

In most ways, going with Kennedy was a logical move. When an apparently powerful player like him made advances, it would have been hard to refuse. He controlled a key venue for them in Belfast, the Maritime Hotel in College Square, and to the teenagers, he must have seemed like someone who might bring their success up a few levels. The rock and blues explosion in Britain and Ireland at this time can be compared in many ways with a gold rush: the 'treasure' was there, the rock phenomenon was a large vein of talent ready for exploitation and this music could be turned into money. The three young men were now entering the tough world of the music business. Kennedy was evidently both a sharp operator and a successful businessman. He had built connections with NEMS, the Beatles' manager Brian Epstein's company, which later became the powerful Robert Stigwood Organisation. Norman Damery looks back on that time: 'Kevin thought we would do better with Eddie Kennedy, but in fact he threw us into the pit.' Yet it was the route to fame.

That summer of 1968 brought musical highs, followed by trauma. Confidence was apparent in the 1 June edition of *New Spotlight*. Norman told the magazine that in Kirkcaldie, a small fishing town in Scotland, 'we found real blues enthusiasts'. Rory was positively gung-ho: 'Going to England was something we had to do. We'd done all we could in Ireland. There's no energy left at home and no one has any "go" about them. We're happy here.'

On 7 July, the band had an afternoon spot at the Woburn Abbey festival in Surrey. The headliners were Jimi Hendrix and John Mayall's Bluesbreakers. Taste's 22-minute set opened with a brief rendering of Gershwin's 'Summertime' (Hendrix had played 'Sgt Pepper's Lonely Hearts Club Band'), before 'Blister on the Moon'. Apparently, Gallagher was so pleased with the reaction to the song he thanked the audience sixteen times. Good fortune followed the gig. The famous BBC DJ John Peel was queuing for food at a motorway services café on his way back to London when he noticed the members of Taste behind him. They got talking; he complimented them on their set and asked them to do a session for his radio show, *Top Gear*. They recorded at the BBC on 8 August. It was one of the last times the three men played together. There may have been a straw in the wind when *New Spotlight*'s B.P. Fallon reviewed their performance at the Sunbury Jazz and Blues Festival, at Windsor, that same week. 'It's impossible to deny that Rory *is* the group', he wrote.

A dramatic line-up change was now under way. A new drummer and bass player had been sourced, respectively John Wilson, from Belfast, and Richard (also known as Charlie) McCracken, from Omagh in County Tyrone, members of a band called Cheese. They now became the new rhythm section. Eric and Norman were unceremoniously dropped. Fifty years on, it is still a sensitive memory for Norman Damery. 'For two years we were constantly together, then we were thrown apart.' The other side of the story is that somebody, maybe Kennedy, maybe Rory Gallagher, was thinking strategically; to make it big, Taste had to up their game. According to Gerry McAvoy, Wilson and McCracken were regarded as the best rhythm section in the country at the time. It is also believed that Polydor Records would give the band a deal only if the bass player and drummer were replaced, which is entirely possible, coupled with the fact that the record company immediately signed Taste Mark 2.

And what of Gallagher's role in the upheaval? Contrary to popular belief over the years, there is strong evidence that he was not an innocent bystander in the events. The headline in *New Spotlight* magazine of 7 September 1968 declared: 'Rory Gallagher Leaves Taste in Shock Group Split'. The writer B.P. Fallon referred to, 'Rory's decision to reform Taste ... "It was a difficult decision", he told me'. Gallagher was so blunt in the article that it could well be that he had in fact instigated the whole thing. 'We took the group to its peak and the Taste didn't get stale, but it *would* have. Time mustn't be wasted, so I'm restarting immediately, taking John and Ritchie to London to see how it works out.'2

John Wilson believes this trauma would have affected Rory because of the kind of person he was, 'but he was also savvy enough to see that this was his time – his chance – and to take it'. He acknowledges the Cork men's role in the Gallagher story. 'They only get credit in passing. But if it weren't for Eric and Norman, there wouldn't be a Rory. They gave their time to let Rory develop. By the time I got to play with him he was ninety-five per cent fully formed.' But such was the impression Gallagher had made in Belfast, Wilson says when he and Charlie (Ritchie) would ask each other what they would really like to do with their music careers, their answers were always the same: 'We used to say, "Could you imagine you and me playing with Rory?"' Eric Bell remembers meeting John Wilson near Belfast City Hall one day that summer. John said, 'I have an audition with Rory Gallagher! Wish me luck.' According to John

Wilson, it all happened very quickly. 'One day it was Eric and Norman, and later that week it was John and Charlie. People just said their goodbyes, and the Cork men headed south.' George Kitteringham, putting family loyalty aside, says 'things go fuzzy with time, but when you see that Isle of Wight performance particularly, I'd nearly go as far as to say that McCracken and Wilson were better than Eric and Norman.' A Cork fan at this time had written a forlorn message on the dust of the Taste van, 'Norman and Eric must stay', B.P. Fallon noted in *New Spotlight*. Pat Egan interviewed Eric Kitteringham for the same magazine a short while after his departure. He was back working as a printer and, displaying no bitterness, told the reporter, 'it happened because Rory was advancing too fast for us. We just couldn't keep up with him.' Kitteringham told Dan Muise that Wilson and McCracken were 'the best Gallagher band of all'. George Kitteringham is philosophical about the fate of the Cork men: 'I think Rory always needed change, so it may have been inevitable, aside from the politics.' Taste Mark 1 played their last gig together in Belfast, at the Tiffany Club on Wednesday 21 August 1968.

That autumn, Taste Mark 2 began their two stellar years. They became regulars at Club Rado in the Maritime Hotel, the venue where Van Morrison and Them's fame had begun. Among Morrison's references to his native city, the song 'Cleaning Windows' recalls hearing Lead Belly and Blind Lemon Jefferson on his street, not unlike Gallagher's musical awakening. Gallagher and Morrison's paths did not cross at this time as Morrison had left Belfast, but they became friendly in later years. It was in Club Rado that Gerry McAvoy, who later became the Rory Gallagher Band's bass player for twenty years, first saw his boss play. In McAvoy's autobiography *Riding Shotgun*, published in 2005, there is considerable insight into Gallagher. He recalled being amazed by how edgy the Taste music was: 'With Cream, for example, there was no danger. Everything Clapton played was perfect and you knew it was going to work, but with Rory it was always teetering on the brink … Clapton may have been a better technician but Rory was certainly more exciting. He would take chances that Eric just wouldn't take.'[3]

Taste was the band's first album, released in April 1969. It opened with 'Blister on the Moon', the song from the earliest days of the band. A curious feature of Gallagher's writing is that he uses surreal imagery and defies the conventional idea of space and time, characteristics of the psychedelic movement of the period. Yet there is no evidence that Gallagher or Taste experimented with mood-altering drugs. Gallagher appears to be embracing a trend:

> But now you want to run away, oh can I see you run,
> Run across the frozen air, try resting on the sun.
> And if you feel it burn you don't yell out in pain,
> Or wish you had a velvet sponge full of soothing rain.

There was an important contrast between Gallagher and many in the rock world. He avoided the amusements of the rock fraternity, especially recreational drugs. 'I won't want to pontificate about it, but I just don't take drugs. In fact in many ways, I don't feel myself part of the rock world at all.'[4]

The next track, the Lead Belly song 'Leavin' Blues', is Gallagher's first recorded blues cover. Interestingly, his version of the song owes more to the recording by the famous English guitarist Davy Graham than to Lead Belly's.[5] Davy Graham was one of the outstanding figures of the English folk revival, bringing an eclectic approach that involved blues, jazz, folk and Indian music. He pioneered a guitar tuning, DADGAD (the standard tuning is EADGBE), which became widely adopted by acoustic players. It shows that Gallagher was not always going to the 'source' of the blues, as it were, and was influenced in this case by someone closer to home. Another song, 'Hail', is Rory completely in 'folkie' mode, revealing the appeal and influence that music had for him. An *Uncut* reviewer described it as 'dazzlingly accomplished for a twenty-year-old'.[6] The lyric begins with a celebration of the folk singer vocation:

> I sing at the corner, my cap at my toes,
> I sing all those songs of joy, sadness and woe.

Then 'Born On the Wrong Side of Time'[7] showcased Gallagher's combination of folk and rock, successfully blending his acoustic and electric playing. Christy

Moore, one of the central figures in Irish music in the past half century, connects Gallagher with the work of three great luminaries of the English folk scene, John Renbourn, Bert Jansch and Martin Carthy: 'Rory sits very easily amongst them. There's nothing even slightly incongruous there.' *Taste* ends in country mode with the Hank Snow song 'I'm Moving On', which Rory had learned from his uncle Jimmy Roche, who had worked in America in the 1950s when the song was a hit. Tony Colton, a confidant of people like Hendrix, Clapton and Page, produced both *Taste* and the follow-up album, *On the Boards*. He was a member of Heads Hands & Feet, which included the legendary English guitarist Albert Lee.

In the summer of 1969 Taste undertook an American tour as part of a star-studded line-up that included Blind Faith, Delaney & Bonnie and Friends, with luminaries like Eric Clapton and Ginger Baker, who had been in Cream, and Steve Winwood of Traffic. The Robert Stigwood Organisation had come up with the idea that they would all share a tour bus. Not surprisingly, touring tensions emerged and, by the end, no one was speaking to anyone else. Gallagher withdrew into his shell and spent most of his time with his head in one of his beloved detective novels.

Dónal Gallagher revealed that one of his jobs on the tour was trying to control Cream's pugnacious drummer, Ginger Baker. He had briefly worked as a roadie for Cream when they were in Northern Ireland, so he knew the form – and egos – of the band members. 'I remember

going into the dressing rooms after one gig and Janis
Joplin was standing there. She said: "Ginger, I got to tell
you, your new band, it sucks, man". I thought he'd swing
at her.'[8] Another incident marred the tour: the singer
Bonnie Bramlett, of Delaney & Bonnie and Friends,
was traumatised when her hairdresser and friend, Jay
Sebring, was murdered along with Sharon Tate in the
infamous Charles Manson killings on 9 August 1969.
The tour bus at one stage also did a bit of humanitarian
work, smuggling two US citizens into Canada to avoid
the US Army draft for the Vietnam War. For Rory
Gallagher, a musical bright side of that tour had been
meeting one of his heroes, Muddy Waters, in a club in
Chicago. Apparently, Clapton and Winwood joined the
great bluesman on the stage, but Gallagher, John Wilson
told Trevor Hodgett, 'for whatever reasons, basically kept
himself to himself on a musical level, at that time'.[9]

If *Taste* made a mark, the follow-up record was a critical
triumph. *On the Boards*, which, unlike *Taste*, contained
no covers, opens with the great Gallagher anthem 'What's
Going On', where he packs much into an economical two
minutes and forty-four seconds. Brian May of Queen
described the famous stop-start opening riff as requiring
serious elasticity with the left hand.[10] 'Railway and Gun'
follows it, with its unusual tempo change.

The album shows Rory's growth as a lyricist, in one
of his tender love songs, 'If the Day Was Any Longer':

If the day was any longer,
Could I change your mind,

If your love was any stronger,
You'd stay behind.

There are several under-three-minute gems, the standout perhaps being 'If I Don't Sing I'll Cry', with its mournful imagery and a lovely falsetto note to end:

If I can't walk, I'll fly,
Well, if I can't sing, I'll cry,
If I can't sing, I'll die.

Another striking song is the longest and most musically adventurous, 'It's Happened Before, It'll Happen Again'. Taste here bring the listener on a whirlwind ride of jazz and rock, when after the second chorus Rory cuts loose first on guitar, then on saxophone. Wilson and McCracken change effortlessly to a rhythm section that could be fresh from the New York bebop scene of the late 1950s, before the guitar returns and all three revert to blues-rock to conclude the song. Gallagher's sax playing began it seems, in the *Taste* period, when he became interested in jazz players like Ornette Coleman. Dónal recalled for Dan Muise's book his brother buying an alto sax (a Selmer) and a 'Play in a Day' type book. 'We were in a very confined flat at the time so he'd play the sax into the wardrobe to absorb the sound. He didn't take any lessons, he was self-taught.'

Arguably, *On the Boards* gets even better on the title track, with its sparse bass and drums rising energetically above bleak, love-lost lyrics:

> Someone has taken my day,
> Turned it to night,
> Who turned out the light?

The famous music writer Lester Bangs said: 'Taste is from the new wave of British blues bands, breaking through the slavish rote of their predecessors into a new form that can only be called progressive blues. In other words, they use black American music as the starting point from which to forge their own song forms and embark on subtle improvisational forays.'[11] Gallagher's performance on the alto saxophone highlighted a strong jazz overtone in Taste's music. Bangs concluded that Rory was 'his own man all the way, even on sax, where his statements are doubly refreshing by their piercing clear tone and the coherence of the ideas'.[12] Several times during his life Gallagher acknowledged the influence of the American saxophonist Ornette Coleman. 'At one point in my life, Ornette Coleman was like my hero. I just admire his free spirit, his sound and his ideas. You can apply some of it to the guitar to an extent.'[13] In August 1969, Gallagher told *Beat Instrumental* that he 'drew energy from such as Ornette Coleman, Howlin' Wolf, Dylan'. In *Sounds* in May 1973, he referred to Coleman as 'one of the top three soloists in the world'. The renowned saxophonist Branford Marsalis wrote that 'Mr Coleman had figured out a way to expand the edges of traditional form, a complete contradiction to the modern definition of innovation'.[14]

John Wilson recalls an incident that again shows Gallagher's shy side. Taste was playing at a jazz festival in Bilzen, Belgium, in August 1969, and Coleman was one of the headliners. They enthused about each other's music and got on to the extent that Coleman arranged to have three chairs put at the side of the stage for them for his gig. Rory's chair stayed empty, despite his regard for the saxophonist. 'He was just too shy.' It was not the only occasion. Gallagher himself described how he nearly met Jimi Hendrix, at the Speakeasy Club in London. In 1992, he was similarly humble about meeting Bob Dylan: 'He walked into the dressing room and I nearly collapsed. He came in with his kids and he was talking about Blind Boy Fuller. It was very interesting – country blues, you know. But I'm still a school boy: I still hero worship people, it's a terrible thing for a man of my age to be like that.'[15]

On the Boards is regarded by many as one of the great achievements of Gallagher's career. According to the writer Colin Harper: 'Displaying all the maturity, variety and power of early Led Zeppelin, it shows the breadth of Gallagher's capabilities, from open-tuned acoustic material to blistering hard-rock anthems and slide-drenched heavy blues.'[16] Brian May described it as 'the most special album of Rory's. It's the rawness. It doesn't feel at all processed. It's like he's in front of you.'[17]

John Wilson says he remembers only two rehearsals in the two years he was in the band. He describes the creative process, in what was a great inventive era, as 'no big discussions ... "here's a couple of ideas ... let's see what happens?" We were more a jazz band than a blues band.' A jazz influence was not unique in the rock music of this period. The great Miles Davis was a hero for many rock followers and was on the bill at the 1970 Isle of Wight Festival. The Dublin-based Skid Row, the trio of Gary Moore, Brush Shiels and Noel Bridgeman (and, briefly, Phil Lynott), skilfully took a similar musical course during their short career. They were often compared very favourably to Taste during 1969 and 1970. According to authors Colin Harper and Trevor Hodgett in their book *Irish Folk, Trad & Blues: A Secret History*, 'Skid Row made music so idiosyncratic, contrary, eclectic and at times, inspired, that it should remain, at the very least, a thing of great fascination to the student of the Sixties.'[18] Gary Moore, from east Belfast, became a huge international star. His career took him south to Dublin, but he remembered Gallagher from the Club Rado days for Trevor Hodgett. 'We didn't have any spare strings between us and he used to leave his guitar on stage for me, if I broke a string, and I'd leave my Telecaster for him if he broke a string. There was a nice vibe between us – there wasn't that horrible thing of trying to blow each other off. I really did look up to him. I'm not influenced by him particularly, but I loved how he played and how graceful he was on stage. He was a great mover – he really had the whole thing down.'[19]

Gallagher said in Dan Hedges' book that his interest in jazz reached its peak during the Taste period. He said that he appreciated the guitar players of the genre, like Wes Montgomery and Kenny Burrell and Django Reinhardt, but he was most inspired by the saxophone players. 'Once I got into jazz, I found I had this terrible hunger to hear something that I didn't hear in rock and blues. I suppose it must have happened to a lot of people when they heard John Coltrane. His lines and the chords are really incredible. The whole era of jazz sort of whetted my appetite and satisfied it. So I veered away from jazz, but not before I'd picked up those ideas along the way. I mean that free-wheeling phrasing I try to get must come from the sax.' Gallagher's interest in jazz and playing saxophone waned during the 1970s, though he played the instrument on studio recordings.

The excitement of this period of rock music's history is conveyed in something the 22-year-old Gallagher said in March 1970. There is the innocence of being suddenly cast into fame, and youthful optimism. 'We don't have a style or a tag, although we are blues based, roughly speaking. I call our style "unpredictable". We are developing all the time, if we recorded an album last night it would be out of date today. That is the way we want it to be, we don't want to be hidebound or pegged down to something we have played before and are expected to play again.'[20] John Wilson paints a romantic picture of the trio's music-making: 'Two and a half hours would seem like two and a half minutes. With Rory, we were gone. We'd left the planet when we started to play, until somebody had to say, "You have to come off now!"'

However, Taste Mark 2 was almost as short-lived as the first incarnation. The band was disintegrating in the summer of 1970, even as they played their legendary Isle of Wight gig. By the end of that year, it was over, and acrimoniously so, by a combination of several things: financial distrust and, apparently, a divide-and-conquer strategy by Eddie Kennedy. A rift developed between Gallagher on the one hand, and McCracken and Wilson on the other. The other factor, the elephant in the room, was the question of whose band Taste really was – Rory Gallagher's or Wilson, McCracken and his? Perhaps in his steely but gentle way, Gallagher was asserting the former. There were spats onstage between the three during this period. In *Irish Folk, Trad & Blues,* John Wilson recalled a gig in Glasgow when he refused to go back onstage for an encore. 'Rory just went out and did it on his own. I made a complete asshole of myself. It was a dumb thing to do. And the point it highlighted was that, although I was the drummer in the band, the main musical movement was Rory.'

Pat Egan, a reporter for *Spotlight* magazine at the time, tends to agree: 'They [Wilson and McCracken] saw it as a band, but Rory saw it differently.' Gallagher later said 'we just came to the end of our natural life. The drummer wanted to play jazz and I wanted to play blues. We also had management problems that went on to cause me terrible legal hassles; I couldn't play for six months after Taste split up because of the contract I was under.'[21] There also may have been a factor not to do with either music or business that contributed to the Taste break-up. Wilson, McCracken and Kennedy were from Belfast; Rory, from the south, was, in a way, the odd person out, though he'd always felt at home in Belfast. John Wilson believes this may have indeed been the case. 'Rory didn't want to break the band up, but he had no alternative if he thought we were going to side with Eddie Kennedy.' Charlie McCracken has rarely spoken about his Taste days, but reminded Dan Muise they were all about twenty years of age: 'The things that are the norm in the business now, that acts, management and record companies take for granted, have evolved over the years. At that time there was no norm. It was cowboy land!' Regarding the whole affair, John Wilson has a similar, probably wise conclusion. 'We were young, we were naive … what can you say?'

But there was triumph awaiting on a small island off the English coast first. For any student of Gallagher's music, the performance at the Isle of Wight Festival in 1970 is more than just essential listening. Here, Gallagher makes a convincing case – debatably his most convincing – for the electric guitar's possibilities. The interaction between the three men is remarkable; the 22-year-old Gallagher is alternately loud, soft, attacking and joyous, as he completely controls the sound he makes from the six strings. The director Murray Lerner's footage is the band's most complete visual record. The animated interaction between the three musicians confounds the apparent turmoil that was going on in their offstage relationship. Though John Wilson insists this was just another gig, he can conjure up the great Taste dynamic. 'You'd see Rory approaching the drum kit, listening. The more "out there" you could be, the happier he was. He'd play something and I'd say to myself, "I know where you're going, but I'll get there before you!" And he'd be playing thinking, "I know where you're going, but I'll get there before *you*!"'

A well-known agent and artists' representative on the rock scene since the 1960s, Paul Charles, believes Taste had world-conquering potential. 'At a Rory gig you couldn't see the join between the musicians and the audience, simply because there wasn't one. He always played *with* the audience as opposed to playing *to* the audience.' He has this recollection of Gallagher's prowess:

> I heard them do a boogie-influenced piece of music that was completely new to my ears. After the gig I asked Wilsie [as John Wilson was also known] what it was called. 'New one to us,' he replied. 'The first time we heard it (nodding towards McCracken) was tonight as we were playing it.' I asked Rory the same question when I caught up with him later. 'Yeah, it's very new; it's called, "I've Bought My Ticket for the Train, but the Luggage Is Going on Ahead". It was unbelievable to me it was a new song, it had sounded as flawless as the rest of the set.

Now that Taste was at the top of the musical premier league, it led to rivalry. John Mayall had a go at the 'young challengers' from Ireland. He told *New Spotlight* magazine reporter Pat Egan, after Taste apparently stole the show from him and his Bluesbreakers at London's Marquee, 'I don't rate The Taste,' and, 'I don't think they will make it.' Of Rory Gallagher, he said: 'He has potential, but that's all.' Cork natives in London were more emphatic about the city's son, as they tracked his progress. Mick O'Leary from the Blarney Street area recalled that, at the Marquee, 'when the MC would announce "Rory Gall-ag-her" – with a hard 'g' sound – "... from Belfast!" – And we'd all shout "Gall-ah-her, from Cork!"'[22] Egan looks back now on that late 1960s period of music, Taste's heyday, with admiration. 'Everything was new. Innovation was everywhere. I know I'm getting old now, but when you listen to bands nowadays, you just think, it's all been done before.'

It's difficult to avoid the conclusion, however, that if Rory Gallagher had wanted Taste to continue, it would have. Just as in the line-up change in 1968, he was not an innocent bystander. With Taste disintegrating, he had decided this was only a phase of his career. The Taste chapter was closing. *Melody Maker* reported from Newry Town Hall at one of the band's last gigs. The reporter, a well-known music journalist, Roy Hollingworth, found the shy, or was it the canny, Gallagher: 'I found Rory in the changing room and he succeeded in talking about everything except the split. You can't help liking the guy because he's so nice. It wasn't a case of him making no comment. He just smiled at questions.' Hollingworth was getting an insight into Gallagher the person: 'I'm not going to say that I'll burst out in tears on Saturday, or say anything, until it's all over. Let it play itself out first.' What was he going to do after Saturday? 'I don't know. What will I do? I don't know. I'll spend time getting things together. Another three piece? I don't know.'[23] But, as it turned out, he did know. Taste played their last gig in Queen's University Belfast just before Christmas 1970. When early the following year, a live album, *Live Taste*, was released by Polydor, the regrets at the band's passing was articulated in a sleeve note by Paul Charles: 'When Taste split we all lost part of ourselves. But life goes on and we have to learn to live with it; this album is going to make living without Taste all that more easy.'

There's little evidence of sentiment on Gallagher's behalf. He was at a turning point, and about to embark on an era where all his line-ups would be 'The Rory Gallagher Band' or 'Rory Gallagher and his Band'. He had also, it seems, decided to eschew 'mogul managers' and settled for the comfort of a family member handling his affairs. It left unfinished business with Eddie Kennedy, which dragged on legally for years. In 2012, his brother Dónal told the *Sunday Times*, 'later, when I became Rory's manager, I insisted that we go to court to get the royalties. Even then, he was reluctant. He didn't like conflict.' Norman Damery recalls meeting his former bandmate in 1971 in Edinburgh and says he was shocked by the amount of money Rory needed to buy out Eddie Kennedy. Gallagher did take 'artistic revenge', however. The songs, 'Bought and Sold' and 'At the Bottom', from *Against the Grain*, are partly about the Kennedy management of Taste. This is confirmed in the notes Dónal Gallagher wrote for the remastered CD in 2012, referring to both and summarising 'Bought and Sold' this way: 'Rory still felt the pain of that time, translating the frustration and disappointment perfectly in this mid-tempo track.'

> I'm feeling bought and sold,
> You're just a three-card trickster.

Rory still took a swipe at Eddie Kennedy in an interview with a Dutch magazine in 1977, while mentioning the legal proceedings. The interviewer told him pointedly that 'he [Gallagher] didn't come over as the ego-tripper he had been portrayed' in the Taste split. Gallagher responded. 'It has nothing to do with ego-tripping. When it came to the music, I wanted to go down a different road than the other two Taste guys. We never had an argument, though. Everything went amicably, but I did want to get rid of my manager, a real bastard. That is when he passed on all those stories, to defame me.'[24] The split was news, and there was a certain amount of 'spinning' going on; in the 16 October 1970 edition of *New Spotlight* John Wilson was quoted as saying that Rory wanted 'the lion's share of the group's earnings'.[25] Several fans got involved in a debate in the magazine's letters page. It didn't go completely Gallagher's way, and was probably the only time in his life he faced fan criticism. One said, 'I would be appalled if I thought he [Rory] was so conceited that he considered himself superior to the other members of Taste.'[26] This would reinforce the view that many fans saw Rory as one of three rather than the main man, something that he was about to change.

Although Gallagher wrote some of his best material in the Taste era, because of regret, stubbornness in his character or just a need to move on, he didn't perform any of the songs recorded by the band for the remainder of his life. And even a full twenty years after the split, he was still touchy about the subject:

> In some respects I regret the group breaking up when it did, but I don't think it would have lasted more than a few months longer in any event. I remember playing the Isle of Wight Festival (August 1970) and we weren't talking to each other then. We took the ferry across, and we put on a reasonable show and got a great reaction, but musically it was all over between us. Other things were happening which shouldn't have been happening, but they were not my fault. Richard and John know the truth. I was made out to be the villain but they know it's simply not true. I got very badly burned there. I've been through the Taste story so many times and I'm sick of it.[27]

Things might have taken a different turn for Gallagher if he had pursued other management options after Taste. Jim Aiken, the successful Belfast concert promoter (who died in 2007), told Gerry McAvoy that his reluctance to take on 'big' management cost Gallagher dearly: 'For U2 to happen they needed Paul McGuinness ... Rory preferred to be in control of his own career rather than passing over some of the rewards to someone else. So possibly he achieved exactly what he wanted, the level he wanted, but he could have achieved so much more if he had allowed himself to give in to the structure of the business.' McAvoy refers to several approaches by Led Zeppelin's manager, Peter Grant, but he concludes that after the Kennedy experience, Rory was not prepared to 'even consider handing his career over to anyone else ever again.'

And what of Eddie Kennedy's side of the Taste story? There are no substantial interviews with him and he died in 1985. But in a short interview clip from that time, he states his *modus operandi* bluntly, if not unreasonably: 'Frankly I have to admit it [music] doesn't affect me other than that I enjoy it. I don't know how it affects them [musicians he manages] personally, or the public in general. My end of the business is to look after the business end.'[28] Sam Smyth worked with Kennedy and did not find him an untypical character in the music business.[29]

Gallagher had softened his stance on the Taste period by a 1992 interview, mentioning Kennedy's passing (but without naming him), and revealing that rather than making money from the band, because of the legal actions, he'd actually lost money: 'I don't give a damn about the money. It's people who let you down that bothers me the most.'[30] Later that year he returned to the subject, mentioning that he was on good terms again with Wilson and McCracken, repeated that it was all in the past, that Eddie Kennedy was 'D.E.A.D.', as he put it, and concluded with a resolution that wasn't to be fulfilled: 'It might be fun one night to do "a" Taste number just for old times sake.'[31]

One thing is undeniable: by the end of the 1960s he was playing at elite level. The next decade would be a highly successful one for Rory Gallagher.

Chapter 7

IT'S THE RORY
GALLAGHER BAND

*'Imagine being last year's superstar. It seems a waste
to me to work and work for years, really gettin' your
music together; then to make it big, as some people do,
and just turn into some sort of personality. You play
less, you perform less, and you circulate less ... that
young retired musician bit doesn't interest me'*

—RORY GALLAGHER[1]

As 1971 began, Taste was probably a combination
of triumph and bad memory for Gallagher. He
was determined to start a new chapter. First, he
needed a band. He knew of a bass player from Belfast
a couple of years younger than himself, named Gerry
McAvoy, from a band called Deep Joy, who had supported
Taste in 1970. Wilgar Campbell, also from Belfast, was

the band's drummer. Rory and Dónal organised a rehearsal/audition session in London. McAvoy recalled in *Riding Shotgun* that 'it just gelled from the word go'. 'Sinner Boy' was one of the numbers they jammed. Little did McAvoy know then that he would spend the next twenty years as Gallagher's sideman, and watch three drummers come and go in the same period. He would also witness the rise and fall of his bandleader. After the audition, McAvoy recalled an anxious three-week wait, during which he heard Rory had tried, among others, two ex-Jimi Hendrix Experience sidemen, Mitch Mitchell and Noel Redding. Then a phone call began what was the most enduring musical association in both Gallagher's and his own life. 'In that lilting Cork accent he spoke the words that made my heart leap: "Gerry, it's Rory. Would you like to make an album, Gerry?"'

What exactly was Gallagher looking for? The name, the Rory Gallagher Band, is the clue; this was not to be a combination of talents coming together in a trio; this was to have a leader – a singer, guitarist and songwriter – who wanted backing musicians, crucially, ones who weren't going to steal the limelight. Colin McClelland has perspective on Gallagher's selection of McAvoy and Campbell: that he was choosing musicians who would complement the guitar blues *led by him*, rather than be virtuosos themselves: 'They wouldn't interfere with the music he was trying to make.' His friend and colleague in the Impact, Johnny Campbell, put it bluntly: 'Rory wanted to take control and after Taste 2 all were backing bands. Before that they were all a band.'[2]

Early in 1971, he, McAvoy and Wilgar Campbell went to Advision Studios at Gosford Street, Marylebone, London, to record an album that was simply called *Rory Gallagher* and is, many would argue, amongst Gallagher's best achievements. He was now self-producing, the pattern for the future with only one exception, but he engaged an engineer, Eddy Offord, who had worked on the recording of *On the Boards*. In 2016, Gerry McAvoy recalled the time: 'It was spring, there was a good feeling, and we were getting to know each other. I was nineteen. I was a fan before that and here I was now working with Rory.' The pattern of the working day was so unlike later recordings, he also remembers. 'It was nine to six, not *starting* at six. 'We'd have half a lager, and then just go home! It's all a lovely memory for me.'[3]

The opening song on the finished product was 'Laundromat', with a riff that made it one of Gallagher's most enduring songs. It was written while Taste members were staying in a bedsit in a house in Earl's Court, south London, with a launderette in the basement. According to Dónal Gallagher, Rory 'used this uninspiring subject matter to create a highly inspirational song'.[4] Of the song 'Sinner Boy', considered to be about their father, the same notes are more circumspect, saying only that 'it exposes Rory's compassion and understanding for his fellow exiled man'. Gallagher told Mick Rock in 1972: 'It's got a bit of a story to it, about an alcoholic. I like that sort of thing, you know, like Woody Guthrie's stuff. I like to mix it. A lot of my stuff is very personal. It's good to get away from it sometimes.' 'For the Last Time', according to Dónal's sleeve notes, is about his brother's treatment 'during the demise of Taste'. The lyric could even be said to be borderline passive-aggressive:

> You've played around
> For the last time
> You've shown your claws
> Now I'm goin' to show mine ...

One of the standout songs, 'I Fall Apart', contains a central metaphor that could well have been inspired by an everyday scene in his mother's house.

> Like a cat that's playing with a ball of twine that you call my heart,
> Oh but baby, is it so hard to tell the two apart
> And so slowly you unwind it
> 'til I fall apart

'Just the Smile' is another tender ballad that shows the bachelor Gallagher to be a sensitive writer of love songs: 'She cools down my mind when she touches my hand / Feels so good, feels so good.'

It is difficult to get a sense of what Gallagher's life was like at this time, when he was not on a stage or in a studio. He was sharing a flat with his brother in south London and returning often to his mother's house in Cork. Socialising does not seem to have been a priority for him, but listening to music was:

Hardly a day goes by without me sticking on a Muddy Waters record – or, if I want to hear a bit of acoustic, Doc Watson. Then I like to listen to Scrapper Blackwell, Blind Blake, Blind Boy Fuller – some of those guys could play the legs off anyone. I often play some old Eddie Cochran, Buddy Holly – I listen to those guys too. People who played guitar on Dylan's mid-period stuff are nice, those tracks with Bloomfield and Robbie Robertson.[5]

Gallagher also talked about his relationship with London: 'I'm domiciled here … it's a place to hang out, but I can't regard it as my home. I'm always thinking about Ireland, but I get home fairly often, so it's not too bad. I mean, that's not to say I don't appreciate London. You'd probably feel the same if you came from Derby.'[6] Cork was still home. And Gallagher sightings were an event in the city in the 1970s. George Kitteringham's wife, Emer, remembers travelling on the number 7 bus towards the south-eastern suburb of Douglas on several occasions in the late 1970s when passengers would spot Gallagher as he strolled along Douglas Road towards the city centre. A cry would go up, 'There's Rory!' People would lunge towards the relevant side of the bus to get a view. Before the Gallaghers moved to a large house, 'Coolfadda', on the Douglas Road in 1978, they lived for six years high above MacCurtain Street, off St Patrick's Hill in the Sydney Park estate. The houses have hardwood floors and art deco touches, like stained-glass internal doors. The medical doctor at the

Cork Ford factory built the several dozen houses as an enterprise in 1950. For the Gallaghers, a corner house, number 11 was a step up from accommodation over the pub on MacCurtain Street. Monica was known for being a reader of tea leaves and George Kitteringham remembers calling to the house with his sister Trish on several occasions to have her fortune read by Mrs Gallagher. Michael Russell, who has lived next door in number 10 since before the Gallaghers and is now in his 80s, recalls that his late wife, Breda, shared an interest with Monica in embroidery. Monica once saw the Russells' son carrying a guitar and no case and offered them one of Rory's. The broadcaster Mark Cagney, who grew up close to the Gallagher home on MacCurtain Street, remembered the local pride: 'Sightings of him would be reported avidly all over our school. You'd never approach him. You'd just stand staring at him with your mouth open.'[7] During the 1970s, Gallagher often visited Eason's shop on St Patrick's Street. Dolores Quinlan, a north-side native who worked there, recalled for *The Archive* Rory going upstairs to the record department, where a woman called Sheila MacCurtain worked (she was the daughter of Cork's Lord Mayor, Tomás MacCurtain, murdered during the Irish War of Independence, and after whom the city street where Rory lived was named):

> We would know through eye contact where he was going. We'd make excuses to go there, and then follow him downstairs when he went to get his

New Musical Express magazine. He always had the correct money, so we never had to give him change. We'd all be giggling to each other, but he was oblivious to all this. I never tried to strike up a conversation, although he was unfailingly polite and friendly. We even knew that he went to 6.30 Sunday evening Mass at Saint Augustine's on Grand Parade with his mother, so we'd go there too.

Before the end of 1971 Gallagher had another album on the shelves, *Deuce*. It was the second of the six he made for Polydor between 1971 and 1974. *Deuce* is where the crowd favourite 'In Your Town' first surfaced and like so many of the enduring Gallagher compositions, it came into its own later in the recorded live version. In 1991, Rory told Shiv Cariappa, writing in the *Christian Science Monitor*, when *Deuce* was being rereleased on CD, that 'I'm Not Awake Yet' was one of his favourites on the record. 'It is an unusual theme, because it was the nearest thing to an Irish-Celtic guitar part with a 12-string and so on. The actual idea was, well not like astral traveling, but quite often where you can control that point where you wake up and where you are still in semi-control dream state. That was the idea.'

As an example of how varied music appraisal can be, these are two verdicts separated by some years. *Rolling Stone* concluded after the release: '*Deuce* is finally a competent piece of basic Anglo-rock, not too heavy, not too light, and not enough to make anybody's year-end poll.' In contrast, the Allmusic.com verdict in 2012 was: 'With bass set on stun, the drums a turbulent wall of sound, and Gallagher's guitar a sonic switchblade, it's a masterpiece of aggressive dynamics, the sound of a band so close to its peak that you can almost touch the electricity.' Was Gallagher trying to do too much by making two albums in one year? An unusually critical – perhaps to fans, heretical – reappraisal of Gallagher's career came in *Guitar World* in 2009. Looking back on *Rory Gallagher* and *Deuce*, the writer suggested that:

> Gallagher hadn't created a distinctive sound for himself ... the albums sound almost painfully anemic. Tighter songwriting might have helped as well. While a decent tunesmith, Gallagher did suffer at times from a lead guitarist's tendency to string a bunch of riffs together, ad hoc, and hope they somehow add up to a song. In retrospect, Gallagher's first two albums might have been more judiciously edited down to a single release, with time taken for higher production values.[8]

Live in Europe followed in May 1972, and unlike most live albums, it contained only two previously released songs, 'Laundromat' and 'In Your Town', either because he was prolific at the time, or it was a gesture to give value for money. The opening number, Junior Wells's 'Messin' with the Kid', became an instant Gallagher classic, a simple twelve-bar blues that makes dynamic use of 7th chords. 'Laundromat', 'I Could Have Had

Religion', a traditional blues song, and 'Pistol Slapper Blues' (by Blind Boy Fuller) complete side one.[9] The album gets into another gear on side two, with Gallagher's traditional-influenced number, 'Going to My Hometown'. Although it has American references, about a person who 'got a job with Henry Ford', it has always been celebrated by people from the city of Cork as a Rory homage to the city because Ford once had a large car-assembly plant there. The song has a simple but infectious crowd-pleasing dynamic between the mandolin and the bass drum. Gallagher often started it by working up the audience with a passionate question, 'Do you want to go?', something tribute bands have ritually adopted.[10]

'In Your Town' is a Gallagher original, a mock-macho song that opens, 'Look out, baby, your man is back in town / Look out, baby, I won't stand no messin' round'. The narrator in the song has done time in Sing Sing prison and his intent is on getting even; he wants to see in turn, the Chief of Police, the Fire Chief and the DA. The refrain is delayed for over six minutes, before it arrives as a triumphant resolution – and an ominous warning: 'Now I'm back / In your town, in your town, in your town ...' The album closes in smouldering style with 'Bullfrog Blues', which Gallagher had heard when he was living in Bangor, County Down, on Canned Heat's first album. He was probably also aware of the original, by William Harris, a country blues singer who recorded in the late 1920s. Gallagher was fond of beginning the song with a repeated call to the audience, 'Well, did you EV-ER?' It's almost like he was saying,

'Strap on your seatbelt, because this song is going to take off!', as it usually did. This straight-ahead twelve-bar blues was given special power by Gallagher throughout his career. According to *NME*: 'Lusty and rocking, quite simply the most exciting rock 'n' roll I've heard in a long time. Listening to it on Saturday night, I think, came as close as a non-disciple can come to experiencing something the other 2,000 Gallagher fanatics present had been feeling all night.'[11]

It was a great year for Gallagher on several levels. *Live in Europe* went into the top ten in the UK album charts (the only time a Gallagher record did). Then *Melody Maker* readers voted him 'Musician of the Year', beating Eric Clapton and Jimmy Page, among others. In the US, *Live in Europe* was his most successful release, yet it was here that Rory's stubbornness in relation to the charts surfaced again. Dónal Gallagher has described how Polydor in the US wanted to release 'Going to My Hometown' as a single. They had got an edit of the song done, but when Rory heard it he apparently hit the roof. Dónal told Dan Muise: 'I recall him [the record company executive] telling Rory, "This is going to be number one!". Rory completely refused. He was quite angry that they had edited it.'

The singles issue was a big bugbear for Gallagher. He said in 1976: 'I could have brought out "Tattoo'd Lady" or "Cradle Rock," not to be hits, but for radio exposure, but I never got the enthusiasm up for it. Then people suggest that you cut three minutes off here, and I'd never do that. LPs, though, that's more my kind of thing. I'd hate to be battling up the charts with John Denver and Helen Reddy. And then if you don't have a hit with your second, everyone thinks you're finished.'[12] He wasn't the only one with this philosophy about singles; he has good company in Bob Dylan, who once recalled how he felt as a young folkie. 'Folk singers, jazz artists and classical musicians made LPs,' he said, therefore they 'forged identities, tipped the scales, gave more of the big picture.'[13]

In 1972 the band had a problem when Wilgar Campbell developed a fear of flying. Rod de'Ath, a Welsh native with Belgian ancestry and a member of a band called Killing Floor, replaced him on several occasions. One of those gigs was Gallagher's famous filmed appearance in the Savoy in Limerick, in May that year. De'Ath later recalled the gig, though perhaps exaggerating a little: 'I got there with about a minute to spare and I didn't know any of Rory's numbers. So I'm in the dressing room changing my trousers and Rory saying, "I'll signal when this number's coming to an end and I'll stamp my foot when this one's starting." We rushed out on stage and I jumped behind this totally strange kit. Then I looked up – straight into a TV camera. They still show it every now and then. I wasn't too bad either!' Another observation would have endeared the drummer to his new boss: 'A lot of drummers get bored playing blues. They think it isn't demanding, and sure, anyone can play it technically well, but not everyone can do it with the right feeling.'[14] When Wilgar Campbell eventually left the band, by mutual agreement, and de'Ath became permanent, it was the start of a downhill slide in Wilgar's fortunes that led to his early death at the age of 43 in 1989, his health declining apparently from a combination of the stress of a marriage break-up and heavy drinking.

There was an accidental witness to that Savoy gig, who later went on to fame as a founding member of the Irish band Moving Hearts. Saxophonist Keith Donald, at that time a member of a showband called the Real McCoy, was passing the Savoy when he just had to stop: 'I heard this fantastic music coming through an open door – an emergency exit. So I saw about half an hour of Rory. And I never forgot it.' A Limerick native, Derry Pennywell, has another recollection of the same gig. He liked to catch rehearsals and soundchecks. On this occasion, de'Ath being delayed, Dónal Gallagher saw Pennywell and, thinking he was a member of the famous Limerick band Granny's Intentions, asked him if he could drum for the soundcheck. 'It was a highlight of my life. I remember going over "Bullfrog Blues" a few times. I couldn't believe I was playing with Gally [the name Limerick city fans gave Rory]. The odd thing is I didn't go to the gig that night; instead I went to see Gary Moore with Skid Row. I have to add that my memory of Rory is one of a quiet and gentle soul.' Pennywell's opportunity meant disappointment for another musician. Len de la Coer was the drummer with the support band, Sleepy Hollow. They had left the venue for something to eat when Gallagher's crew were looking for him to step in for the soundcheck. 'I missed the opportunity to play with God!' he says.

The last member to join that Rory Gallagher Band

line-up was a keyboard player and Belfast native: Lou Martin, born in 1949. He became a stalwart of the band's sound for most of the 1970s. Classically trained, he could handle everything from boogie to Beethoven. Gallagher fans will remember him stooped over the keyboard, his long hair trailing over the keys but seemingly causing no impediment to his proficiency. A *Sounds* reviewer described one of the first gigs with Martin as he played on 'Should Have Learned My Lesson': 'a stunning, tripping solo which brought a mean expression of effort to Rory's face as he pitched his guitar against it.'[15]

In 1972, the guitar hero became the fan himself, when Rory recorded with Muddy Waters on *The London Muddy Waters Sessions*. Gallagher was one of several players from this side of the Atlantic to contribute to the record released by Chess, Steve Winwood, Ric Gretch and Georgie Fame[16] among them. Gallagher felt extremely honoured by Waters. 'The whole thing has stuck in my memory like a video. I can plug it in at any time and replay it in my head. I only wish I could do it again with my experience now because Muddy taught me an awful lot during those sessions and I came out a much better player than I went in.'[17]

Perhaps the greatest measure of Gallagher's fondness for Waters concerns a car, the one in which he drove Muddy back to his London hotel. He said: 'I've kept that car ever since as a sort of shrine because Muddy sat in it. It's an old Ford Executive, a real Hawaii 5-0 car with stars and stripes down the side, and it's sitting at home in front of our house in Cork. It's falling apart at the seams but I refuse to scrap it or anything. I can still see Muddy in the front seat, smoking these cigars with a big plastic tip on them.'[18]

A year later, Gallagher guested on Jerry Lee Lewis's London recordings, playing on three numbers. On RTÉ, he remembered feeling trepidation when it came to doing 'Whole Lotta Shakin''. 'We had to come up with the goods, to impress him.' When the interviewer, B.P. Fallon, compliments Gallagher on the slide solo, the Cork man's modesty is again revealed: 'It stands up fairly well.'[19]

In 1973 Gallagher was prolific in the studio, despite the demands of touring, producing both *Blueprint* and *Tattoo*. The former would be the less regarded of the two works, though its opener, 'Walk on Hot Coals' is among the most popular Gallagher songs, not least among the tribute bands. This studio cut was later eclipsed, though, by the *Irish Tour '74* version. The song is one of love and loss in a gambling setting, where Gallagher's superstitious side again emerges as he resolves, in the last verse, to throw away his 'lucky penny, rabbit's foot and gypsy ring'. 'If I Had a Reason' has a waltz time, which belies the song's serious intent. Like other writers have done, Rory drew from the train tradition in rock 'n' roll on 'Race the Breeze',[20] the band's groove suggesting metal on metal rolling into the night:

> Well, that sounds like the night train,
> blowin' its stack
> Spreading its wings on homeward track

Another song, 'Seventh Son of a Seventh Son', explores a folk belief, and was inspired by the life of the healer Finbar Nolan, born in Dublin in 1952. It was later published in book form after Gallagher's death.[21] One of the extra tracks on the 2000 reissue is a throwback to Rory's early Cork days, with a version of the Roy Head song 'Treat Her Right', from his days with Impact.

The follow-up album that year, *Tattoo*, is among Gallagher's best recording achievements. It opens with the celebration of the burlesque in 'Tattoo'd Lady'. The song has often been referred to as Gallagher's ode to life on the road, but it has more – an invoking of the excitement of the fairground, with a nostalgic tone (for those who, for example, remember letting their scarce pennies disappear down the arcade chute in forlorn hope):

> Tattoo'd Lady, bearded baby, they're my family,
> When I was lonely, something told me where I could always be
> Where I could push the penny, if you got any
> You'll meet me down at the shooting gallery ...

On *Tattoo*, Gallagher ventures into swing for the first time with 'They Don't Make Them Like You Anymore'.

The record was well received: 'Most of the tunes on this album are, again, based on well-entrenched blues forms, but they are now augmented with fillips, hooks, bridges and phrases that transcend De Blooze and make them Rory's personal property. *Tattoo* is Gallagher's closest attempt at a true pop album. It is his brightest and most joyful work, but still contains that streak of meanness, which makes his live sets so powerful.'[22] 'Sleep on a Clothes Line' is a joyous boogie, where Gallagher and Lou Martin swop solos with abandon. 'Who's That Coming' celebrates the power of human attraction, at one point using a religious image:

> Well, those words she's saying
> Could make even the devil start praying
> On his knees down upon the ground.

The *pièce de resistance* is probably 'A Million Miles Away', a meditation on alienation, with its central image of driftwood once observed by Rory off the Cork coast.

Gallagher was not generally one to boast about his work, but he was confident and upbeat when asked about *Tattoo* in December 1973: 'I'm very proud of it; I think it's the most vibrant of the albums. There's a mixture of forms on it, but it's less diverse than *Blueprint*. There's not so much a common lyrical feel going through it, but a rhythmic one. It does slow down here and there, but even the slow ones have a slight … *click* to them, you know?'[23]

Gallagher fans have always discussed what the high point of his recording career was. Some believe it was the Taste period and *On the Boards*. Probably more would opt for the mid 1970s, and the release of *Irish Tour '74*, a double album bristling with all Gallagher's attributes as an entertainer and guitar player. The concert documentary film by Tony Palmer captures the sheer joy of the gigs, but the audio recording is the key. 'Tattoo'd Lady' was a good studio cut, but here it's on fire. One of the record's many 'sublime moments', as *Mojo* magazine referred to them in reviews, comes during Rory's second solo when he and Rod de'Ath sound completely as one as the guitar seems to follow the drummer's roll across his kit. 'A Million Miles Away' takes on a new life, too, in this recording, where he pulls the volume back to near silence before erupting again with an inspired, wailing note, deftly using the guitar's volume control. But the highlight must surely be 'Walk on Hot Coals', where, in an elongated solo, the Strat advances and retreats in volume several times, orchestra-like, before it finishes dramatically with Gallagher's left-hand fingers all cascading notes from the top of the fret board, as the crowd cheer him on. The recording was described by writer Mark Prendergast in 1990 as 'a fifteen-minute revelation – precision picking, harmonic wah-wah, fuzztone – you name it, it's involved here. The more he plays, the more the instrument plays him.'[24]

A weaker song (but only by comparison), 'Back on My Stompin' Ground', driven by a funky slide riff, contains a hint of darkness in the lyrics' metaphor that contradicts the song's otherwise joyous message. Gallagher is celebrating being back in Cork, perhaps, after some professional trials:

> I've been bitten,
> Lord, I've been stung.
> Well I was cornered,

And I was almost hung.
Well, I sure made a getaway,
And I'm almost back on my stompin' ground.

The *Irish Tour* film ends with a sing-song in the Cork Boat Club. Art Lorigan, one of the participants, recalls that the night of the filming was a long, high-spirited one. In his own case, he got into such good form and inebriation that late into the night he went outside and jumped into an empty Garda car and pretended to drive it away. Needless to say, when this was discovered he made a hasty retreat, before being chased and caught by the policemen involved. He recalls Gallagher's reaction to the incident, revealing again the faith element in his persona: According to Rory, Art was 'suffering for all our sins'.

Overall, *Irish Tour '74* is, arguably, Gallagher's showcase, littered with great examples of his artistry. In the *Lexington Post* in 2011, Walter Tunis described what he called a 'blissful little blues moment'. 'The passage centers on a dialogue between guitar and voice that eases into Muddy Waters' "I Wonder Who". It's almost like a séance, an artist communing so keenly with a muse that the guitar voice completes a solo conversation of restless and relentless urgency.'

At the end of the *Irish Tour '74* film, Gallagher gives a summing-up of his musical purpose, of his life: 'It happens that you have two hours a night on a stage. You're lucky enough to have an audience to play for. For me, it's the important hour and a half or two hours of the day.' He made a similar point to Mick Rock in *Rolling Stone* in 1972: 'Some people get all worried about this fantasy and reality thing, the stage only being the fantasy. I don't see it like that. It makes things easier if you treat the stage as reality. Reality is the thing you're best at.'

The road was, after all, what Gallagher lived for.

Chapter 8

THE THERAPY OF TOURING

> *'To me, doing 12 gigs a year is crazy. I couldn't work like that. I'm against musicians getting that lazy if they suddenly become successful. You've got to work at what you play. It's my hobby; it's my hobby and has been since I was a kid. I'm too restless and nervous a person to let the reputation take over. Nothing is a forgone conclusion. I don't like saying, "We'll sell out tonight, no sweat". THAT is death.'*
>
> — RORY GALLAGHER[1]

Touring, being on the road, getting onto a stage as often as possible was an imperative for Rory Gallagher, almost to the point of obsession. By the 1970s, he was not catching sleep lying on equipment in the back of a van, as in the Fontana days, but the road went on and on for him. The band's touring schedule was particularly intense throughout the 1970s. In 1972, there were 130 dates, including Verona, home of the famous Romeo and Juliet balcony, where a passionate fan enthused, aware of the Shakespearian connection: 'This night, Rory starts off with a blistering "Laundromat", boogies on down with an inspired "Tore Down" and doesn't turn loose till the final sliding licks of "Sinnerboy". Truly, a guitarist with any other name would not sound half as sweet as Rory did on this night.'[2]

The peak was 1973, when the band played 160 gigs, beginning that year in Düsseldorf and finishing in the Carlton Cinema in Dublin. The gruelling schedule started with dates in Germany and the Benelux countries, before they headed for the US, with dates in the east, south, Midwest and west. Gallagher took a couple of weeks off the road, but it was spent preparing for the *Tattoo* album. The band rehearsed in his old haunt, Cork Rowing Club, in July before returning to London to record the album in early August. There were two UK gigs that month before another long US tour that took them into October. German dates followed, before a 22-gig UK tour, then another hop over to Netherlands, Paris and Zurich, before finishing with an Irish tour that lasted into 1974.

Melody Maker described the climax of the gig at the Roundhouse in Dagenham, London, in April:

> 'Bullfrog Blues' comes tearing out of the P.A. and the place goes even pottier. I notice that when the solos come in, that's the moment for cathedral-like hush followed by wild approval.

What these guys like is pure physical effort. Bass solos must be mile-a-minute and drummers have to expend enough energy to push a Ford Transit halfway up Ben Nevis.

There's a cleverly written, candid account of Rory Gallagher Band 'road life', penned by Angie Errigo in 1979:

'I'm sorry, you'll have to excuse me,' Rory announces. 'I'm just having a bowl of soup and then I'm going to bed. You can go on drinking all night, but I have a tour to do.' He's doing his boy-next-door stuff, see. The rest of the band greet this with knowing laughs and start telling each other, 'Well, I don't know about you but I have to get some sleep, I have a tour to do.' A bowl of soup, six lamb chops and numerous beers later, Rory is still with us. 'I always feel really hungry after playing,' he says between chews, reaching over to take another chop from Gerry McAvoy's plate and resuming a lengthy discussion of Irish politics. He accepts a chop from me and tells us all again he's going straight to bed.

He's still sticking to that story at 6 a.m. This is after he's finished eating, discovered a piano in the cellar of the restaurant and hauled everyone down for a sing-along taking in most of the band's considerable repertoire of Irish tearjerkers. He's also done a Maurice Chevalier song and dance routine to 'Chattanooga Choo Choo' before being flung out at four and bundled shakily back to the hotel. 'I'm goin' to bed,' he insists, slurring. 'I've 'n 'Merican tour to do.'[3]

Gallagher once summed up what touring meant to him. 'I think music has something to do with playing and people and sweating and dressing rooms and breaking strings. That's music to me.'[4]

'The road', as it's called, could be a hard slog, too. Gigs weren't always triumphant. Gallagher wasn't always the headline act. There could be problems, as in Roanoke, Virginia, in the winter of 1976. Gallagher was supporting the Doobie Brothers, a band then riding high. A local journalist, Guy Sterling, reported that the sound wasn't great; there had been no soundcheck because Gallagher's equipment had arrived late; the audience was somewhat indifferent, Gallagher a little crestfallen, the reporter noted backstage. Sterling was an observant type, noticing some of his subject's key personality traits as the night wore on: 'Gallagher continues. His talk is animated, sometimes contemplative, but rarely personal. He finds great delight in reading a press release issued on him by his record company. There is something in it about the gods making guitarists. Rory is laughing. His team is laughing.' Sterling notes that Gallagher, as he leaves the room, bows to the women and shakes hands with the men, before the report concludes: 'Outside it has begun to rain. For Rory Gallagher, a man from the land of fog and bogs, it is familiar. If nothing else, it has been just another night in another city.'5

Gallagher was canny enough to notice when he was being patronised about his relentless touring. He hit back robustly on one occasion in *Melody Maker* in 1975: 'Journalists have been using the hard-working Rory thing as a backhanded compliment for years. I hate that tag of being "the hardest working guy" in the business because it's an easy cop-out. I'd prefer them to say that they don't like my music, rather than say that. "Hardworking" doesn't mean anything. Our music thrives on touring. It gets slicker. It's that kind of music.'6 It's also quite likely that Gallagher realised, though it was never stated, that he was much more successful as a live performer than a studio artist. It is not a coincidence that his two most successful records were *Live in Europe* and *Irish Tour '74.*

For some, the memory of Gallagher gigs has a transcendent quality. Eamonn Wall, a County Wexford native, now Smurfit-Stone Professor of Irish Studies and Professor of English at the University of Missouri–St Louis, evokes both his Gallagher memories and train romance – Irish style – in 'Blues for Rory':

> From the Slaney Co. Wexford Mississippi Delta
> rode the rails in flannel shirts, warm CIE beer
> in hands, in the smoking carriage by big muddy
> cities Gorey/Chicago, Arklow/St Louis, moving on
> mile by mile marker by great rivers getting closer
> still to hearing the legendary bluesman from Cork
> City play on his battered Strat the blues, and sing
> I could've had religion but my little girl wouldn't

let me pray, that kind of girl hard to come by in
the Slaney Co. Wexford Mississippi Delta though
neither did we pray too much being all prayed out
since Confirmation[7]

Kieran Dempsey and his pals from Ballymun on the
north side of Dublin saved diligently for Rory's gig in
the Carlton Cinema in December 1973 by bringing
empty bottles back to their local pub, The Autobahn.
The night didn't disappoint.

> It was better than the sex we never had. We couldn't
> hear ourselves think. Saturated in teenage sweat –
> and Gallagher's too every time he flicked his hair
> back – it was the best night of our young lives. No
> drink, no drugs, just high on the music and atmos-
> phere with the occasional Major cigarette to calm
> the nerves. When Rod de'Ath threw his drumsticks
> into the crowd in triumph, one of the group caught
> one, took a belt in the stomach in the melee that
> followed, dropped the prized piece of wood, and
> his assailant made off with it.

A key feature of a Gallagher performance was movement.
Showmanship. He liked to run, to duck-walk gleefully, as
he eyed the audience. He had a particular ritual, during
the late 1970s, which climaxed with him dragging the
Strat across the stage by its cable. Though he didn't
continue with these particular theatrics, his ability to
move on stage contrasts with Eric Clapton, who always

stands virtually static. Gallagher took up this subject in 1972: 'You know, after the big blues boom influenced by Mayall, it became a crime to move onstage, but American artists have always been fond of a show and quite honestly, I think that a lot of artists over here just found that they *couldn't* put on a show. But the basic music we play is from the jungle and it makes it so you've got to move on stage.'[8] This is how a *Times* writer, Michael Wale, described a gig in 1971:

> He has an instant communication with his audience, whipped up by his movements on the stage. At one moment he is playing thunderously into the path of the drummer's sticks, then with a peacock-like leap, he turns upon his audience, stalking towards them, guitar slung low, hair hiding his face. A musical mating performance. Then as suddenly as he has turned towards them, he is off again, in quick little bounds, across the stage to join Gerry McAvoy, all the time urging his two fellow musicians to more and more effort.[9]

Gallagher also had a sense of the dramatic potential of contrast; when he had worked the crowd up to a frenzy, the band would leave the stage and Gallagher, alone, would change the dynamic in the hall and cast a spell with an acoustic guitar, before the band re-entered and all hell broke loose.

And what of Rory Gallagher between the tours? He revealed very little about his domestic life, except in the way it related to touring. When Michael Wale interviewed him for *The Times* in 1973, he described him as 'the ultimate anti-hero, he's still living in a bed-sitter in Earls Court. "Yes, I must leave it, but I never seem to have the time to do anything about it!" When you ring him up an uninviting Irish lady answers the phone. You say you want Mr. Gallagher in room 16 and you hear the number echo up the stairs as he is called.'[10] The Irish journalist John Spain got something of a glimpse in 1978, Gallagher briefly describing his lifestyle at his London home at that stage, in the Fulham Road area: 'I don't have any relaxing hobbies – the way Bing had his golf – and, in fact, I usually relax by mending guitars and amps: my bedroom is full of them. There are always a lot of mundane things that need to be done after a tour – clothes to be cleaned and equipment to be repaired. I see some movies and read a bit, but I'm never very far from the music. It's a labour of love for me.'[11] One event paused the touring in June 1975, when Danny Gallagher died in Derry. His sons returned for the wake in Orchard Row, the superstar's presence causing quite a stir on the street. According to Antoin O'Hara, 'Rory bought a lot of crates of Guinness to give his father a send-off.'

In early 1975, there was a celebrated – perhaps over-celebrated – encounter in Rory Gallagher's life, his 'audition' for the Rolling Stones. Mick Taylor had left the band at the end of 1974, so Jagger and Richards invited Gallagher to come to where they were rehearsing in Rotterdam in January. They were working on their album *Black and Blue*, released later that year. Rory jammed with them, waited to hear back, before leaving for Japan where he had a tour commitment. But there's little evidence to suggest that Gallagher actually joining the Stones was on the cards. In 2011, the former Stone, Bill Wyman, said: 'Rory stayed two or three days there and played some nice stuff. We had a good time with him, but I think Mick and Keith felt that he wasn't the kind of character that would have fit. If he'd have been in the Stones, he wouldn't have been singing and that was one of his strong points. He would have just been playing [guitar] solos … and learning to be subservient to two big egos. I don't think it would have worked.'[12] Over the years the subject has been tossed around. Bob Geldof had a colourful view in the documentary *Ghost Blues*:[13] 'He could never have put up with the b**locks of Mick and Keith, never in a thousand years … Up against Mick and Keith, he would have shot himself.' The Wexford musician and writer Larry Kirwan had another view: 'He could have single-handedly revived their creative spark. Imagine Keef trying to keep up with this bluesy dynamo? What a power duo they would have made. Talk about intertwining rhythm and lead lines – they were born for each other.'[14]

Gallagher was later asked the obvious question: could he see himself as a guitarist in another person's band? 'I could, yeah. If somebody needed a guitar player for a tour, and I was free and it was the right situation, I'd do it and it would be good fun. There would be so much less pressure if I just had to stand there and play leads, yeah, it would be good fun. But to do it in the long term, I think not. I like singing too much.'[15] The Rolling Stones story has reappeared in the press over the years and many Gallagher followers might have been surprised that Dónal Gallagher, as late as 2012, did not pour cold water on the idea of his brother becoming effectively a sideman as a 'Stone', seeing it more as an opportunity (perhaps thinking more of Rory guesting with the band): 'At the time, he was outselling the Stones across Europe, so it's not like he needed the gig. But, in retrospect, I wish he had communicated more with them [Jagger and Richards], as it could have worked.'[16]

There is a less talked about, possibly missed opportunity in 1976. Martin Scorsese was filming the farewell concert by the great American 1970s ensemble, The Band, on Thanksgiving Day at the Winterland Ballroom in San Francisco, a recording that became probably the most famous rock film of all time, *The Last Waltz*. According to Gerry McAvoy, Bill Graham, the promoter of the event, asked Rory to join the line-up, as Robbie Robertson was a fan. Gallagher turned it down, despite pleas from his bass player, because he had two shows booked in Portland and Seattle. McAvoy asked the rhetorical question in *Riding Shotgun*: 'What would an appearance in *The Last Waltz* have done for him?' However, Eliott Mazer, who worked later with Rory as producer, said that it was unlikely that Robertson and Scorsese would have added someone at this late stage in the planning. And, of course, Eric Clapton already had the gig.

Rory Gallagher's passion for music extended beyond blues. He had a great interest in folk music and counted among his friends a giant of the English folk revival, Martin Carthy. A distinguished and innovative guitarist, Carthy has brought a unique style to the accompaniment of English traditional songs. Simon and Garfunkel recorded his version of 'Scarborough Fair'. Carthy is arguably the greatest living interpreter of English folk song. His relationship with Gallagher began, Carthy recalls, when Rory came to see him play a gig in Earls Court, sometime in the early 1970s. 'He gave me a telling-off for playing using an open tuning. Peculiarly, I had never done this before, and, though not because of Rory's criticism, since!' Gallagher later became an enthusiast for such tuning. (Dave McHugh believes that Gallagher perhaps still had to discover 'the harmonic possibilities of different tuning'.)

Martin Carthy remembers 'a very, very gifted, very fluent guitar player.' He was touched when Gallagher wrote to him after Carthy's 1987 LP, *Right of Passage*, was released. Carthy appreciated being endorsed for striking out. 'I remember he wrote, "Let me congratulate you. It's a fine piece of work."' Martin Carthy also acknowledges Gallagher's connection with the other pioneering English guitarists: 'I know he had enormous sympathy with all of us, Davy [Graham], Bert [Jansch] and I.' Carthy offers a piece of conjecture: 'If he had started doing Irish material, who knows what might have happened?' Larry Kirwan had a similar thought in his *History of Irish Music*, having heard Gallagher sing 'Dan O'Hara' and 'She Moved Through the Fair' in 1994. 'It's not outside the bounds of possibility that he would have tackled some of the compositions of another Cork blow-in, Seán Ó Riada, and worked his considerable magic on them', he concluded, however speculatively.[17]

Gallagher made another lasting friendship with someone in the folk world about this time. It was Ronnie Drew of the Dubliners. They met by chance in a bar in Berlin, the Dubliner not having a clue who this young man he was talking to was. 'I thought he was one of the young fellas that were going over to Germany to work. So I said, "What are you doing yourself?" He said, "I'm doing a few gigs", and I said, "You're doing gigs, what's your name"? He said "Rory Gallagher". I nearly died because I knew the name. So we got drunk that day, we went on the piss. We had a great day!'[18] Over the years they exchanged books, recordings and poetry and the Dubliners released Gallagher's song, 'Barley and Grape Rag'. In 2005, Drew mentioned Rory expressing interest in records by Margaret Barry, the Cork balladeer, and the sean-nós singer from Carna, County Galway, Seosamh Ó hÉanaí.[19] 'We struck up a nice friendship, without living in each other's pockets,' Ronnie told the *Sunday Independent* in 2005.

In his most successful decade, Gallagher's work was not universally praised, however. A programme called *Messing With the Kids,* made for RTÉ in 1977, took a different angle, attempting to get to grips with the world of pop music and the negative effect it was having, as the programme saw it, on young people. Using footage of a Gallagher gig, the opening script stated, a little quaintly, perhaps:

Many older people who listen to Rory Gallagher perform may not agree with Samuel Johnson that music is the least-repellent form of noise. But for the hundreds of young people who clamour to get to Gallagher concerts, his music whips them into ecstasy. They dance, jive, sing, let their hair down, ape every move and turn he makes. However, his concerts typify all that is hard to fathom in pop. For many parents, pop represents all that is loud, brash and rebellious in their children. In their view, the songs, the singers and the confused world of pop really are ... messing with their kids.[20]

A significant aspect of Rory Gallagher's career in the 1970s was his commitment to his audience in Northern Ireland. His childhood in Derry, his Taste days in Belfast and a general humanity may have all played their part in this. When the IRA's bombing campaign was continuing to cause death and destruction in Belfast in January 1972, Gallagher told *Melody Maker*: 'I see no reason for not playing Belfast. Kids still live here.' It is acknowledged that his concerts in that city, like the punk movement later, were cathartic events, where Catholics and Protestants could gather in a conflict-free arena. Roy Hollingworth reported for *Melody Maker*:

I've never seen anything quite so wonderful, so stirring, so uplifting, so joyous as when Gallagher and the band walked on stage. The whole place erupted, they all stood and they cheered and they yelled, and screamed, and they put their arms up, and they embraced. Then as one unit they put their arms into the air and gave peace signs. Without being silly, or overemotional, it was one of the most memorable moments of my life.[21]

At Macroom in 1978, Gallagher agreed to become the Northern Ireland Guitar Society's Honorary President. The society's founder, Joe Cohen, worked in Crymbles,[22] a music store in Wellington Place in the 1970s, and remembers selling Gallagher a Hohner harmonica microphone, proudly watching it used that same night in the Ulster Hall for 'All Around Man'. Liz Reeves was a teenager in the 1980s when she heard about 'a guitar player from the south' who always came back to play in the darkest times, which Van Morrison didn't. 'That's my man', she decided, and became a devoted fan and one of those behind the project to erect a statue of Gallagher at the Ulster Hall. Clifford Goliger, a taxi driver in the city, still remembers the way the 'whole place used to shake' as people pounded the Ulster Hall's floor for Gallagher to come on. 'He came to play for us all through the Troubles … it was like an escape. And we knew he was from the south, and a Catholic, but he was *our God!*'

Gallagher kept his counsel as far as commenting on the Troubles was concerned. 'Rory would not take sides in the dispute,' Dónal Gallagher told the *Sunday Times* in 2012: 'He insisted we tour there because he believed in the positive power of music. While Tony Palmer filmed the 1974 Irish tour, he tried to push Rory into taking a stance,

but he refused. He was there to bring joy, not politics.'
Rory was questioned at the Ruisrock Festival in Finland in
1975: 'Are you handling the situation of Northern Ireland
in your music?' 'No, I don't write political lyrics' was his
reply. 'I'm an Irishman, I play there a couple of times a year,
play in the north of Ireland.' The interviewer kept pushing
the point, but Gallagher answered firmly – and probably
wisely: 'I have strong emotional feelings about Ireland.
But I don't try to make my songs political platforms. I
don't think that would be any good for anybody.'[23] He
was asked once about Billy Bragg's protest music: 'I like
Billy Bragg as a musician and I even agree with some of
his views, but I would find that a very narrow area to
work in, to be always left of centre and always writing
from a socialist point of view. I might agree with him on
certain things, but I don't have that vocation.'[24]

Yet he had a quite pointed comment about U2 in 1984,
when asked about their political stance:

Actually, they're almost radically apolitical from an
Irish viewpoint. I admire them as a group, musically
and so on. But that 'white flag' thing – that radical
peace sort of thing is troublesome because the whole
Irish issue is just so complex. They're all genuine
about it. They're into the better nature of humanity
and genuinely very nice people. I don't want you
to think I'm being catty and talking about them,
because I admire them greatly as a group. But I tend
to be a bit more gritty about the way things really
are over here.[25]

Yet there is what could be seen as an oblique reference to Northern Ireland by Rory in 'Whole Lot of People', on *Deuce* in 1972:

> A whole lot of people talking, trying to make sense
> Seems everybody's living on a barbed-wire fence
> Whole lotta people too proud to call
> 'Cause it won't get no help at all.

By the late 1970s, Gallagher's music, particularly the energy and commitment of his concert performances, had made him a superstar. But there would be trouble ahead for his career. A sense of the tide turning comes from the words of a fellow musician, Larry Kirwan. In his 2015 book, he quotes his 1998 song, 'Rory'. It begins nostalgically in the triumphant Gallagher years with lines like, 'Volts of lightnin' in your fingers'. Kirwan's book then adds a more sombre reflection. 'Does that song seem bittersweet with a whole dollop of regret, and not a little sorrow wrapped around it? Well, that's how I feel about Rory when I recall the love and energy he injected into each of his shows.' But in the last verse of 'Rory', the elation has gone:

> What the hell happened, head?
> Where did the lightnin' go?

However, Kirwan's song is retrospective. Gallagher in the late 1970s was still riding that crest of a wave.

Chapter 9

A GENTLE GAFFER

'Once the lights go down and the crowd roars,
something magical happens.'

– STATUS QUO'S RICK PARFITT (1948–2016)[1]

When the punters had gone home, and the tour on the move to the next town, what kind of experience was it to work closely with Rory Gallagher? Firstly, it wasn't called the Rory Gallagher Band for nothing. 'Complete control, but always with a smile on his face!' is how Gerry McAvoy described it in *Riding Shotgun*. There was, for example, an imaginary line on the stage that the man with the bass guitar was not allowed to cross, the only exception being permission to step forward to sing on the chorus of 'Follow Me'. Gallagher was the boss. McAvoy had another recollection of the firm side of Gallagher; he was in the back seat of the van with the band's then drummer, Wilgar Campbell, when a *Melody Maker* journalist, who was travelling with them, casually asked Campbell about the band's choice of songs. 'Rory in the front seat quickly turned around and said, "I decide which songs we play".'

There are precedents for this approach. Bruce Springsteen, for example, believes that making the E Street Band *his* band was 'one of the smartest decisions of my young life'. He continued: 'Everyone knew their job, their boundaries, their blessings and limitations. My bandmates weren't always happy with the decisions I made and may have been angered by some of them, but nobody debated my right to make them.'[2]

So what was Gallagher, the bandleader's, *modus operandi*? Spontaneity, but driven by his own instincts, was Gallagher's way onstage. No fuss, just play. In 1983 he described it this way when asked about his stage show:

> You have to play what you feel. If something feels stagey or made up, or too tricky, I don't like it. With a lot of bands the whole thing is too much like a military operation. Obviously, you get the other end of the scale where everything's totally disorganized and being messed up – but I think there's a happy medium where it still feels semi-natural. Just grooving along. We've toured with some of those big, sort of programmed rock bands and I don't envy the people in them. I don't like the heaviness, the pressure about them.[3]

Shiv Cariappa brought up this subject when he talked to Dónal Gallagher in 2003 at the time of the release of *Wheels Within Wheels*:

> I would tell Rory to do ninety-minute sets, some encores, and Rory would get upset even if I suggested a set list. I mean a lot of the shows evolved and remained quite similar a lot of times. Rory would not allow a set list, and he wouldn't even tell the rest of the musicians on stage what the opening number was. He wanted to keep the spontaneity in that situation. He wanted an electric feel and keep everyone on their toes, including himself.[4]

Vivian Campbell, the Belfast-born guitarist who joined Def Leppard in 1992, was a music writer when he interviewed Gallagher in 1991. He had a practitioner's type of question: 'When you improvise from night to night, do you play different solos in the same songs, or do you pretty much work around a structure?' Gallagher replied:

> I'd say about 75 per cent improvised. There'd be 10 per cent that are worth re-doing every night, 'cause they're pretty or they work well. There's always that 5 per cent of things that you have to include every night because they're nice, but they might not always be in the same part of the solo. It depends on how hot you are as a player that night. It's not that you dodge anything, but you're not gonna foul up something. There are certain nights that we all

have where you know that, 'God, these hands will do anything tonight!' And you take yourself right to the edge, the limit. And then other nights where, subconsciously, you know that you're playing OK and think, 'Make a good job of this, be tidy.' But then, even on a bad night, you might play badly for a number or two, but then make up for it in some other. I don't have any formal technique. I've developed quasi-kinds of techniques. I still can play very primitive and brutal, which is just as important to me as being super-clever on the guitar.[5]

Phil McDonnell, who worked as tour manager and engineer with Gallagher during the 1980s, described for Dan Muise's book being at the sound desk: 'Rory would whip me up into a frenzy, same as he could whip up the audience. He just had that way about him where when he started to rock, you started to rock. And you used to say to yourself, "OK, if you want to go there, let's go there!"' In 1984, Gallagher used a religious metaphor to describe the imperative in his performances: 'The Blues is the first commandment. The second commandment is, "let it rock". The third commandment is to have something in between, a mixture, folk, or whatever.'[6] The interviewer then asked him how the previous night's show in London had gone, he said: 'I'm very superstitious about judging my own shows.'

Gerry McAvoy discussed Rory as a musical director, saying he would never give chord sheets for any of the songs, or tell the band that it was in a particular key.

At rehearsals, he'd just start the song and they would work around his chords. 'Rory was a great band leader in that respect because he was always extremely patient with us and would allow us to find our own way within the song, although, obviously, after years of playing together, we could usually pick things up pretty quickly anyway.' McAvoy, in Ballyshannon with Band of Friends in June 2016, recalled this aspect of his boss: 'Rory was able to write to suit the band,' he says. 'It was one of his great features. He recognised a changed dynamic when people left and others joined, and he could exploit that.' Between the drumming styles of Wilgar Campbell and Rod de'Ath, he noticed a change in the writing. 'Then when Ted [McKenna] joined, the writing reflected that big drum sound that he had brought – like "Mississippi Sheiks", or "Shadow Play".'

The sound Gallagher was given in his stage monitors was, of course, crucial to the performance. Joe O'Herlihy, a Cork man who went on to great fame as soundman and later 'audio director' for U2, told Dan Muise: 'Depending on the environment, the condition on the night, what the stage and the venue was like, if you were getting slap back or spill or something like that, he would go off on a rant. But it was always to better the actual stage sound.' Phil McDonnell told Dan Muise how exciting he found the job: 'Rory would just hit one string on his guitar and those guys [the band] – and I did too, just knew what was coming next. Whatever tone he was putting on his guitar, how he was tuning, and whatever guitar he was changing to, you knew what song was coming. So there was never any need for a set list. We were all totally educated in sounds and guitars and tunings and stuff. So it all worked like that.'

Gallagher's relationship with Gerry McAvoy was enduring. No other musician came close to the Belfast man's twenty-year record of service. Many have speculated as to why this was so. Gallagher had this to say when interviewed in the *Cork Examiner* of 26 June 1978, on the occasion of the band's line-up change that year: 'I wanted Gerry McAvoy to stay with the band because we've always had a great understanding for each other when we were on stage. His play inspires me. I don't know why, it's hard to explain. But when you play with someone like Gerry, there's just his electrifying spark on stage here and there. However, he's an excellent bass man.' The Belfast man was once described in a way that people who saw the band will appreciate: 'McAvoy may be the best current proponent of the Phil "look, my feet are on two different continents" Lynott bass-player stance.'[7]

In the twenty years McAvoy was with Gallagher, there were three changes of drummer. Ted McKenna was the man behind the kit between 1978 and 1981, who found playing with Gallagher great, but somewhat taxing too. The Scotsman left the band, he says, 'to stretch himself a bit'. Rory was demanding and would often gesture wildly to drummers to play louder, an artistic foible of his, it seems: 'I only realised this later, but it was because he only had guitar in his monitor. That was what he was used to. He was dyed-in-the-wool in that regard. So he'd come over to me trying to get me to play louder and I'd be trying to say "I'm playing as loud as I always play!"'[8] According to McAvoy's book, Brendan O'Neill, who succeeded McKenna as Gallagher's drummer, found things no less demanding: 'Rory had very specific ideas of where the beat should be – there were only three places: behind the beat, on the beat, or ahead of the beat. With Rory, you always had to be in front of the beat, but try to do it without speeding up.'

Gerry McAvoy mentions another factor that could really account for his own longevity as a Gallagher sideman. He did what he was told. In describing Rod de'Ath having arguments with Rory about what direction the band should go, he admits to having already learnt where his place was: 'In my entire time with Rory I had never questioned his musical judgement; he was the man, Rory Gallagher, and you just didn't do that.' In *Riding Shotgun*, McAvoy raises a thorny issue, suggesting he contributed to the writing of some Gallagher songs, something that Gallagher did not acknowledge. This is a fraught subject in music in general; what constitutes creative input into a song, and where or when is credit due to another person? McAvoy asserted they did collaborate. Referring to the mid 1970s, he wrote: 'There were songs created during this period that I feel I deserved some credit for, but there was no way I was ever going to get it.'

Gallagher had definite ideas about studio recording, never liking, as he saw it, overproduction. He was specific about this for Shiv Cariappa in the *Christian Science Monitor*:

I like Muddy Waters' [records] because they were so rough and echoey, but the right kind of echoes, you know what I mean? Even to this day I don't like some of the mixes that people do. They take the rough edges of some very good pieces of music. A lot of the new equipment is designed to do that in fact, whereas some of the older recording equipment and echo machines – their deficiencies helped make the sound of that time. So when I go to the studio, I always look around for the older bits of equipment and compressors and things like that, you know.

However by 1993, Gallagher's relationship with recording had become more fraught:

I don't want to repeat certain errors of the past by spending an incredible amount of time in the studio abusing my physical and mental health by thinking and rethinking what will work and what won't. An album that takes six months of work to record isn't worth the effort in my opinion. The problem today is the technicians and sound engineers. With the advent of digital, they constantly have the desire to redo this or rework that, by natural reflex.[9]

One person who observed Rory Gallagher at work was Dieter Dierks, a musician, recording engineer and owner of the studio where Gallagher recorded three albums, *Photo-Finish*, *Top Priority* and *Jinx*. The studio is in Stommeln, a small village to the north-west of Cologne, where Dierks was born in 1943. Gallagher and he became friends and, like so many others, he found his client 'a most warm-hearted and friendly person' who liked the studio's equipment and its sound, 'and my mother, who was a really good cook, the family feeling and the peaceful surroundings of the little village'. Dierks gives a rare glimpse of the artist in his free time. 'He was married to his guitar and his music, but we often went to the pub next door, called Anno 1900, and he loved to play darts. He even started a team, 'Kamikaze Dart Team Stommeln'.

While describing Gallagher as 'an outstanding musician, great composer, guitar player', Dierks singles him out as, 'a very special singer'. Regarding the working methods he observed, he has sympathy for the singular Gallagher approach: 'He was the man in charge. He always knew exactly what he wanted. Rory and Alan O'Duffy [a co-producer on *Photo-Finish* and *Top Priority*] were a great team. Alan always knew how to get what Rory wanted.'

Gallagher was a worrier, as he admitted to Vivian Campbell in 1991:

> I've always gotten nervous about everything. The monitors, the band, myself, the heat, the length of the show, what to play, what not to play. I've tried to train myself, to give myself pep talks and say, 'What is this, you've been playing 20-odd years. You know enough tricks now to

get through it. You know how to play. You know
they're good players. You know you've played
this gig before.' All those factors just go out the
window when I'm in the dressing room. I just
get wired up, and it's probably a good thing,
because when you hit the stage it sort of ignites.
I wouldn't mind being a little bit cooler and
calmer, but I'm still as nervous as I was when
I was 18.[10]

Yet many would regard Gallagher's dislike of allowing
others to make recording decisions about his music
as a flaw. He felt he was always right, albeit in his gentle
way. He engaged a producer, other than someone in
a co-producer role, only twice in his post-Taste
days, and one of those became the disaster in San
Francisco in early 1978, when he binned Elliot
Mazer's expensive work. Dieter Dierks has no doubts
on this question! 'I think Rory was an outstanding
artist. He didn't need an additional producer. For
him it worked perfectly.'

Yet music history is littered with artist/producer
collaborations that changed the course of careers: U2
and Daniel Lanois, or Rick Rubin and Johnny Cash,
being just two celebrated examples. Gallagher was
rarely questioned about this. But an Irish journalist,
'Famous Shamus', took the matter more journalistically
in 1973. This is what Gallagher began by saying: 'In days
gone by, I used other producers on my albums. In fact,
the last couple of times I had a producer, but it wasn't

what I needed and I don't think it really worked. A lot
depends on the right mood and the right engineer. It's
not that I'm anti-producer, but sometimes there is so
much aggression that you need to put it down without
discussion.'

The interviewer then cut to the chase: 'But isn't there
a danger that a man can become deaf to his own failings
and weaknesses?' It was a reasonable question, to which
Gallagher replied: 'That was something I gave way to
and that's why I got the producer, because someone else
can say "that was a better take than the last one", or
whatever. But I think if you're a singer who hasn't got
material and who isn't used to singing into a mike in a
studio, then a producer is right. Or if you want to change
everything round, a producer is right.'[11]

Members of Rory's band had to deal with at least one
aspect of their boss's personality not related to music –
his superstitious side. Mark Feltham recalled, for Dan
Muise, Rory on a tour bus spotting one magpie and
getting anxious till he saw another. There were many
occasions, too, when Gallagher would come into his
dressing room and notice the position of Feltham's
boots. If the right boot was on the left or the left boot
on the right, he would, 'go absolutely ape shit! "C'mon
man! Bad luck! Bad luck!" I would have to change them
around.' McAvoy's book confirmed this aspect of their
bandleader. 'You couldn't put a pair of boots on a table in
a dressing room. "No, don't do it! Take them off the table
fast!"' McAvoy added, knowingly: 'His mother is very
superstitious. His mother actually reads cards.' In 1990,

Gallagher confirmed this superstitious side for David Sinclair in Q magazine's July issue:

> I'm trying to cure it. If I throw a shirt on the couch and I should tidy up ... I might look at it and think, No, I'll leave that. Even the position of a piece of paper at home, or where you leave your shoes ... It's actually dangerous to get that psychotic about it, but I am. I'm also into the zodiac, unfortunately. I try to avoid it because that's bad luck. Numbers and stuff. I think it may be an Irish thing. It's a Druidic, pre-Celtic thing that creeps into Irish Christianity. It's something that you have to conquer because it is very unhealthy mentally. It can control your mind.

Gallagher made a noteworthy revelation towards the end of his life. He said he suffered from very sensitive hearing: 'I can hear something moving from the corridor. I can hear a telephone ring in a hotel, two rooms away. Which is ... it sounds very ... big and clever, but it's actually, when you're trying to get a night's sleep, it's not that much fun for you. My hearing is too acute, if you know what I mean.'[12]

Gallagher had an aversion to bad language and profanity. Phil McDonnell told Dan Muise that he only heard his boss use the F-word twice. 'He never liked bad language when there were women about. And he didn't really like it when there weren't women about.' McDonnell told Dan Muise that Gallagher saw the lighter side of this. 'When we all had a good ol' skinful, it used to make him laugh. We used to go, "Oh for fuck's sake!" And he'd go, "Oh, ho ho ho!". It was almost like a mischievous little boy side to him.'

Rory was sometimes referred to as 'Doctor' by his bandmates, both for positive and negative reasons. Mark Feltham elaborated for Muise: 'He was a famous hypochondriac. He used to worry about all sorts of ills. He used to carry balms and things for his skin. And then he'd have oils. He'd be a great one for old wives' remedies! "Rub this on that. That's great for that."'

Yet, the overwhelming picture of Gallagher as a boss is positive. Feltham, who continued to play harmonica in the later Gallagher line-ups, discussed Rory candidly in September 1998 with Shiv Cariappa, who asked if Gallagher could be tough onstage. 'It was very much "keep your eyes on my back, and don't wander farther on stage than me. I am very much the governor," which he was. You had to have a leader out there. But in saying that, you could go to him before a show or after and everything was forgotten if you made a fluff or an error in some way. It was all forgotten after the show. He was never a man to hold grudges. I think he was deeply religious, deeply superstitious, and very humble, extremely humble.'[13]

And Rory Gallagher would not be the first to discover that the music world was tough.

Chapter 10

THE CHRYSALIS YEARS

> 'The minute I feel anywhere near content, I hear
> something on a record or go and see a certain act and
> I think ... ahhh. I feel like I've only been at it for about
> five years. But the older you get, the more you find new
> angles on things, maybe play them a different way, but
> you still want to keep the feeling of a crazy 16-year-old
> when you get down to the rhythm. I'm certainly not
> satisfied or fed up. No way.'
>
> — RORY GALLAGHER, IN 1987[1]

Despite all the triumph, some clouds were
gathering in 1975 as Gallagher completed his
Polydor contract with *Irish Tour '74*, and began
a six-album deal with Chrysalis Records. There was a
sense of opportunity at this time; others were courting
him, but he decided to join the British label created in

1969, its name combining a stage of the butterfly's life with the names of its founders, Chris Wright and Terry Ellis. In *Rolling Stone*, later–to-be-famous Cameron Crowe quoted Ellis on 'landing' Gallagher: 'He knew that Chrysalis wanted to give him the close, personal attention that he never really had before. We wanted to go all-out with him.' Despite the ambition, and commercial efforts, some musical highlights, the five years with the label were, instead, where the ebb in Rory Gallagher's career began.

The Chrysalis contract began on an optimistic note with *Against the Grain*, the cover shot showing the bare wood grain on the Stratocaster, but the phrase was also something of a defiant gesture to the rock world. Gallagher, McAvoy, de'Ath and Martin had become a tight unit, and Dónal Gallagher said, for the reissue of the album in 2012, that the record 'perfectly captures the enthusiasm and emotion of that time'. Many regard it as an album where he came closer to being a more successful studio artist. But *Against the Grain* didn't have anything like the impact of *Irish Tour*.

It was another attempt by Gallagher to crack the studio, with mixed results. One standout was a cover, 'Out on the Western Plain', which featured in practically every Gallagher gig after this release (one theory was that he became superstitious about leaving it out). It's the Lead Belly semi-fantasy story of cowboy life, name checking Jesse James and Buffalo Bill. Talking about the song in 1976, Gallagher remarked to *Circus* that it was unusual for a black American to write a cowboy song, going on to make an interesting musical observation: 'In working out an approach to the tune one night, I started fooling around with a drone tuning, a bagpipe tuning. It produces strange chords – they're neither major nor minor – but every chord comes out waiting for another to fall on top of it.' This is how Mark Prendergast in *Isle of Noises* pictured what the song evoked: 'sounds of cowboys, horses, campfires, firearms flare up in tune with Rory's picking and booming on the bass strings – gliding from one chord to the other – changing key and bringing you with it, his voice the husky colour of a woodman.'

Interestingly, 'At the Bottom' is not a new composition but was performed in the Taste years. It's considered by many to be about the tensions in that band. Rory himself told *Circus*: 'it's supposed to communicate the feeling of walking around on the ocean floor – a bit of a simile, as they say.'[2] Another of the cover songs was Bo Carter's 'All Around Man'. Despite his admiration for the writer, a member of the Mississippi Sheiks, Rory found some of the lyrics 'a little pornographic', he told *Circus* magazine, and changed them. The original had contained couplets like this one: 'Now I ain't no milkman, no milkman's son / I can pull your titties 'til the milkman comes …' Rory's rewrite fairly sanitised the song; gone were the original's 'plumbing', 'milling' and 'milk' references, and he brought a more 'professional' tone:

> I ain't no doctor, I ain't no doctor's son,
> But I'll fill your prescription,
> Till the real doctor comes

Of 'Souped-Up Ford', he had this to say to Richard Gold: 'I had that one in my head for a long while and really wanted to get it out. I don't like songs that are just "he and she and you and me" and all that. I wanted to get right into that sense of movement and machine-power going off into the horizon.'[3]

This is what Simon Frith had to say about *Against the Grain* in *Rolling Stone*: 'Gallagher is obsessed, like all great lovers, but *Against the Grain* will get your hands twitching too, even if you ain't Joe Cocker! If a man can play this good standing still, why should he progress?'[4]

For the first time since Taste, Gallagher allowed someone else to produce the next album, *Calling Card*, which came a year later. It was another musician, Roger Glover, Deep Purple's bass player, who had produced for the Spencer Davis Group and Nazareth. Though some regard it as his best-produced record, Gerry McAvoy described it as 'too clinical and clean, to the point of being a little boring'. He also describes, in *Riding Shotgun*, tensions between the artist and Glover during the recording, with Rory resisting the producer's efforts to make a cleaner sound. Then Gallagher was unhappy at the mixing stage, and the famous American producer Elliot Mazer was called in to remix the songs. As an indication of a control-freak aspect to Gallagher, he rejected the Mazer mixes,[5] though the Neil Young producer was invited to play an even more significant role in a Gallagher recording only a year later. Chrysalis then tried unsuccessfully to get Rory to agree to edit one of the hookier songs, 'Edged in Blue' (it clocks in at five minutes and thirty seconds), for a single release. Dónal told Dan Muise that Chris Wright wanted to cut the guitar intro, edit the solo and they'd 'have a top 10 hit in the U.S.', and retitle the album *Edged in Blue*. 'I proposed that to Rory and he hit the roof!'

Calling Card's title song is a return – the last he made – to the jazz that influenced him so much in the Taste days. In the song, 'the blues comes calling' with its 'calling card'. He talked on RTÉ Radio about how the song came about: 'I had this line, "the blues ain't fussy about where it lands". It's just one of those things that the blues are going to get you in any case. They're not too fussy whether you're rich or poor. It's set in that kind of mood, anyway.'[6] The interview was about songwriting. Gallagher spoke gently, but had a critical comment to make: 'I don't like laid back. I like music that's laid back, but it has to have tension. A lot of people in the same field as myself ... they've watered down ... over the years it has become sleepy music. The most essential ingredient, to my ears, is getting a good, tough rhythmic edge to it.'[7]

The year 1977 brought both triumph and trouble for Rory Gallagher. The triumph came with a much-recalled headline gig at the Macroom Mountain Dew Festival in June (said to be the first open-air rock concert in Ireland, though there had been a one-day event in September 1970 in Dublin at Richmond Park football ground, with Mungo Jerry headlining, supported by a fledgling Thin Lizzy). The Macroom event was held in the grounds of Macroom Castle in the west Cork town, not entirely coincidentally close to where Rory's maternal forebears came from in Cúil Aodha. Gallagher played the festival in both 1977 and 1978. (Peadar Ó Riada has recalled that first cousins of Rory's, from his mother's side, sang at a Mass during the 1978 festival as members of the choir Ó Riada directs, Cór Cúil Aodha.[8])

The facilities were rough and ready by today's festival standards – just a stage in a field and no frills. The festival had begun in 1976, with events like dances, a pig race and cultural talks, but it seems the festival's promoters decided to think bigger for the following year by securing an act that could bring the festival to another level. So Rory Gallagher was invited to the castle grounds. People of a certain age recall that June day with great fondness. The RTÉ broadcaster John Creedon told Roz Crowley for her 2016 book, *Macroom Mountain Dew*: 'It was boys meet girls, add music and stir – you have a great time.' All the logistics and crowd-control issues that visited the organising committee must have seemed worth it when, to an ecstatic crowd, Gallagher – in a straw hat and brown suede jacket – bounded onto the stage at 5.30 that Sunday evening. The gig was recalled in a refreshingly non-aficionado way in Crowley's book. 'My own particular verdict is that it was a deafening success, and if anyone disagreed with me, I can honestly plead that I cannot hear a word he says. I found the music weird and wild and unwillingly found it spellbinding.'[9] Coincidentally, the first band onstage that day was Sunset, from Cork, whose bass player was Rory's old sideman, Eric Kitteringham. John Waters, the writer and columnist, summed up Gallagher devotees' passion with a nostalgic reflection in *Hot Press* in 1992, when he and his pals missed their bus home:

> But ask me was our joy diminished? No chance. And oh, what stories we had to tell of the man in the cowboy hat who strode the boards like a Strat-totin' Butch Cassidy. And boy, was his aim true.

One person in the crowd at the 1977 festival was destined to be its most famous punter: a fifteen-year-old Dublin north-sider of Welsh stock, called David Howell Evans, who later became world famous as the Edge. Bob Geldof, then making waves with the Boomtown Rats, was in the crowd for the 1978 event.

Gallagher has passionate fans. Pat 'Boots' Healy was a seventeen-year-old when his odyssey began at Macroom in 1977. He later felt compelled to sneak in to soundchecks when his hero was playing in Cork, and remembers one particular encounter that impressed him, in the city's Everyman theatre in 1992: 'Rory stopped playing and actually asked *us*, "Does that sound ok?"' The living room of Boots's home in Midleton is like a Gallagher shrine. For him, it's simply a fan's imperative. 'It's part of me. It always came first.' In 1997, he was asked to formally open the Rory Gallagher Bar in the Meeting Place pub in Midleton. Not used to public speaking, he expressed himself using Gallagher album and song titles: '*As the Crow Flies*, Rory, we all know you are not *A Million Miles Away* and even though you left us all your *Calling Card*, the *Blueprint* is there for one massive gig *Out on the Western Plain* ...'

With Macroom over, what could be called a fork in the road came in Gallagher's recording career that autumn. Chrysalis Records had at this stage released two albums, *Against the Grain* and *Calling Card*, both only moderately successful commercially. He was known as a live performer. His albums were mostly well reviewed, but did not sell in the quantities that other acts enjoyed. They only bubbled briefly at the bottom of charts. So there was a plan afoot to try and seriously take on America with the next record. The veteran producer Elliott Mazer, who had been brought in to do remixes on *Calling Card* – work Gallagher had rejected – was the choice. Mazer had worked with Bob Dylan, The Band and Neil Young among others, so he was a proven producer, and had a US Number 1 single with Young's 'Heart of Gold'. Such was the importance of the project that Mazer and Roy Eldridge, managing director at Chrysalis, travelled to Cork in 1977 to meet Gallagher. The plan was for 'an American album', to be recorded in the US, with an American sound, one that would give Gallagher a breakthrough on that continent, something it seems even the modest artist himself desired.

When Dónal Gallagher released the album in 2011, under the title *Notes From San Francisco* (along with a second CD of live recordings made at the same time), Rory followers could speculate and analyse. They would have immediately recognised more produced versions of songs that had appeared on *Photo-Finish* in 1978. The

San Francisco record had a more layered sound than Gallagher's normal 'rugged purity' approach. It was only the second time in his post-Taste career that he had allowed someone else to produce him in the studio.

At this remove it is difficult to see into the past and decide whether or not, if this album had been released, Rory Gallagher would have achieved greater commercial heights on the North American continent. One argument is that, since five of the actual songs, though sounding different in the Mazer versions, appeared later on *Photo-Finish*, this was not a lost opportunity. In other words, maybe it was the songs themselves that were not capable of catapulting him to greater success, that he lacked a 'Springsteen touch'. The other side of the argument is that under Mazer's influence, a more commercial sounding Gallagher emerged from the sessions and that this might have been a hit album, or at least gotten him more airplay. We can only speculate.

Gallagher and the band spent the last few weeks of 1977 living in the Pacific Heights area of the city, and working on the recordings at Mazer's Master's Wheels Studios. A considerable budget was involved. In early 1978 there was a mixing process that eventually produced an album, which then got to the stage of a test pressing. Then everything changed, much to Dónal Gallagher's horror, as he described on the sleeve notes of the 2011 release:

> As both our tensions and voices rose, Rory made his point and stance clear: 'This is what I think of the sessions', as he released his fingers' grip on

the disc, allowing it to descend to the trash bin.
'I'm going to re-record the whole album and with
different people', Rory concluded. In horror and
shock I exclaimed, 'I feel like breaking every bone
in your ...' and left his room to head for Chrysalis's
office to try and blag my way out of the mess – I
now had stage-fright office style!

Why Gallagher had changed his mind after all the work
is a matter of speculation. Gerry McAvoy still believes
that a Sex Pistols gig they attended in San Francisco
during their stay was a significant factor.[10] Rory was
apparently very impressed with the Londoners and
their direct approach when they played the Winterland
on 14 January 1978, and saw the success that the raw
guitar energy of punk was having (significantly, too, its
minimalist approach to production), and so decided to
change his own course. Joe O'Herlihy echoed this view,
describing the binning of the album as 'a complete bolt
from the blue' in Marcus Connaughton's book.

Was the album the 'one that got away'? We'll never
know. Mazer himself concluded: 'I don't think any of
those tunes would have been a hit. They would have
gotten him a lot of radio play.'[11] The original album, by
agreement between Rory and Mazer, had opened with
'Overnight Bag', perhaps indicating some belief in its
hit potential. An examination of the song is useful in
assessing the fidelity of Gallagher to what could be
called a guitar ideal: the chorus is very strong, but
it doesn't come till two minutes into the song. There

are two guitar solos, where, thinking commercially, an edit (for a single release) might have dropped one and cut to the chorus after the first verse. This is purely speculative, of course, because, as Chrysalis had already discovered with *Calling Card*, editing Rory Gallagher's work was not an option.

There are four songs on *Notes From San Francisco* that were never featured again during Gallagher's lifetime: 'Persuasion', 'Rue the Day', 'B Girl' and, arguably the gem among them, 'Wheels Within Wheels', where Rory is almost in pop-ballad mode. However, as for the album itself, was the Elliot Mazer approach really Rory Gallagher? *Shadowplays'* writer, Milo, concluded in a 2011 article: 'He was not willing to change his sound to accommodate what others felt he should do. In some ways that makes him the ultimate guitar hero.' And as for Elliot Mazer, despite their chequered relationship, 33 years later he was glowing about his client on the sleeve notes for *Notes From San Francisco*: 'Rory is an amazing singer, songwriter, guitarist and performer. I speak of him in the present tense because his spirit lives on through his music.'

There's a curious footnote to the San Francisco debacle, and recounted in the *Ghost Blues* documentary.[12] On the day that Dónal Gallagher travelled to LA to inform the record company that his brother had effectively scrapped the album, Rory, still in San Francisco, and returning from the cinema, caught his thumb in a taxi door and had to have hospital treatment. He again reveals his superstitious side by connecting the incident with his rejection of the album; he is heard saying in the documentary, 'It was an omen from the ghost of Django Reinhardt[13]... to appreciate what you've got.' The cover of *Notes* is perhaps an evocative reminder to Gallagher followers of what might have been; San Francisco Bay at sundown, all golden, suggesting a lost world, a utopia of musical fulfilment. But, for Gallagher, between his rejection of the album and then the hand injury, it was not an idyllic sojourn.

After his return to London and recovery from injury, Gallagher set about making an album from some of the remnants of the San Francisco recordings. Firstly, there were changes made. Rod de'Ath was no longer the drummer. Lou Martin and his keyboards were also dispensed with. Gerry McAvoy remained the constant. In the spring of 1978, Gallagher auditioned several drummers, before choosing the former Alex Harvey Band member and Glasgow native, Ted McKenna. Gallagher had now reverted to the power trio idea. One of their first gigs was that year's Macroom Festival. McKenna was still learning the repertoire. A German TV channel, Sender Freies Berlin (SFB), sent a crew to make a documentary about the event. In it there is a rehearsal sequence where Rory is explaining the groove he wants his new drummer to get on 'Brute Force and Ignorance', which appeared on the album *Photo-Finish* later that year.

Gallagher and the band spent July and August in Dieter Dierk's studio near Cologne working on the album. Five of the songs from the San Francisco recording ended up on the new record, called *Photo-Finish* because of the deadline pressure involved. Three new songs were added, including 'Shadow Play'. That song became a Gallagher 'hit', though he would not have liked that word. It has hard-rock majesty about it and is probably the most successful example of the turn that Gallagher's music took at this stage. But the song also has great lyrical subtlety. And despite the fact that Gallagher had rejected the earlier album apparently because of its highly produced sound, this one is not exactly raw punk either, with plenty of overdubs.

Overall, the relative light and shade of *Calling Card* was gone, and both *Photo-Finish* and its successor, *Top Priority*, are harder musically, less diverse, though they contain several songs that became Gallagher live favourites; as well as 'Shadow Play', there are 'Shin Kicker', 'Follow Me' and 'Philby'. *Melody Maker* had this to say about *Top Priority*: 'The album kicks off with a winner in 'Follow Me' but, alas, then gradually slides downhill over the ensuing eight compositions.' The review concluded a little ominously – with a mixed compliment: 'The songs themselves, however, never really match the magic of the guitar playing.' Gallagher himself had no doubts about the record when Dave Fanning interviewed him after its release. 'It's a record I can play and not wince at it.' Fanning's follow-up question was gentle, but firm: 'It didn't have an acoustic track – why's that?' Gallagher replied that, firstly, he had no acoustic song ready. 'Second of all,' he said, 'I wanted to keep it electric, to keep it sort of hard and harsh.'[14]

Chrysalis clearly still had an ambition to 'crack' America with these releases, but it was not to be. How much their artist did, and how much he was prepared to compromise, is another matter. Yet he called his last studio album with that label *Top Priority*, apparently to remind them of a promise to give the record's promotion just that.

A more controversial view of this late 1970s phase of Gallagher's career comes from Dave McHugh, a Dublin guitarist who has performed Gallagher material for over twenty years and is a keen observer of Gallagher's career. 'This celebrated period is his most barren, musically,' is his blunt assessment. He views songs like 'Follow Me' and 'Shadow Play' as Gallagher at his least subtle, musically, though lyrically they tell a different story. These compositions are, without doubt, much more straight-ahead rock than blues. They are also among Gallagher's most popular songs, but McHugh's dissenting voice is a determined one: 'The tempos were the same, the songs lending themselves to a commercial air in terms of production and duration, and the blues was largely absent. It was an unrecognisable trio to Taste.' McHugh believes that Gallagher's late 1970s material was written around the drumming style of Ted McKenna. There was definitely a contrast between his style and Rod de'Ath's. In 1980, when Dave Fanning asked about the difference, Gallagher was reluctant to compare the two men's styles, but offered this perspective: 'Rod was a busier drummer. I hate comparing them ... but Ted has a lot of power and drive, though he can be flamboyant when necessary. He can be

A photo believed to be of Danny Gallagher.

A picture of Rory taken by Oliver Tobin on a camera he had bought in a pawn-shop in London. The bubble car was parked across the road from the band's digs. 'I asked Rory to pose for me,' he said in his book, describing it as a picture of a 'solitary man on his way to fame'. (*Courtesy of Frances Tobin and Choice Publishing*)

FORMERLY
FONTANA
SHOWBAND
CORK

A flyer for Impact. (L–R): Oliver Tobin, bass; Eamonn O'Sullivan, drums; Bernie Tobin, sax; John Lehane, sax; Declan O'Keeffe, rhythm guitar; in front, Rory Gallagher, lead guitar. It has been assumed that Rory was making a statement by not wearing a suit like the other members, but according to Declan O'Keeffe, his suit was not ready in time for the picture. (*Courtesy of Declan O'Keeffe*)

These pictures were taken either the winter of 1963 or 1964. In the first shot, the person in the middle is John Lehane of the Fontana. (*Courtesy of Gill Bond*)

A playful band. This shot of the Fontana was taken on their way to play at Dingle Regatta in August 1963. Clockwise from top right: Rory (with short hair), Bernie Tobin, Declan O'Keeffe, Eamonn O'Sullivan, John Lehane and Oliver Tobin. (*Courtesy of Declan O'Keeffe*)

Impact on Pickin' the Pops, Teilifís Éireann, 22 April 1965. (*Courtesy of Declan O'Keeffe*)

Rory, with Oliver Tobin, does some weeding in the garden of the guesthouse in Amhurst Park, Stamford Hill, where the Fontana stayed on several occasions when they were in London. The photo was taken by Oliver's brother Bernie. (*Courtesy of Frances Tobin and Choice Publishing*)

Rory and friends in the early Taste days. (*Courtesy of the Kitteringham family*)

Rory Gallaghe She Isn't Worth it. KEY F

She isn't worth it you know she's not
That kind of girl is better off forgot
She didn't treat you good anyway
Please believe in what I say

The opening lines of what may be Rory Gallagher's first song, 'She Isn't Worth It', handwritten by him. (*Courtesy of Declan O'Keeffe*)

Rory's drawing of Bob Dylan that he gave to Trish Kitteringham. The badge refers to the famous Cork actor Joe Lynch. (*Courtesy of Tara Hynes*)

Roy Esmonde's portrait of Taste in 1970: McCracken (top), Gallagher and Wilson. (*Courtesy of Roy Esmonde*)

Rory photographed in London in 1970.
(*Courtesy of Roy Esmonde*)

'Two and a half hours would seem like two and a half minutes,' said John Wilson. Taste at the Isle of Wight. (© *Charles Everest, courtesy Cameron Life Photo Library*)

Scene from a 1974 tour: Gerry McAvoy on the far left, Dónal Gallagher on the far right. Note Dónal's ZZ Top sticker; the Texan band at this stage was a blues outfit, their chart-topping career coming much later with Eliminator. (*Courtesy of Frans Verpoorten*)

Gallagher pictured with his famous Stratocaster in 1974. (*Courtesy of Frans Verpoorten*)

Rory and his band in the Ulster Hall, 4 January 1975. (*Courtesy of Joe Cohen*)

Gallagher on St Patrick's Hill, Cork, in 1976. (*Courtesy of Irish Examiner Archive*)

Rory at the Winterland Ballroom, San Francisco, in November 1975. (*Courtesy of Ben Upham, www.magicalmomentphotos.com*)

Liam Quigley, a well-known Irish rock photographer, took this famous photo of Rory with young fans in 1976. They were (L–R): Aidan O'Shea, Nicky O'Connell, Philip Long and Ger Coughlan. (*Courtesy of Liam Quigley Photography*)

Rory Gallagher performing at the Free Trade Hall, Manchester, January 1977. (*Courtesy of Steve Smith, with thanks to the Rory Gallagher Music Library, Cork*)

The Rory Gallagher Band in New York in 1979. (L–R): Rory, Gerry McAvoy and Ted McKenna. (*Courtesy of Patrick Brocklebank*)

'Going to My Hometown' in the Apollo Theatre, Manchester, in April 1978.
(*Courtesy of Steve Smith, with thanks to the Rory Gallagher Music Library, Cork*)

Gallagher drags his Stratocaster by its cable at Montreux Jazz Festival, Switzerland, in July 1979 in a ritual he performed several times in the late 1970s.

Rory Gallagher and Gerry McAvoy in Philadelphia on 29 September 1982. (*Courtesy of Jon Hahn*)

Gallagher at the Ripley Hall, Philadelphia, September 1982. (*Courtesy of Jon Hahn*)

Rory playing a Gibson guitar in Dinkelsbühl, Germany, in July 1986. (*Courtesy of Wolfgang Gürster*)

Rory Gallagher at Circus Krone in Munich in November 1987. (*Courtesy of Wolfgang Gürster*)

Rory under strain at the Temple Bar Blues Festival, 15 August 1992. (*Courtesy of Kyran O'Brien*)

Towards the end: Rory in Munich, December 1994. (*Courtesy of Wolfgang Gürster*)

The Rory Gallagher monument at the Diamond, Ballyshannon, was sculpted by a Scottish artist, David Annand, and was unveiled in 2010.

rock steady too, which in a three piece is really important. A drummer has to hold the whole thing down like a magnet.'[15] That relationship between an artist and the person who controls the percussive elements of performance is an alluring one. In his memoir *Broken Music*, Sting gives a sense of what makes musical chemistry between musicians in recalling his excitement when he first played with the man who became the Police's drummer, Stewart Copeland. He describes 'a rapport and a tension between the amphetamine pulse of his kick drum and the shifting, rolling ground of the bass. It is like two dancers finding a sudden and unexpected harmony in the glide of their steps, or the sexual rhythms of natural lovers, or the synchronised strokes of a rowing team in the flow of a fast river.'[16]

When Gallagher did an interview for a British magazine, *Beat Instrumental*, at the time of *Photo-Finish*, the interview was ostensibly about equipment, but Adam Sweeting was provocative as he questioned his subject on a more career-defining topic:

> Would he agree that a lot of his tunes are custom built for the purposes of guitar wizardry? Perhaps this wasn't tactful. 'No, never [Gallagher replied]. It's a constant problem, people sort of think that I write songs as guitar vehicles, which I don't. Some songs I think could be done by other people with other, you know ...' (I think Rory meant that some of his songs could successfully be given a different treatment to his own by other artists. Sounds feasible).[17]

Another writer, Peter Archer, seemed aware of this artistic dilemma for Gallagher in the late 1970s. 'It's Rory Gallagher's misfortune to be caught in a stifling triangle of possibilities. His live audience demand sonic demolition, but his musical knowledge points to a devoted expedition through evergreen forests. His solution is to pull off at 45 degrees and catapult his urban and country blues into loud acceptability.'[18]

Dónal Gallagher made a revealing comment in 2000: 'The record company, Chrysalis, saw how the new wave of British Heavy Metal was spreading at that time. They tried to push Rory in that direction, and to make a real hard rock musician out of him. I think Rory tried the best he could, but his heart was much more in the traditional music styles such as folk, blues and country.'[19]

This view of Gallagher's 'musical soul' is borne out by his frequent reference to country blues and also the influence Davy Graham and Bert Jansch had on him, but also by an interview he gave to *Hot Press* in June 1978, where he described himself to Niall Stokes, tellingly perhaps, as a 'folk-type person in a rock world':

> Maybe I'm just too cynical about the whole system. Maybe with the new album I'll have a bash and see what happens. You can get so hung up on ethics and idealism to the point where it outweighs the whole issue anyway. I don't set out to be a pill about the whole music business. I just try to do my own thing – the old cliché – and it turns out like I'm at odds with a lot of what goes on. I don't have any

crucifixion complex about it. I have a big following. I can do what I want on the albums. I can play what I want on the shows … it could be that I'm a folk-type person in a rock world. The other side of it is too time-consuming.'

One of the songs from *Top Priority*, 'Last of the Independents', is a fitting bookend to Rory Gallagher's 1970s. Again, crime fiction was the backdrop for something more personal:

> I'm the Last of the Independents
> Well, I play by my own rules
> Yes, I'm the Last of the Independents
> The Syndicate, well, it don't approve
> Well, I'm the Last of the Independents
> Well, I got to keep on the move …'

Gallagher has admitted a personal dimension to the lyric, though the song idea came from *Charlie Varrick*, a film starring Walter Matthau. Further on in the interview with Mark Stevens, he returned to that 'independent' theme, as he admitted an ambition about America, one that in the end he would not realise:

> I'd love to be as big as Springsteen or Seeger [Bob Seeger, a huge act at the time] by all means. My long-term ambition is to have a top-ten album in America, and to get that you have to be ambitious. But if the ambition overrides the fun of it, you're

in trouble. Some people see me as the last crusader of the blues or some kind of independent because I do a certain amount of things my own way. I don't mind being an independent, but I don't want to be the last of anything.[20]

But in relation to a big commercial breakthrough in the United States for his music, the chance had probably come and gone. And the challenges were not going away. His career was about to plateau – and his health was about to deteriorate. He was still only in his early 30s.

Chapter 11

THE 1980S: UNCERTAINTY AND RESURGENCE

> 'I can't go away and vanish like some people want. In the '80s, I felt adrift because I was doing something that wasn't part of the new wave or punk thing. It wasn't MTV video material. I was developing my music, but I didn't fit in the music press or in a social way.'
>
> — RORY GALLAGHER[1]

In 1970, the world had been Gallagher's oyster. By the early 1980s, he was, to some extent, a lone figure holding out against the march of pop glamour, the ever-present synthesiser and the decline of guitar rock. A decade earlier, his work with Taste had been bold and innovative and a challenge to the mighty Hendrix and Clapton. But the rock music world had now moved on. Guitar bands, and blues-inspired music, were in decline. There was punk, of course, in the late 1970s, which Gallagher appeared to embrace, mainly for its back-to-basics approach. Dave Fanning asked in their March 1980 encounter, might he have survived the onslaught of bands like the Sex Pistols better than others of his vintage. 'I always like to stay somewhere near the ground and play for the fun of it. This business of living in a mansion and only doing one gig ... you'd get bored. I just love playing ... I love the energy ... I like rock to be aggressive. I don't like when it gets too ... complacent.'

It was not just changing fashion that was challenging him. A warning sign may have been this critical *NME* review: 'his solos are numbingly predictable because the end of a verse usually amounts to a trigger for guitar to see red and leap into high register where the stage front army are already floating in anticipation. There's a lack of surprise that levels out his playing like a steamroller and this, by current standards, represents a narrow view that no amount of pumping-up can salvage. That it comes from the guitar of Gallagher is doubly condemning simply because his resources are so enviable.'[2] It was the great artistic dilemma – how was he going to move on? Where could he bring blues music? He wasn't going to start performing wearing a suit as Eric Clapton did, so where to for his career?

Gallagher output in the 1980s began with a live album, *Stagestruck*, perhaps the least delicate recording of his career. There was little of the light and shade of *Live in Europe* and *Irish Tour '74*. One review said

Gallagher was 'pumping out blues-rockers with requisite aggression, yet none of the charm and subtlety that made his previous concert recordings so essential'. It went on, in what sounds like a critique of this whole period of Gallagher's career: 'Where both previous live discs added a few acoustic tunes as well as digging into deep blues to vary the sound and show Gallagher's versatility, this one stays firmly rooted in straightforward sluggish rock, with precious little roll.'[3]

Reflecting on the album with Shiv Cariappa in 1991, Gallagher said: 'I would've liked to have some more different – different shades in it, you know.'[4] In places, the recording raises the question of where hard rock ends and heavy metal begins. Rory looked like he might be heading down a hard-rock road, which Gerry McAvoy described in *Riding Shotgun* as 'the mood in the camp'. It was certainly a phase of the Rory Gallagher Band's career: 'Ted was a big, loud rock drummer who played the songs in a full-on rock style, which suited Rory at the time. This had a knock-on effect on the audience, as denim jackets covered in badges – Status Quo, Uriah Heap, Motorhead, Black Sabbath – began to appear more and more, and we reacted accordingly.' Doug Collette reviewed with measured enthusiasm: 'Opening with a frenzied rendition of "Shin Kicker", Gallagher and his stalwart rhythm section of bassist Gerry McAvoy and drummer Ted McKenna play with such abandon, it sounds as if they've been deprived of taking the stage in front of an audience for months.'[5] Niall Stokes was more diplomatic in *Hot Press*: 'This is an album of gut Rock 'n' Roll, and Gallagher underlines definitively that on this territory he can mix it with the bare knuckle boys.'

The hard-rock issue was a very tender spot with him, Gallagher said in 1984.

> I'm terrified of becoming a heavy metal act. I don't ever want to be that. By the same token, I don't mind HM fans coming to our shows because I'd rather listen to metal than disco or pop. At least there's some connection with the organic nut case element of rock 'n' roll. I suppose that between Hendrix, Cream, Mountain, Vanilla Fudge and the Yardbirds – they sort of set rock on the road to heavy metal, but I thinks it's nice if it stops somewhere around ultra hard rock. It wasn't leather and chains, all that sort of uniform of heavy metal, which all sounds the same to me. I still regard myself as a blues player – rock 'n' roll cum R&B-ish. It just so happens that – even going back to Taste – we've always rocked hard on the rock numbers. I'd rather be known as an R&B player, but if you play with a lot of drive and grit, it's very hard not to attract some heavy metal fans. I'm sure that Eddie Cochran or Chuck Berry wouldn't have kicked them out of the hall because they liked metal.[6]

Gallagher returned to the studio in 1981 and the following year the album with the somewhat gloomy title *Jinx* was released. It was his last before the uncharacteristic (for him, at least) fallow period of five years.

There was a line-up change for the recording when Brendan O'Neill[7] from Belfast joined on drums after Ted McKenna's departure. On *Jinx*, Gallagher could be described as treading water musically, rather than striking out in any new direction.

It was Gallagher's last recording for the Chrysalis label, released by that company in the UK but by Mercury in the US, as the Chrysalis operation had ended there. The album could be described as a halfway house between his blues-driven instincts and the harder turn he had taken in the late 1970s. 'The Devil Made Me Do It' is catchy, and one of the few Gallagher songs that come in under three minutes. The raucous 'Big Guns' could have been a great crowd pleaser – but in a different era. A ballad comes in the form of 'Easy Come, Easy Go'. He paid homage to another bluesman with a cover, 'Ride On, Red, Ride On', a song about 'escaping' from the American south, in this case by the singer and writer of the song, Iverson Minter, known as Louisiana Red. Albinos are referred to as 'reds' in the southern states. He was born in Alabama in 1934, lost his mother through pneumonia when he was an infant, and the Ku Klux Klan lynched his father when he was five years of age.

Paul Strange in *Melody Maker* called the album a Gallagher classic, and had this to say about the song 'Signals': 'A compassionate, bravely argued theory about life's misfortunes and lost love.' The writer was flippant, however: 'Whaddya mean, you thought he was dead? And stop sniggering at the back there! Listen. *Jinx* is one of the finest examples of a man rising from the grave, and nearly 2,000 years ago that made you a saviour.'

But *Jinx* had a generally muted critical reception. Following its release, Gallagher's five 'lost years' began. After the Chrysalis label dropped him, no other record company came on board and Gallagher eventually started his own label, Capo Records, in 1985. It was another fork in the road for his career.

A gap of five winters between recordings was unheard of for him, someone who had twice released two albums in the same year. Was this a creative block? Had a serious doubt set in? Or was there an undisclosed personal issue? Gerry McAvoy puts it down to the decade that it was: 'After *Jinx* it was a strange period. It was the Eighties. This was the fourth line-up of the band. Electronic music and disco ruled the airwaves. I think Rory just took a step back, and instead of competing he waited and bided his time.' Dónal Gallagher's sleeve notes went as far as to suggest that the title *Jinx* hinted that Rory 'had become quite frustrated at the way life was unfolding for him at this time'.

Bruce Springsteen wrote about this challenge of longevity, and the failure of so many rock artists to outlive what he calls 'their expiration date'. He describes a rock world of addictive personalities, 'fired by a compulsion, narcissism, license, passion and inbred entitlement, all slammed over a world of fear, hunger and insecurity.' This 'Molotov Cocktail of confusion', as he calls it, 'can leave you unable to make, or resistant to making, the leap of consciousness that a life in the field demands'.[8] One of Gallagher's crime-novelist heroes, Dashiell Hammett, suffered a writer's block of 27 years. In Hammett's case the question has been asked: 'did he want to write a different kind of book from his characteristic brand of crime, but was unable to do so?'[9] The parallel with Gallagher's life are the discarded recordings of the mid 1980s, where he was never satisfied, despite countless hours in studios. In discussing his brother's death, Dónal Gallagher said in 1998: 'He had been under strain during his time off the road in London, trying to create new music. It had become counter-productive.'[10] Perhaps Gallagher was someone who lived so much for his music that deep down he was not prepared to accept that his more creative days had passed. He wanted to keep striving. He was not going to be content with past glories celebrated in 'greatest hits' tours. There are parallels: Bob Dylan has described experiencing a creative crisis. In 1987, his songs had 'become strangers' to him. 'I didn't have the skill to touch their raw nerves, couldn't penetrate the surfaces.'[11] He says he 'couldn't wait to retire and fold the tent'. Yet, of course, he is still recording and performing over 30 years later.

In March 1988, Bill Graham of *Hot Press* interrogated Gallagher about this 'career break'. Graham used the words 'mysterious' and 'careful' when describing his subject's explanation of these years. 'Maybe people thought I was sheep-farming', he told the writer, ruefully. After Chrysalis dropped him, there were talks with different companies, but discussions broke down on several occasions, Gallagher said, 'because a lot of record company people would be suspicious of me for not being too commercial or being too obstinate'. He then added, revealingly: 'So a lot of deals fell down, which caused a lot of tension for me, in myself.' In the early 1980s Gallagher was to some extent suffering the same fate, in terms of Irish rock, as Thin Lizzy. Hard rock was out of favour. U2 were having hits with a different music; songs like 'Gloria', 'Sunday Bloody Sunday' and 'Pride', were starting to fill stadiums worldwide. Graeme Thompson reflected on Lizzy's decline and U2's rise in *Cowboy Song*: 'They started having hits, as Thin Lizzy stopped. Fervour was in; ragged intemperance was out.' But as a measure of the status he still had in Ireland, temporarily at least, Gallagher was the headline act at *Hot Press*'s fifth birthday gig at Punchestown Racecourse in the summer of 1982. He was supported by U2 (though they were advertised as Bono, Edge and friends), before their meteoric rise would have made such a billing impossible even a year later. That day, Gallagher joined forces with Phil Lynott and Paul Brady to perform a Brady song, 'Night Hunting Time'.

The year 1983 was the quietest in Gallagher's touring career, with little more than a dozen gigs, five of them in Ireland. He and Van Morrison had top billing at what was the last of the six Lisdoonvarna Festivals in County Clare in July. That year's event was marred by the deaths by drowning of eight young men on a nearby beach at Doolin, and the running-amok by Hell's Angels, who had been, inexplicably to those attending, hired as security during the weekend. But the festival's place in cultural history was later assured by Christy Moore's surreal, acerbic take on Ireland in the 1980s in his song 'Lisdoonvarna'.

In 1985 there was an attempt to break into new markets. The Rory Gallagher Band played a series of dates in January in what was then Yugoslavia, playing Ljubljana, Sarajevo, Novi Sad and Zagreb, followed by gigs in Hungary, in Pécs, Budapest and Miskolc, finishing on 24 January in Debrecen. (They had played three gigs in Poland in September 1976). It has been said over the years that Gallagher had a big following in Communist-era Eastern Europe. However, these touring forays into the east were never repeated. In May, they were back in the familiar US for a long tour. Gallagher was interviewed for television while in Houston, Texas. He was more candid than usual and was critical of artists who were more willing, more, as he put it, 'light-footed' about changing their style. This wasn't for him; to be R&B one minute, and then a New Romantic: 'I work from day to day, from week to week, as opposed to having the album, the video, the tour, the ... stew! I don't like big projects.' But he added, ruefully: 'that's not the Dale Carnegie way of living. I'm happy as long as I can proceed. I play with my heart and soul, and respect the roots of the music.'

Self-Aid, the Irish follow-up to Live Aid, was held in Dublin on 17 May 1986. U2 were the headliners. But Gallagher appeared, as did Van Morrison, making a case for veteran rockers. Gallagher bounded onto the stage to open with 'Follow Me', then successfully risked the slow blues 'I Wonder Who' with the hyped-up, mainly young audience, before 'Messin' With the Kid' and 'Shadow Play'. It was an energetic performance, but cracks were now showing; tuning and vocal pitching were an issue, and he stumbled on the words in the first verse of 'Shadow Play'.

Andy Kershaw has recalled this part of Gallagher's career, and in the process has complimented the Gallagher *modus operandi*. In the early 1980s, Kershaw was Entertainment Secretary of Leeds University Union. Other bands, he says, would insist on all manner of pampering, demanding 'a spread to be laid out worthy of a state occasion'. Not only the type of wine could be specified, but also the temperature, he says in his autobiography, *No Off Switch*. But the Gallagher dressing-room requirements, in contrast, were a crate of Guinness and a big plate of cheese sandwiches. 'After enjoying a couple of these, and leaving the rest for later, Rory would pick up his Fender and amble, almost shyly, to the stage and, for the next hour and a half, play his arse off.'[12] As proof of this attitude, Gallagher said in 1983: 'I have no time for that sort of messing. Although some bands have the most ridiculous riders to their contracts ... too Sodom and Gomorrah altogether.'[13] Keith Donald remembers an example of the Gallagher brothers' generosity. Moving Hearts were supporting Rory in Paris in May 1983. The tour company promoting the Hearts had gone bankrupt and the band were left high and dry. When Donald met Rory and Dónal to 'settle up', Dónal said he'd heard about the band's misfortune, so they'd made a small adjustment to the fee. In fact, the envelope contained exactly double the agreed fee. 'In my experience, that's unprecedented,' he says.

Gallagher's five-year recording hiatus ended when *Defender* was released in the summer of 1987 – with less acclaim than it might have got, the roots-based music that had propelled his earlier career being less in favour. Some Gallagher followers maybe expected something stronger after the long wait; others would applaud his more roots turn. *Defender* is not Gallagher pushing any boundaries, yet the album is full of what can be termed Gallagher musical integrity. There is, however, both a unifying theme and a worrying feature: nearly every song on the record is concerned with the area of fictional crime or political corruption. That's not to say some of the songs aren't strong: 'Continental Op', a tribute to Dashiell Hammett, became a standard in his set – and those of tribute bands that arrived after his death. As for the album's title, it's hard to avoid the conclusion that he's 'defending' a certain musical ethic, defending the blues against the ravages of pop, 'defending the faith' – his faith. The title is also a reference to the *Chicago Defender* newspaper, a black America oriented publication, which was often sold by blues men to earn money, as many waited to get recording work. Dermot Stokes lauded Gallagher's earthiness in *Hot Press*: 'People need to feel they can touch and be touched, reach and be reached. *Defender* finds Gallagher right in tune with those sentiments. It is his most primal album in a decade and a half, based on his love for and faith in the blues, his encyclopaedic knowledge of elemental American music and his own direct and earthy sensibility.'

Gallagher told Spencer Leigh in 1998 that 'Loanshark Blues' was his favourite on *Defender,* mentioning that, in keeping with his cinema passion, the film *On the Waterfront*, starring Marlon Brando, had inspired the song. 'It is a story about a fairly reasonable guy. He doesn't want to mix with the Mob and he has to borrow from a loan shark all the time and he gets beyond the part where he can pay it back so he is made an offer he can't refuse. In other words, he will commit a crime for them so that he can square up.'

Getting *Defender* completed had been difficult, he admitted in the *Q* interview that year. 'If you produce, write and play on an album, you lose all perspective. I get terrible doubts. The predecessor of *Defender* was put in the bin. The recordings went on and on and eventually I just turned against it. This happened before. We did a complete album in the '70s and then scrapped it [the San Francisco album]. That was the album before *Photo-Finish*. This is the constant danger. If you're working for months on end in the studio you lose the joy of it and in the end you turn against it. I've just got this one finished in time. I'm happy enough with it now.'

Torch was the title of the scrapped album, the one that became *Defender.* The similar titles could suggest a somewhat embattled artist, as if he's 'carrying a torch' and being a 'defender'. In a later interview about it, he was less self-deprecating than usual. The pain of completing it seemed to have dulled his critical faculties.

'It was blood on the tracks ... If I retired from the stage tomorrow I think *Defender* would stand up as, at least, a semi-important album, in years to come. When I was recording "Loanshark Blues", I thought if I die tomorrow I'd be proud of that one.' Then he added a familiar line: 'But it's bad luck, with the gypsies, to analyse yourself.'[14] The truth is that in this year Gallagher was fairly overshadowed; U2 became megastars with *The Joshua Tree*. Guns N' Roses launched what became the biggest-selling debut, *Appetite for Destruction*. And that's before Michael Jackson came along in August to mop up both the singles and album charts with *Bad*. Despite five different studios and many, many hours, this was one judgement on Gallagher's effort: 'By-the-books crunch-rockers like "Failsafe Day" and the unfortunately titled "Road to Hell" don't bode well for Gallagher moving out from an increasingly formulaic pigeonhole.'[15]

Despite Gallagher's own upbeat attitude at this stage, there is evidence that he was having doubts, perhaps about the whole career project. A kind of gloom had set in. In Bill Graham's March 1988 interview in *Hot Press*, in more than a hint of uncharacteristic bitterness, he said: 'You see, if I was living up in Buckinghamshire with a huge mansion and seventeen Alsatian dogs and a limo and acting the guitar-hero thing, I'd probably get more respect. But we've stayed on the street, within reason, we've been touring. I think it's kind of the story of my life in that I'm certainly not part of the mainstream here.'

Rock and roll has its brutality. As an artist, you get your years in the sun, some getting more time than others. Then the great days are gone. You replay the hits to smaller and smaller crowds. Some are content with that. Big music 'brands' like the Rolling Stones keep everything going by corporate means. When the touring is less frequent, when the adulation is less apparent, when your fingers may no longer have the dexterity they had, what do you do if you're not taken up with family or investments or golf? How does the sensitive human being 'come down' from fame? With difficulty, perhaps, is the answer. In 1983, Gallagher was asked what his 'Biggest Fear' was. He answered: 'Electrocution and early retirement.'[16]

In an Irish television interview in 1988, there were signs that this was not the confident Rory Gallagher of old: 'I get more worn out when I'm off the road, in nervous tension. I'm better off when I'm touring – I become fit. Whereas, if I'm rehearsing or doing bits in a studio, I become less together than when I'm on tour.'[17] Bruce Springsteen discussed this predicament, saying 'off the road life was a puzzle'. Then still in his 30s, Springsteen had to take stock of his life: 'Eventually I had to come to grips with the fact that at rest I was not at ease, and to be at ease, I could not rest.'[18]

There were certainly health issues for Gallagher in the 1980s, a physical decline that set in when the tours became less frequent and the prolific creativity of the 1970s was no more. Whether alcohol dependency triggered this or was the result of it is a matter for debate. But there is no doubt that by the late 1980s, he had a serious drink problem. Gerry McAvoy, among others, has testified to that. He described a meeting they had in Crosshaven, County Cork, in 1980, when Rory was 'off the drink', an indication that the problem had begun some years before. With a combination of alcohol and various prescription drugs for different ailments, Gallagher had also become bloated, too much so for a man just over 40 years of age. In a year where the band played only nineteen gigs, McAvoy's description of one in Germany is a telling account of deterioration:

> I remember one night in Hamburg in 1989 we played for three and a half hours and every minute of it was like hell. He couldn't even remember which songs we'd already played and went into 'The Loop' for the second time. It was totally unlike him; he was normally so honed in, so sharp. Then he went into 'The Loop' for the third time and I went over to him and said, 'we've done it twice already'. He just looked at me blankly. It was so sad.[19]

McAvoy describes another occasion when the band were rehearsing and Rory just couldn't play the opening riff of 'Shin Kicker', something he'd done thousands of times. Gallagher became emotional. They knew he needed help. Then, McAvoy admits, 'like an idiot, I piped up, "Forget rehearsals. Let's go to the pub and have a drink."' An old pal of Rory's from Belfast, Billy McCoy, also testified to the decline, for Trevor Hodgett in 2000. Before Rory's gig in the Ulster Hall, in January 1984, McCoy went to the dressing room: 'He was pacing up and down and he never spoke to me and I said, "Hey boy, what's wrong?" And he says "I always get really nervous before I go on". We went back to the Europa Hotel that night. He had hit the bottle by then and we drank till four in the morning. [Before] he would have sat with a Coke.'[20] Brendan O'Neill recalled for McAvoy a festival gig sometime in the 1980s where Rory was 'the worse for wear'. He kept asking O'Neill to play harder and harder, he recalled. 'I had blisters on my fingers like open sores but whatever I did was never enough – "Harder! Harder!" – and I just turned to him and said, "Fuck away off!" and he didn't speak to me for a week after that.' O'Neill, who had joined the band in 1981, told Gerry McAvoy that by the late 1980s, 'he just wasn't functioning as Rory Gallagher. When I joined first, he was so imposing, a wild cat on stage – so intense, so inspiring and so conclusive. He drained every last bit of energy out of the band and himself. And to see him go from that to a man who was finding it difficult even to play. It was hard to watch.'

Further evidence of a serious alcohol problem comes from a friend of Gallagher's from Germany, Rudi Gerlach, a cameraman he met at his first Rockpalast gig in 1977.[21] They stayed friends for the remainder of Rory's life, Gerlach apparently becoming a counsellor on the drink problem that Gallagher had developed. Gerlach told Dan Muise in 2002 how he gave his friend advice, based on his own experience, and it was the main reason they had so much contact. Gerlach said that he himself had at one stage been consuming three bottles of vodka a day. He told Muise that he had recorded their conversations on the subject. 'The first question he asked me was, "Do you still drink?" I said, "No". And then he made the sign of the cross on his body and said, "Good God, how did you do this?" Gerlach in Dan Muise's book mentioned long phone calls between Cologne and London during which he tried to persuade Gallagher to give up the drinking and the pills. He recalled a time in Belgium when he found Gallagher in his room before a gig in an agitated state. When Dónal intervened and took away pills, his brother's rage continued onto the stage where he raised his guitar in a threatening gesture saying, 'Dónal, this one's for you!'

There were still many triumphant nights for Gallagher in the 1980s, however. There's a breathless account of a New York gig in 1985 by one audience member:

> Lone Star Café June 1985 New York City. Me and girlfriend … she'd never seen Rory before … 'Shinkicker' cranks … Rory leaps from the stage onto the stairs and stops right in front of us … he leans back and pins us against the wall … plays a bit (I couldn't see anything, cause his hairs in my face) … turns to us and nods a thank you and leaps back onto the stage! By the end of the night … second or third encore … Rory jumps into the crowd and to the floor … out the exit door and onto the Manhattan sidewalk …

> playing outside to a crowd that had gathered and
> back in again and onto the stage ... The crowd
> could hardly contain itself ... my girlfriend was out
> of her mind insane over the whole thing ... then
> she really went nuts and became my wife ... thanks,
> Rory ... I guess! Charlie.[22]

Gallagher had what amounted to another affliction in
the 1980s. His adherence to folk belief had become more
pronounced. He was open about it to Anil Prasad, when
the India-born journalist asked him if being superstitious affected his life:

> It has affected me very much in the last 10 years. I
> get it from my grandmother. She was very superstitious as well. I'm funny about numbers. It's become
> a phobia, so I have to watch it. It affects your day a
> lot. Before I go on stage, there are certain things I
> do that are semi-sort of gypsy superstitious things,
> but I'm coping with them. It hasn't affected the
> music, thank God. If you got really bad, you'd say
> 'I'll pick that note instead of that one or sing this
> song before that.'[23]

Gallagher developed a fear of flying in the 1970s,
which was apparently cured eventually by medication.
In reflecting on this in 1991, when he had apparently
overcome the problem, Gallagher revealed:

I had a couple of bad flights and I got my Buddy Holly complex. It got so bad I couldn't even fly to Ireland, which is only an hour away [from London]. Then to play on the Continent, I would have to fly out the night before so I'd be okay on the date. It was not so much a fear of death thing, but a mixture of claustrophobia and a few other things. This is a miracle – I flew from London to Tokyo, Japan to Australia, Australia to L.A., L.A. to San Francisco, and so on. We'd have to make our way cross-country and then back to London. So far, so good. My prayers have been answered, then. To beat that flying phobia was quite an ordeal for me, I can tell you, because it's the last thing I needed after all those years of touring and flying two times a day.[24]

In 1987, he made a triumphant return to Cork, for a gig in the Opera House, part of a series recorded for RTÉ television. The producer of the show, Avril MacRory, still remembers the reception he got on that 'homecoming' night. 'It was amazing to be there to see that pride and emotion in the crowd. I saw people in tears.' Gallagher played four nights at the Olympia Theatre in Dublin in February 1988 to enthusiastic crowds, though a reviewer suggested that nostalgia was a significant factor motivating the attendees. 'He's a little fatter now. A little older and no doubt wiser, but Rory Gallagher's skill when it comes to guitar playing, together with his genuine love of the blues, brought simplicity and craftsmanship back to the Irish stage last night.' The reviewer, Paul Russell, continued, revealingly: 'Sometimes it is hard to imagine there was Irish rock before U2.' And this was his conclusion: 'One things is for sure, the venue was littered with guitar players, if the gasps and cheers during his solo acoustics spot were anything to go by. It was clear Rory was quite taken aback by their knowledge and enthusiasm. "It's been a long time, thanks for waiting for me," he told them.'[25]

Carmel Murphy worked in *Hot Press* in the 1980s and she and others in the magazine got to know Gallagher socially around this time. She still has a memento of their friendship, from one of the Olympia gigs in 1988. Vulnerability is revealed. 'He approached me and took off his navy stage bandana and signalled to me for mine. It just so happened I was wearing a navy one too and we both put each other's on. Rory told me his was Mexican, a good-luck one. The next time we met I asked if he wanted it back, knowing his superstition of certain things, but he said "not at all". Over the years I've brought it with me when flying, knowing how Rory, much like myself, felt anxious when having to board a plane.'

Gallagher was never the aloof superstar, and always maintained a fondness and connection with the Irish scene. In 1988, he guested with a blues outfit, the Mary Stokes Band, in a now-defunct Dublin club, the Waterfront. Brian Palm, the band's harmonica player, Stokes's husband and a native of Hartford, Connecticut, recalls this as the band's 'highest celebrity peak', as both

Rory and Van Morrison were in the audience. Their guitarist at the time, Beki Brindle,[26] stepped aside and Gallagher took her Strat to play on a Little Walter song, 'Can't Hold Out Much Longer'.

Bill Graham of *Hot Press*, in a measured way, summed up the predicament for Gallagher at this point in his life, his great years probably behind him: 'Rory Gallagher could justifiably be anxious that he's become a kind of historical figure – an icon unknown and unapproachable to a new generation of Irish music consumers who presumably associate him with check shirts and their own hazily-remembered pre-pubertal Seventies, when the guitar was God *and* video-pop purely a science-fiction concept.' Graham concluded his article with a quote from the Cork man: 'I never blended in with the Led Zeppelin situation. Or even the Thin Lizzy situation, or whomever you care to mention. Anyone who knows me knows what the origins of the music are. Though I'm not St Francis, I don't make an easy path for myself. When I'm 65, I might say you silly fool, you could have saved yourself all that anxiety.'[27]

There was some welcome light at the end of the decade, as far as recording was concerned, in the form of the album *Fresh Evidence*, released in May 1990. If *Defender* had been for his fans something of a return to form, this was an artistic triumph, proving his creativity was still intact, as he explored various blues styles. The opener is a dynamic straight-ahead rocker, 'Kid Gloves', and many consider the album's closer, 'Slumming Angel', a Rory classic. On 'Heaven's Gate', inspired by the film of the same name, he plays two intense solos, which stand up with his best. 'The Loop', a jazz-meets-Chicago-Blues style instrumental, takes its name from the elevated rail line in central Chicago and it comes with train sound effects. The other instrumental, 'Alexis', is a tribute to Alexis Korner, the British blues musician and broadcaster. Further musical homage, in this case to the Louisiana accordion player, Clifton Chenier comes on 'The King of Zydeco'.[28]

Melody Maker was highly complimentary: 'Simply, he is making a return trip to those places which originally fired his imagination, is re-exploring old fields of influence with the authority of someone who has all of the experience to be confident in his craft.' Gallagher would surely have been pleased to hear that he was again 'among the sugar cane, the lonesome town, the barrel-house and down at the station'.[29] David Sinclair wrote: 'Gallagher's neurotic attention to detail has paid off and *Fresh Evidence* is a considered and varied collection without an ounce of spare flesh on its wiry frame.'[30]

Arguably, the standout five minutes on *Fresh Evidence* is when Gallagher, alone with his National acoustic, recreates the Son House song, 'Empire State Express'. House recorded it in 1965 when he worked for the company that runs the celebrated passenger train that ran from New York to Cleveland. This recording is unadorned, and captured in one take, with the mature Gallagher, as if in full retreat from the commercial music world, going back to the kernel of the music he found so inspirational. The song celebrates the potency

of trains, something that may have aroused the young
Gallagher's imagination as far back as in Derry in the
early 1950s. The train is an object of wonder, becoming
almost otherworldly ('The Empire State, you know / She
rides on Eastern Time'). In his homage to the song and
its writer, he brings a starker, more desolate tone than
on the original: a forlorn vocal, jarring sounds from the
instrument animating the steel giant, and ending with
resignation as the lyric laments the train's power over
the individual:

> I'm going to tell you what that mean
> ol' train will do,
> Take your woman away,
> And shoot black smoke back at you.

At this time there was something of a resurgence of blues-
rock, a tide that might have brought opportunities for
Gallagher. Bonnie Raitt had just topped the American
chart. John Lee Hooker was more successful than he
had been for several decades. Gary Moore returned
to blues in 1990 with *Still Got the Blues*, with Albert
King, among others, guesting. David Sinclair's Q article
added: 'Gallagher has, of course, occupied the one fixed
point all along and smiles at the thought of everyone
else once more coming round to his way of thinking.'[31]
Arty McGlynn recalls an aspect of Gallagher's commitment to this music. While talking to him after a Van
Morrison gig in Croydon, he detected misgivings about
some of the set Morrison had performed, the more

mystical material, such as 'In the Garden'. Rory had regarded Van as a fellow bluesman.[32] Dave McHugh believes that *Fresh Evidence* was 'the starting point of the new Rory that would have emerged.'

But Rory Gallagher at that stage was perhaps past caring enough. It's doubtful he had the will or the energy left to capitalise on this apparent resurgence of blues and associated music. Or had his time just passed? He had set out his 'blues stall' with the *Fresh Evidence* album, reasserting his commitment to the genre. In doing so, for one thing he put clear water between himself and Clapton, as he told Anil Prasad: 'I suppose he's the successful face of what the blues is and I'm probably the guy on the sidelines. He's working in a different area from me now. And even in the blues field, I cover different blues tangents than Eric does. I work in country blues and even though I do some numbers that are in the B.B. King and Albert King area, I work in a lot of other influences in as well. My blues roots are all over the place, where Eric's tend to be a little narrower.'[33]

Despite *Fresh Evidence* exploring morbid themes, Rory Gallagher could hardly have thought in 1990 that he had only five more years to live. Or might he? Long before *Fresh Evidence*, 'Shadow Play' had already given a clue to the troubled state of mind that contributed to his early death. The shadows were now closing in on Gallagher's life.

Not very much is known about that life, about Rory Gallagher, the person, when each tour was over, and the star was alone again in his London home ...

Chapter 12

THE OTHER RORY GALLAGHER

*'I'm a private person, not just in terms of the media,
but also with my friends. I don't even discuss my
relationships or feelings with them.'*

– RORY GALLAGHER[1]

Rory Gallagher made a candid remark when asked about his stage manner in 1978. 'Sometimes I don't recognize myself up there, and sometimes I don't recognize myself when I come off the stage. I don't know. I am not aware of this Jekyll and Hyde change. I mean, if I were as crazy offstage as I am onstage, people would lock me up or they wouldn't talk to me.'[2] Here Gallagher was actually stating a problem, one that would grow and grow for him.

We know he lived a solitary life, and that he may have been 'isolated by the white heat of his talent', as

Michael Ross put it in a *Sunday Times* article in 1998. 'He was like two completely different people on stage and off,' Dónal Gallagher told the writer on the same occasion. He made a revealing statement to Ross: 'I can't say that we ever had an in-depth personal conversation. There wasn't a lot said between us. There was a kind of telepathy between us though.' He went on: 'He was tremendously melancholic and he was never satisfied with anything he did.'[3] Dónal made another comment in *The Sunday Times* in 2012, which might have been a throwaway remark, but if true, could explain much. 'My wife wonders if he was autistic. That's possible.'[4]

In 2005, Bono had this reflection on dealing with talent and fame. 'You don't become a rock star unless you've got something missing somewhere, that is obvious to me. If you were of sound mind or a more complete person, you could feel normal without 70,000 people a night screaming their love for you.'[5]

From the mid 1980s, Gallagher was living in an apartment he had bought in south London, 4 Brompton Cottages, at the junction of Hollywood and Fulham Road in SW10. It is quite small and very modest in comparison to the elegant period houses in this part of London. Dónal Gallagher had his office in the apartment for a period. The famous pianist Liberace was a former resident. This is the area of the city that Rory always favoured, from the house that inspired 'Laundromat', to addresses such as Philbeach Gardens and Cluny Mews[6] nearby. An extra track on the reissued *Jinx*, 'Lonely Mile', was dedicated to a section of the Fulham Road that he used to walk to try to deal with insomnia, the 2012 sleeve notes reveal. In contrast to his small apartment, Gallagher made a bigger investment in his native city. He bought his mother a large house, 'Greenbanks', on a three-quarter acre site off the Well Road on the south side of Cork city, bordering the Lee estuary. (Following her death in 2005, the property fetched €2.9 million.)

Avril MacRory, a television producer who later had executive roles in RTÉ and the BBC, got to know Rory Gallagher in London, and recalls both a troubled and contented person, but firstly somebody of remarkable gentleness: 'He had a wonderful old-fashioned courtesy – he would always stand up and give you his chair.' She describes Gallagher as someone who was content to live alone. He socialised sometimes and could really engage in conversation on occasions. But this was not his routine. 'He led a solitary life. He would go for long walks, mostly on his own. Rory had a vulnerability about him that was really touching. On the rare occasions when he did open up, you felt really privileged.'

The accounts of Gallagher's personality in Gerry McAvoy's book, given their twenty years on the road together, have to be regarded as reliable. He describes the so-called 'rock 'n' roll lifestyle' he experienced: the drinking, the casual relationships, the adulation and availability of young women for male rockers. What's clear, however, is that Rory, despite being the star and attractive and charming (a pin-up in *Jackie* magazine at one stage), was not interested in this part of life on the road. He didn't 'play the celebrity' at all, it seems.

Sitting at a bar bragging or cracking jokes till the small hours simply was not for him. One of McAvoy's Belfast friends, Jim Ferguson, testified: 'It was like trying to have a casual conversation with a nun. He didn't talk about women or football or drinking – just music. He wasn't a good storyteller, so he didn't come up with anecdotes. He wasn't a man's man, but he could talk to women very easily.' And, as evidence of a gracefulness in Gallagher's personality, Ferguson's wife, Eithne, told McAvoy: 'I could sit and talk to him for hours. What was really attractive about him was that he didn't come on to you, unlike most of the other men in Belfast!'

There has been speculation as to whether sexual orientation was an issue. We know that Trish, Eric Kitteringham's sister, was very fond of him in the early Taste days, but that the feelings were not reciprocated. Gerry McAvoy's book describes Rory being close to a Belgian woman, a photographer and model, Catherine Mattelaer, in the mid 1970s, describing her as 'the girl Rory should have married'. The Gallagher brothers, having become wealthy, were then living as tax exiles for a period of some months in the house she shared with a fellow musician, Roland Van Campenhout, in a village called Sint-Martens-Latem, on the River Lys, close to the Belgian city of Ghent. It seems romance blossomed between the two and they grew to love each other. They never declared themselves as a couple, though McAvoy, and also Avril MacRory, believe there was a bond between them right up to Rory's death. Apparently, their relationship was something more than just friendship, but Rory either did not allow himself or know how to take it any further. A significant insight concerning Rory's emotional life comes in Dan Muise's book: Ted McKenna told the author that, at some point before he joined the band in 1978, Rory had a girlfriend who 'broke his heart'. Muise follows this with a dramatic quote[7] from Rory:

> A certain lady, who I had a great thing for, right, went off and married this guy. Then she went off and had his child. And she introduced me to the husband who showed me pictures of the child right in front of my face. And I couldn't take it. I really couldn't take it. The only reason I didn't move is that she was a musician friend of mine. She must have no feelings. I mean, how do you do that? He's a nice guy; I'm not sayin'. But I spent two years in a terrible state over that.

Gallagher was also close to a woman called Christine Fox, who died in 2017. She had spent time in Cork and become acquainted with Gallagher's mother, Monica.

Of course, no human being is obliged to be intimate with, or marry, or form partnerships with another. It may suit certain people, for various reasons, not to. In the many interviews he did in his lifetime, Gallagher could rarely be drawn on this subject. This very brief exchange from an interview is an example of his reticence:

> TP: Do you have a family?

RG: Well, I'm not married.[8]

And this is how the *NME* writing style dealt with the issue on another occasion:

> Bear with us as we investigate The Rory Enigma.
> Uh, Rory, are you married? Do you have a girlfriend?
> 'No –,' (blushes). 'I'm on the loose. Free.'
> A sympathetic workman in an adjoining room nixes this Embarrassing Moment by drilling noisily.[9]

Probably because there was never a woman closely associated with him publicly, the suggestion persisted that he might have been gay, and either did not realise it, or want to disclose it, but there is no evidence to support this. And according to Norman Damery, Rory 'wasn't interested in men, women, or drugs. He definitely wasn't homosexual.' In 1972, Gallagher gave a youthful, swaggering answer to the marriage question on RTÉ: 'I'd think about it, but I'm in no hurry. I'd like to stay footloose for a while.' This is a normal enough reaction for a 24-year-old. Then he added, more tellingly: 'But you can never tell when you're going to be … caught.'[10]

The question came up again in 1986. 'This whole marriage question is a pop star question, you know. "When are you getting married, Rod?"; "When are ya getting married, Elton?": You know? The world is full of people, and certain people marry at different stages but I'm not the jet set type. If you bump into someone, and marriage is the route you want to take; fine, and if not, that's fine too. But I imagine it'll happen along the way.'[11] However, a remark he made to journalist Michael Ross in 1992 sounds more like resignation than light-heartedness: 'Everybody wants other things in their lives, but I don't dwell on that.'[12]

Because of their long association, Gerry McAvoy's conclusion on this aspect of Gallagher has to be taken into account: 'In my opinion, the real reason for Rory's reluctance to let anyone into his life is that he was simply so focused on his music that he wouldn't allow women – or anything else for that matter – to interfere with that.' In 1988, Gallagher was asked by Dave Fanning if he had read Chuck Berry's recently published autobiography. He had, and Little Richard's also, but for him, the music was the focus, so he was critical of exploration of other matters: 'I don't care what they did in the dressing rooms, or the hotel rooms.'[13]

One woman Gallagher was very close to was his mother. His postcards to her, sent prolifically from many locations around the world, give a glimpse of this particular mother–son relationship, and the sense of obligation he felt towards her. After her death in 2005, Dónal Gallagher found dozens of the cards, and later that year the Triskel Arts Centre in Cork featured them as an exhibition. Firstly, he addressed the cards to 'Mrs D. Gallagher' until his father Danny's death, after which he used 'Mrs M. Gallagher'. A common feature of the writing was, though the messages were short, that he always enquired about his mother's health and about a particular family pet. It is noteworthy too that, even at the height of his fame, he never bragged about the audiences' reaction to him or how big the hall was. Terms like 'show went well' was a frequent, modest appraisal. His diligence with regard to postcards may be evidence of obligation, too, that his mother had a strong possessiveness towards her sons. This may have been the result of her deciding to return with them to Cork in 1958, effectively facing life as a lone parent. His mother's liking for telling the future from the pattern of tealeaves left at the bottom of a cup, making her well known around Cork, even found its way into her son's writing, in 'Maybe I Will', from *Deuce* in 1971, which has a reference to 'reading leaves' in a cup to start the day.

There is an interesting parallel between Gallagher's life and that of another music figure – from a contrasting genre – Johannes Brahms. The great nineteenth-century German composer, at several crucial stages in his life, rejected personal commitment. When his fellow composer Robert Schumann was admitted to a sanatorium, a romance developed between Schumann's wife, Clara, and the young Brahms. When Schumann died in July 1856, rather than Brahms and she becoming closer, their friendship, so often passionately declared, cooled. Brahms later met Agathe von Siebold, and clearly fell in love with her to the extent that in one of his works, a string sextet, the first and second violins famously invoke her by playing the musical notes that spell her name. Yet Brahms, despite what the social norms of the period expected, would not take the relationship any further. Agathe forgave him, writing that 'his immortal work has contributed to her happiness'. Also, Brahms was offered many professional posts during his life, which he turned down, rather than be 'fettered'. Biographer Karl Geringer's conclusion on the composer's life refers to Agathe von Siebold's words. It could also apply to Rory Gallagher's life: 'Brahms could not belong to one alone. Unwedded and childless, he had to tread life's paths, that he might bestow on all, the riches of his soul, his mind and his art.'[14]

There are hundreds of press interviews with Rory Gallagher, and virtually none contains any insight into his life outside music. This was an exchange reported by one journalist who tried to probe in 1973:

> Gallagher is a Catholic and refuses to be drawn further on the subject of religion and politics, believing apparently that musicians should stick to talking about music. I pushed him on the subject of personal information and significantly got nowhere. 'I really don't lead a very spectacular life and so it is really more interesting to ask me about my music and my guitar ... I haven't many interesting things to say about myself that I would want printed.[15]

Gallagher's sideman, Ted McKenna, reflected on this subject as a TV programme panellist in 2009: 'People need to celebrate ability, as opposed to notoriety' he said, continuing: 'Because of the speed of media nowadays we constantly need something new to write about. Notoriety is becoming easier to get hold of than talent.'[16]

To his credit, Dónal Gallagher has, on several occasions, spoken candidly about this aspect of his brother. In 2012, Shiv Cariappa asked him a blunt question: 'At what point did you realize that something was amiss with him?' The answer is significant.

> Since I knew him as a child. He was very different from the norm right from his early formative years. He seemed to have more wisdom than my pals or his pals. Rory seemed to have a destiny about him. Rory seemed to harbor a terrible depression hidden inside him. I first became concerned during the split up of Taste – as far back as then, when he returned from the UK to Cork. He went in to retreat. It took a while to get him out of a shell to which he seemed to get himself in. He was somebody who could hide his feelings. Even with alcohol, the rest of us would get super silly and do stupid things, Rory would be still very together. He wasn't overtly falling over. And illness-wise, I suppose in the 1980s. Even with so many days on the road, we would take some long gaps like six months. Rory would go back to Ireland and write. The difficulty with that was that Rory off the road was a totally different person because he would become very insular. He would become very depressed. Yeah, it was great to take a break (from touring), but he wasn't a person I felt who

was doing anything constructive on his time off. He wouldn't go off on holiday. He didn't have a hobby he would pursue or other interests. Then we realized that this was the wrong thing to do with his languishing till we got back on the road. He didn't have a set of friends to hook up with. His friends were musicians on the road. It was a gypsy lifestyle.'[17]

There has been speculation on the Internet about the possibility of a Rory Gallagher son or daughter. This kind of conjecture is, of course, not uncommon in the world of popular music. Intimate encounters have produced love children all through music history. The implications for the Gallagher estate are, of course, obvious. In Rory Gallagher's case, this remains purely in the realm of speculation. Not surprisingly, there has been at least one Gallagher 'lookalike' identified since his death. And the Internet has featured claims, and disbelief and anger at the same claims, by some fans. The accounts of the private lives of artists have always been a fascination; biographers have explored at length the nature of James Joyce's relationship with Nora Barnacle. Academics have wondered why Jonathan Swift had two women who were close to him but whom he kept secret. Literary assessment of Oscar Wilde's work has gone hand in hand with examination of his sexual life.

As for Rory Gallagher and this relatively unexplored aspect of his life, Martin Carthy sees it sympathetically as something of a paradox: 'He loved humanity, but didn't find anybody for himself.' The musician and academic Mícheál Ó Súilleabháin of University of Limerick may have had the measure of what drove Gallagher, with an observation in a tribute in *Hot Press* in 1995: 'The music he made sounded so personal – almost as if it was a necessary healing that he constantly pursued.'

He was resolutely private, but there is one place to uncover the inner Rory Gallagher: his songs.

Chapter 13

'THIS SHADOW PLAY ...'

'Through his songs Rory was an open book'.
— DÓNAL GALLAGHER[1]

Rory Gallagher wrote songs about many subjects: gambling, crime, cars, corruption, alcohol, a fairground and a launderette, among others. Many of the songs were joyous, rocking, anthems. But there was also a deeper, expressive side to his writing. This was when he wrote about himself. Here, he could be revealing.

A piece of driftwood in the Atlantic Ocean off County Cork inspired the central metaphor in his meditation on alienation, 'A Million Miles Away', written for *Tattoo* in 1973. The song's narrator (Rory himself, perhaps) describes a happy hotel bar with a good piano player, but asks why, therefore, 'should I wear a frown?'

> The joint is jumping all around me and my mood
> is really not in style
> Right now the blues want to surround me but I'll
> break out after a while
> Well, I'm a million miles away, I'm a million miles
> away
> I'm sailing like a driftwood on a windy bay.

Dónal Gallagher recounted the song's conception for Ivan Little in the *Belfast Telegraph* in 2015. He and his brother were once walking by the sea near Ballycotton, when they became separated. He called for Rory in vain. 'I was about to raise the alarm with the Ballycotton lifeboat, when Rory shouted to me. He told me he hadn't been able to answer me immediately, because he was writing a song which he had to get down on paper.' 'A Million Miles Away' had been spawned.

In 'Philby', one of his best-known 1970s songs, he chose to directly compare himself to an outsider, in this case a *persona non grata*. Kim Philby was one of the famous 'Cambridge Five', graduates of that university who worked for British intelligence but became Soviet spies, mostly out of idealism. The first line of the song is something of a revelation, when he says, 'there's a stranger in my soul'. Perhaps the stranger was Gallagher himself? The verse continues, in the first person, 'I'm disconnected but I don't need pity / The night's gonna burn on slow'.

Philby's secret life as a double agent was exposed in 1963, and he defected to the Soviet Union. The story had fascinated people; the crime writer John le Carré created a Philby-like upper-class traitor, Bill Haydon, in his 1974 novel, *Tinker, Tailor, Soldier, Spy*. Philby was also the inspiration for the Harry Lime character in Graham Greene's novel *The Third Man*. Gallagher would probably have been aware of both works. His song 'Philby' reflected the intrigue and distrust involved in this world of intelligence and espionage, and coincidentally was perhaps the song in which Gallagher got the closest to a pop-type chorus, with a 'Yeah, yeah, yeah' punctuated with his playing of an electric sitar. Choosing this unpopular figure, in the West at least, showed something of Gallagher the outsider, perhaps also, the egalitarian. He was asked about the song in 1987.

> One day I felt harassed as there were a lot of things going on and I thought that I felt like Philby, just before he went over the Albanian border. I had read a book about him and though I'm not over-sympathetic to his plight, he is a fascinating character. The song is not strictly about him, but I tried to bring in some of that twilight zone that was in his life into the song. When you're on the road for a long time, living in hotels, it's a bit like the life of a spy.[2]

In 1991, Gallagher said, 'I don't agree with spying and so on, but he was so audacious. I never heard a song before that on a spy or a specific spy. I often wondered if he [Philby] ever heard it.'[3]

Dave McHugh's view is that Gallagher's lyric writing 'drifted from tender, optimistic introspection, to a sense of isolation. By the late 1970s, he was writing about himself as an outsider.' McHugh says 'Off the Handle' from *Top Priority* is starker than 'Philby' in revealing Gallagher's sense of himself:

> Well, my cat won't scratch or show its claws
> It just prowls around the house all day
> for the last night or two
> I can't eat or drink
> I think I'm gonna fade away

Another song from that album, 'Overnight Bag', takes up a similar theme:

> Too many sleepless nights put my soul on edge
> And so many restless moods lay heavy in my head

In 2003, when Dónal Gallagher was asked about the portrayal of his brother in the Muise and McAvoy books, he said though they were 'good factual accounts, there's still more under the surface of Rory'. His brother's writing was the key: 'If you read through his lyrics he's wearing his heart on his sleeve. To me, it's very obvious. Perhaps I know a bit better – I can sort of identify all the songs having huge significance, or what he's actually getting at.'[4]

Philip Chevron, the highly regarded Dublin songwriter and member of The Radiators and The Pogues, once said that Gallagher's songwriting was overlooked because he played the guitar so well. According to Roy Hollingworth: 'He could play loud and exciting guitar, but the guy was also a poet in the Irish tradition.'[5] Gallagher had admitted once that 'people sort of think that I write songs as guitar vehicles'.[6] Perhaps he was lumbered with this. Though many of his songs have an undoubted lyricism, they don't tend to get covered by others. But Stephen Hunter, of University College Cork's folklore publication, *The Archive*, had no doubt about this question: 'His lyrics are masterly in their descriptive power and expressive range, although to remove them from their musical context does them less than justice. They are essentially Romantic in origin, in the sense that they suggest a world of adventure and possibilities lying in wait at our doorsteps, of everyday reality transformed into a more magical dimension. They draw extensively on the folkloric motifs typical of the vast open spaces of North America, almost, I would suggest, an America of the mind.'[7]

Louis de Paor, the Cork-born poet, now Director of the Centre for Irish Studies at NUI Galway, believes Gallagher was underrated as a lyricist, by himself as much as anyone else. 'They're unusually well written, with the words working against the natural rhythm of speech on the one hand and the tight structure of the music on the other. So many of them play on that idea of holding your ground against the system, against the odds. There's often mention of the themes of *noir*, and covert things in the songs, but there's also a great sense of uncertainty he explores in his writing that's really interesting.' While living in Melbourne, Australia, during the 1990s, de Paor interviewed Rory on radio, and recalls him confirming there was a personal dimension to his writing, but at the same time, he didn't want to 'unload things on other people'.[8]

The *pièce de résistance* of this confessional side of Gallagher's writing must be 'Shadow Play', a fiery rock anthem that hides an inner angst. The song is set during a kind of dark night of the soul, where lights, noise, lack of sleep and troubling memories torment the narrator, presumably Gallagher himself. In 2015, Dónal Gallagher referred to the song's meaning, suggesting the personal dimension, and quoting the lines: 'I feel a little strange inside / A little bit of Jekyll, a little Mr Hyde.'[9] The song's theme of a creative person's turmoil, anguish and uncertainty at night has an echo in music history. 'At Midnight' by the German poet Friedrich Ruckert was set to music by Gustav Mahler in 1901: 'No thoughts of light / brought me comfort / at midnight'. The obvious theme is restlessness, but the term 'shadow play' also refers to an ancient form of storytelling, originating in Asia, which uses shadows made by cutout human figures, which are held between a source of light and a translucent screen. Gallagher made this a central metaphor in the song: 'Shadows run, in full flight, to run, seek and hide / Well, I'm still not sure what part I play …' This, one of his most energetic songs, has a sophistication and delicacy in its imagery, a suggestion of human alienation and vulnerability to fate.

The opening rocker from his next album, *Top Priority*, a song that became a standard in his set, 'Follow Me', actually sounds like a plea:

> Won't you follow me
> Where I'm bound
> Time's for borrowing now
> Won't you follow me
> Time is tight
> Before things swallow me down

This feature of his writing, up-tempo songs that hide personal unease was apparent even in the early 1970s. On 'Crest of a Wave' from *Deuce*, he suggests that success – perhaps his own – can have a downside:

> Well, you can ride on the crest of a wave
> If that's where you want to be
> But does the look on your face
> Mean you're really feeling happy?

Gallagher told Shiv Cariappa about the song: 'Well, the idea is in the song title itself that you don't walk on people when you are flying high.' But this song also has more than a hint of 'Shadow Play'.

Gallagher, of course, wrote love songs. Here he could both express tenderness and describe trauma. His description of love, loss and depressive feelings goes right back to his Taste days, with a song like 'On the Boards':

> Someone has taken my day,
> Turned it to night,
> Who turned out the light?

In the early 1970s he wrote several what could be termed more generic boy-meets-girl scenario, like 'Used To Be' and 'I'm Not Awake Yet', both from *Deuce*. Then in 'I'll Admit You're Gone', from *Calling Card* in 1976, the writing is more candid, more telling. It's hard not to believe this sensitive expression is not born out of some personal experience, maybe the relationship described in the Dan Muise book. Whether Rory had been heartbroken or not, he could certainly imagine it:

> Where do I belong, I just keep on searching?
> I want to see the dawn of the day when I stop hurting.

'I'll Admit You're Gone' was the last explicitly love-themed song that appears in Gallagher's work. *Calling Card* contained four such songs out of nine, something he did not repeat. 'Moonchild' was one. He was somewhat candid in discussing it with a music writer, Darcy Diamond: "'The song is sort of an open refrain to a fantasy woman I know," he says, winking his eye and giving the old Irish shrug. "It also addresses itself to the child in all of us, the innocent in us, in me. I am a Pisces, a water sign, and I flow about quite freely.'"[10] Gallagher was more what could be termed romantically robust in another of the songs, 'Secret

Agent'. 'My baby's got a secret agent / to watch me like a hawk'. The narrator (is it Rory himself?) 'slips around', but he's 'too quick to catch in the morning'. Is it a more cloak-and-dagger Gallagher, or was the crime fiction milieu already attracting him? In 'Edged in Blue' he's more vulnerable, and seems to cry out as he sings, 'Here I am, where are you / All my days are edged in blue.'[11]

There were later songs describing personal pain, like 'Easy Come, Easy Go' on *Jinx* and 'Walking Wounded' on his last record. In 'Fuel to the Fire' from *Photo-Finish*, he intimates experiencing loss, and describes the torment he feels:

> I call out your name, so you might hear it,
> But it only adds fuel, to the fire,
> In my soul ... yeah[12]

The posthumously released tour de force 'Wheels Within Wheels' can be added to Gallagher's canon of reflective songs. A great mystery of his career is why he turned his back on what many regard as one of his best compositions. With a reflective melancholy in the downward chord progression, the song is reminiscent of the elegant, understated lyric writing of his early twenties. Yet for whatever reason, he never resurrected it after recording it during the cancelled San Francisco album in 1978. The song demonstrates that Gallagher could go to the 'middle of the road' and retain subtlety. In the lyric, he is appealing, somewhat ironically given his own life, to someone not to walk away, not to fear commitment: 'If you keep your heart closed / You'll live out in the cold'.

Many have been drawn to this song and its resonance since it was uncovered. Adi Roche, well known and recognised for her humanitarian work, primarily as founder of Chernobyl Children International, and who has lived in Cork most of her life, admits to falling in love with Rory Gallagher when she was thirteen. She says the song 'touches a raw nerve … it's musically delicate and poignant and the long intro sets up for the complex, yet simple story of love and life and how despite when we may lose both that we can still carry on, how we take the risk, maybe get let down but we still carry on.' It is possible that, given his belief that music should be tough, Gallagher may have feared this might have been his 'Wonderful Tonight'.

Dónal Gallagher was candid with Shiv Cariappa about this song, and revealing about his brother: 'To me, "Wheels" was such a beautiful, melancholic song that could have been a turning point perhaps in Rory's life. The sadness that checked in there. He wouldn't perform the song. He did attempt it back in Germany, but it wasn't a song with which he wanted to get involved. From a spiritual standpoint, Rory also probably knew of his own destiny. He refers to it often about fading away, about being taken away by depression. And "Wheels Within Wheels" is no exception in that case.'[13]

Gallagher was never sentimental, however. Even when he was lyrically tender, he was musically robust. 'Daughter of the Everglades' is an example: gentle verse, energetic chorus. On his notes for the reissued CD *Blueprint*, Dónal Gallagher describes it as 'one of the most beautiful songs [Rory] ever wrote'. It is certainly one of Gallagher's most eloquent. And one of his most musically sophisticated, with subtle major-to-minor turns. Romance and mystery combine. The 'Daughter' is someone taken from her natural environment, with tragic consequences:

> I should not have brought you here
> So far from the bayou
> Down in the low, low land
> Don't know why you left me
> But now I think I understand.

Barry Barnes, who has performed Gallagher songs for many years with his band, Sinnerboy, has a particular fondness for the song and its story. To him it is reminiscent of Alfred Lord Tennyson's poem 'The Lady of Shalott'. In the poem, the lady lives on an island on a river near Camelot, suffering from a mysterious curse and must only look at the world through a mirror. When she sees Lancelot passing, she looks directly, so the power of the curse consumes her. Gallagher's song, Barnes says, 'has a quality of writing that's really quite magical'.

In 2012, another song from the sessions for 1973's *Blueprint* came to light, as an additional song on the reissued *Calling Card*: 'Where Was I Going To?' It is Gallagher as a vulnerable human being, quite unlike the album's other material. Nostalgia – with a hint of regret:

> I've been thinking about where I come from,
> For so long.
> But now those days are past,
> and that time is gone ...

The themes of anguish and uncertainty were explored again on *Jinx* in 1982. The track 'Jinxed' harks back to his superstitious side, and also sounds like a cry from a troubled soul:

> Everything I try just crumbles before I start
> Feel like a lost child, I'm searching in the dark
> Will I swim or will I sink?
> This must be some kind of jinx.

His soul is 'on fire', he says in the next verse, and he asks for someone to come and be the 'ice'. Was he speaking here of someone in particular? We'll probably never know.

Dave McHugh compares Gallagher's situation to the scene in one of the twentieth-century's most famous realist paintings, *Nighthawks*, painted by Edward Hopper in 1942. Hopper painted an 'outsider' sitting in shade in a diner, while life goes on in light around him. 'It's the idea of the artist observing the outsider, when the outsider is really the artist himself.'

As he got older, something else had a big bearing on Gallagher's writing. He became increasingly attracted to crime and thriller fiction. It became more and more a pervasive theme in his songwriting. Out went introspection and in came intrigue. What did he find so attractive about the work of authors like Patricia Highsmith, Raymond Chandler and Dashiell Hammett, with characters typically trapped or on the edge of some kind of calamity? He told Bill Graham in 1988: 'I'm not interested in the violence, it's the characters, the remarks they make and the loyalties: particularly the code of honour between police and thieves in the French gangster movies. I mean there's eating and drinking in all that stuff.'[14]

'Continental Op' from *Defender* is probably his best-known song set in this milieu. He dedicated it to Hammett, the master of the hard-boiled detective story, a kind of dark fiction popular from the 1920s to the 1950s. The Continental Op was a detective working for the fictional Continental Agency, in San Francisco.

> So who they gonna get
> When the trouble's got to stop
> Here's my card
> I'm the Continental Op

Gallagher would probably have been flattered to know that this hobby led to at least one academic study. A scholar, Wesley Callihan, began by noting Rory's fascination with the genre: 'Perhaps Rory Gallagher was drawn to someone else who was essentially a loner, someone who had obtained a certain emotional distance from others in order to do what he had to do the way he had to do it. Or perhaps he just plain liked the stories.'[15] Callihan notes that the *Cambridge Companion to Crime Fiction* describes this kind of writing as 'deriving from the Romantic tradition, which emphasized the emotions of apprehension, or terror and awe. Hard-boiled fiction differs from that tradition in the narrator's cynical attitude to those emotions.' In the 18 March 1988 edition of *Hot Press*, Gallagher told Bill Graham candidly: 'The guys in these books appeal because they're up all night, so it's really a parallel life to an insomniac musician.' Later that year, he talked more about the subject: 'If you look at rhythm and blues, whatever that means, compared to the pop scene, and then just look at a hard-boiled detective story with sort of amoral crime in it, there's a kind of funny connection. Plus, the writing in a crime thriller is very sparse, sharp and bittersweet – usually bitter. And I can see some kind of connection myself, you know.'[16] At the same time, many would find it fascinating that the gentle, mild-mannered Gallagher was drawn to the work of Patricia Highsmith, whose most famous character, Tom Ripley, is a charming psychopath, a cold-blooded killer, but with a taste for the finer things in life (Gallagher's favourite book, he told *Hot Press* in 1983 was *The Talented Mr Ripley*). This is much darker than the relatively playful detective-in-the-trench-coat novels. One biographer put it bluntly: 'Behaviour or destiny, Highsmith felt, could not be predicted and deterministic readings of life leached man of the very things that differentiated him from lower forms of life.'[17]

Gallagher's 'comeback' album of 1987, *Defender*, was almost exclusively concerned with the milieu and themes of crime fiction. The confessional songs of the late 1970s had given way completely to the world of conspiracy and corruption. This could be called being thematically consistent, but could be deemed over-infatuation too. Bill Graham seemed to opt for the former, suggesting Gallagher was combining his two great obsessions: '*Defender* chases down grittily realistic and not deglamourized versions of the Outlaw Blues myth. In the past, Rory Gallagher may not have been the obvious Irish candidate for song-poet status but on *Defender* his characters exist on a credible border-line of the law, trapped in "Kickback City" with the "Loanshark Blues" where "morality" is the property of the prosperous.'[18]

Hammett's work 'propelled the mystery genre into literature', according to one biographer, Sally Cline.[19] The books also suggest a view about humanity, a negative but, to many, a coherent one. According to Cline, 'Hammett's books, which attempt to get to the truth behind crimes, only to find that there isn't any one "truth", offer the view that the world is ruled by meaningless, blind chance.' A liberal or left-wing outlook has often been associated with crime fiction (Dashiell Hammett was a victim of the McCarthy era in America because of his liberal views. The globally successful Swedish crime writer Stieg Larsson wrote for a left-wing magazine before he began his famous [if short] career as a crime writer.) For his part, Rory

Gallagher told Liam Fay in 1992 that he had 'given up on television since the Tories won the last election'.[20]

Dónal Gallagher confirmed his brother's attention to detail in regard to current affairs for the music writer Trevor Hodgett. 'He'd get a few newspapers every day and in America, no matter what state you were in, he'd know the name of the Governor, what party were in power and what the dirty laundry was.'[21] Gallagher was not forgetting his home turf, either, and had an ear for detail in Irish politics, as he told Liam Fay in July 1992, mentioning a veteran Irish historian and broadcaster: 'You can get RTÉ radio as far south as Munich. I was in Paris during the last general election and it was great to hear John Bowman doing his broadcasting.' Gallagher got a political endorsement after his death in 1995 from the *Socialist Review*: 'I haven't a clue what politics Gallagher had, but his genius combined with his dedication to his art, his lack of airs, graces and pretensions, and his unwillingness to sink into the mire of showbiz, all rightly earned this exceedingly nice man the title "The People's Guitarist".'[22] Avril MacRory remembers Gallagher's apartment being full of VHS tapes, as he was an insatiable film buff as well as an avid reader. His interest was not only in commercial thriller and spy material, she points out, but in European art films also. He admired the work of the Polish director Andrzej Wajda, in particular his 1954 film, *Ashes and Diamonds*, considered to be one of the great masterpieces of Polish cinema.

As part of his ongoing commitment to preserving his brother's legacy, Dónal Gallagher released *Kickback City* in 2013, an 'immersive album', as it was described. It features a specially compiled CD of Gallagher's crime novel-influenced music, and a novella by Ian Rankin, illustrated by graphic artist Timothy Truman. The BBC Radio 4 programme *Front Row* in October 2013 featured the release. Rankin's character in the novella, Rivas, listens to Gallagher songs, Rankin explained. The Shadowplays website questioned Daniel Gallagher about the evident similarities between his uncle's life and how Hammett's fiction looks at political corruption and class warfare, suggesting it could easily translate to the 'underbelly of the record industry and the London-centric music scene that Rory had to contend with'. Rory's nephew responded:

> I think he [Gallagher] does refer to the music industry as being the villain/mob type, which he has to duck and weave in and out of to survive. Songs like 'Kid Gloves', where the boxing character is told to take a dive, strikes me as Rory being told to release a single, it'll earn him money, but won't help his soul. I think in 'Kickback City' as a track you can really hear Rory's despondency with having to exist in the business side of music where, 'you try to learn all your lines / And you try to play the part / With all this double dealing / I tell you brother, you get smart.'

On the *Front Row* programme, Dónal Gallagher described taking care on tour of Rory's cases, which were 'literally full of these kind of books', adding, a touch ominously: 'He'd lock himself in the room for days when we were off a tour … distressingly so, in a way.'

By the end of the 1980s, Rory Gallagher's art and his life were becoming more entangled. In his last album, *Fresh Evidence*, he becomes confessional again with themes of mortality and ill health. 'Heaven's Gate' is a song with bleak overtones, about life's end. There's a strong religious reference:

> You'll never get to Heaven
> Putting money in the plate
> Can't bribe St Peter
> When you're at Heaven's gate.

'Walking Wounded' was written when Rory's health was not so good, he told Anil Prasad in 1991: 'It's not written in the first person as such, but I suppose it's written from the point of view that if you're at a very low ebb, you still have fighting spirit. That's the basic message in it. The song has a nice riff and a bittersweet flavor to it.'[23] The song contains one of Gallagher's references to Cork, when he touchingly resolves that 'if he had some sense' he'd 'move back to the Southern Coast.' In the last verse, he has decided to do just that.[24]

Perhaps the most autobiographical cut on the album is 'Ghost Blues', a song about alcohol dependency and all that goes with it.

> Came home this morning,
> Looking half-way like a ghost.
> Walked in this morning,
> Feeling half-way like a ghost.

There are suggestions later in the song of domestic strife, a reference to coming home and finding a woman crying at the door. Could Gallagher have been thinking of his own home in Derry in the 1950s? Could the 'ghost' in the song be the ghost of Danny Gallagher? It can also be seen as a throwback to a song from the Taste period; but while 'Sinner Boy', all those years ago, was written in the third person, this song is an alcoholic's confession, in the first person. In *Guitar* magazine, Gallagher was expansive about that song and the recording of it, before hinting it had a personal resonance:

> I always find the first song you write after New Year is an important one and 'Ghost Blues' was no exception. It's a lonely time of year in many ways and if I'd been in Ireland with all the family, I'm sure it'd never have been written. The melancholy you feel that time of year brings on good songs though, which was one consolation ...

> I sang it in one take, but then with emotional songs it's always easier if you're in the right mood. The feel on that track is specific to that day I recorded it. I recall I had a serious bout of the flu when we came to cut it in the studio and I was feeling very

weak. That tends to polarise you and make you more open to strong emotion. It all seemed to combine into this huge haze but I had to do the track, get it out. Almost like some sort of purification ...[25]

Chapter 14

THE RORY GALLAGHER LEGACY

'I've always believed that the best music should be
dangerous. It's like taking it to the edge where a riot
could break out. Even in gospel music, you get the mad
ecstasy. I'm no fan of cocktail music, the best blues and
rock is a collision.'

– RORY GALLAGHER IN 1988[1]

Rory Gallagher surely believed that he would come face to face with his maker. What would he be asked at the celebrated gates of heaven? What did you leave for humanity, for art? We could answer for him. He undoubtedly brought joy to people all over the world. From the time he picked up the four-stringed plastic guitar, from the moment AFN first reached his ears, Rory Gallagher was following a vocation.

Gallagher was, firstly, a bluesman. He flirted with hard rock, flirted with commercial rock, but he said many times his immovable ethic was to be true to the pure black music of the American south, particularly country blues. 'A lot of the young rock guitarists who turn on to the blues think it ends and begins, with all due respect, with Albert King, Freddie King, B.B. King and maybe Muddy Waters,' Gallagher said. 'They don't delve back into the country blues or the borderline where country blues turned into electric country blues. If anything, even though I can play in the sort of standard string-bending style, in the B.B. King mold and all of that, I've always had a great interest in the more primitive playing, the open chord playing, rhythm and figures.'[2]

In 1982, he was strident when asked if his style of blues playing came easily to him.

> It's easy in as much as you could throw me in at the deep end at almost any Blues session, and I could provide what was required. If someone wanted a Chicago Blues style, or Delta Slide, or Detroit or North Carolina, I'd know what they were talking about, so in that sense it's easy for me; but by the same token, playing the Blues is one of the hardest things to do because it's the one music that is so emotional that if you can't summon up the feeling, you can't play the Blues; it sounds false and hollow. That applies to the real Bluesmen as well: I mean, even Muddy has to work at it every night and you can't get more of a giant than that. Rock 'n' roll's

more of an aggressive, rhythmic thing, but with
the Blues you've got to summon up an atmosphere
– you can't act it.[3]

Gallagher was not an academic, but he could discuss
blues history. He believed, for example, that among
Mississippi players, Son House[4] had been somewhat
overlooked in comparison to Robert Johnson. 'Everyone's
stating that Robert Johnson is the virtuoso of that era, but
Son House was very important at the time.'[5] In a detailed
discussion with Stefan Grossman, where he analysed
different phases of Blind Boy Fuller's career and said that
Howlin' Wolf's lead-guitar player, Hubert Humlin, had
been underrated, he said of House: 'In terms of intensity,
Son House has to be listened to. Of all the blues players,
that's probably the closest connection with Africa.'[6]
A factor in the popularity of Johnson was, Gallagher
believed, 'the mystique, the death thing and the devil
connection'. Johnson was supposed to have made a pact
with the devil at the famous crossroads in Clarksdale,
Mississippi, in order to gain musical mastery. (Son House
apparently said, 'he [Johnson] must have sold his soul to
play like that'). Gallagher was once asked if he believed
in this aspect of the Robert Johnson story: 'I think it's
possible. I heard the same thing about John Lennon that
when he was in Hamburg, he made some kind of deal.
And if you look at his death and his effect on people and
life in general, you have to wonder, but then I'm a little
bit superstitious anyway.'[7] He described the two Robert
Johnson records on Columbia as 'cornerstones' when

Grossman asked him what the essential recordings were. 'You'd have to get at least one of those.'[8] Interestingly, Gallagher's composition 'Hell Cat' (a bonus track on the reissued *Top Priority*), is thematically very close to the famous Johnson number, 'Hell Hound on My Trail'. In Johnson's song, the devil in the form of a hellhound is catching up with him, as if it was time to repay his debt. In Gallagher's song, there is a reference to playing 'dice with the devil' and 'having a hell cat on your tail'. This all shows Gallagher being immersed in blues culture as well as the music. He would surely have identified with this kind of folk legend. Dónal Gallagher described 'Hell Cat' as a 'spooky track', his brother 'contemplating his superstitious nature and wondering whether he himself is jinxed'.[9]

Yet Gallagher took issue with one aspect of blues music, the violence towards women present in so many of the songs, referring once to 'worrying questions about sexism in blues lyrics', he told a journalist, 'by Big Bill Broonzy and company'.[10] (Robert Johnson's famous 'Me and the Devil Blues' had included the line 'And I'm going to beat my woman till I'm satisfied.') Gallagher continued: 'As a white European, I have tried to take the songs to areas beyond that "I am a Little Red Rooster" department. And I feel proud of at least attempting that, even if the songs aren't hits.'[11]

So where did Gallagher get *his* blues? According to Philip King, a musician and singer himself with a career in the presentation of music on screen, who can remember as far back as the 006 Club in Cork: 'Gallagher understood, at a deep, deep level, the revelatory power of the blues. He inhabited that music, not just as a voyeur; he sought to be inside it.' Gallagher said in 1976: 'I don't think you get it from anywhere. You're born with that love ... for that feeling, that mood that the blues gives you. I don't think it has to be a purist sort of approach, or academic. You just feel it ... you just want to express yourself – through the instrument, or vocally. I don't think it's an American thing or a European thing. You just do it.'[12] In the end, for Rory Gallagher, blues was personal, something more than just music. He told Dave Fanning in 1988: 'what makes it [the blues] more important ... it gets right into your veins, as a lifestyle and as a mind[set] ... a little beacon in your life, you know.'[13] Paul Charles puts it this way: 'You couldn't possibly play the blues like Rory played the blues without being connected to the blues.'

Gallagher was blunt about blues music played on his side of the Atlantic. The 'British Blues Boom', he said, had 'both good and bad moments. It was a very London thing with John Mayall, Fleetwood Mac and Chicken Shack and they were so po-faced about it. Good players but professors of the Blues – so a lot of them missed the emotion of it. Americans like Mike Bloomfield and John Hammond were looser about it.'[14] Mike Bloomfield was a Chicago-born guitarist, a member of the Paul Butterfield Band in the mid 1960s, who became a much sought-after guitarist. He played on Bob Dylan's album *Highway 61 Revisited* and in Dylan's band at the famous Newport Folk Festival gig in 1965 when the folk hero first turned electric.[15] Gallagher described Bloomfield in 1991 as, 'a very nice, modest guy, and a beautiful player. A really soulful player.'[16]

The accepted view of Gallagher's relationship with blues is that he went to the original sources for material, discovering old recordings in music shops in Belfast or London. But this view may not be the whole story. When some song connections are examined, there's no doubting that Mike Bloomfield's recordings were a significant influence. Gallagher's version of Big Bill Broonzy's 'I Feel So Good', which featured on both live Taste albums, owes much more to Bloomfield's version of the song than to Broonzy's original 1941 recording. There are at least four other songs recorded by Gallagher that had been recorded by Bloomfield in the mid 1960s, so they pre-date Gallagher's recording career – 'It Takes Time', 'Gamblin' Blues', 'Messin' With the Kid' and 'I Wonder Who' – suggesting the connection is not mere coincidence. Does this amount to influence or plagiarism, some might ask? Dave McHugh, who has studied Gallagher's relationship to American blues, sees it this way: 'Many people see Bloomfield as "that fella who played with Dylan", but he and his Chicago blues background were clearly a significant influence on Rory.'

'The blues are the roots and the other musics are the fruits', the Mississippi-born Willie Dixon once said, gently highlighting a modern issue. To his credit, Rory Gallagher's treatment of original blues songwriters was entirely honourable. This was not always the case during the White Blues boom. A well-known example concerns

Led Zeppelin's most successful song, 'Whole Lotta Love'. It bears a strong resemblance to Willie Dixon's 1962 song, 'You Need Love'. After an out-of-court settlement in 1987, Dixon's name was added to the song credits. Dónal told Dan Muise that Rory was asked to be a witness in the case, to say that this was 'the done thing at that time'. Gallagher evidently refused.

* * *

For his audience, Gallagher was, first and foremost, a guitar player. Each night as the strap went across his shoulder and his fingers reached for the strings, he created great expectation. What were – what are – the qualities that made the legend? Stephen Hunter of University College Cork identified a crucial quality in his playing: warmth. 'He might unleash an explosive flurry of growling, bent notes, yet there always seems to be at the back of this a sensitivity, a kind of aesthetic precision that prevents his work ever straying into the more self-indulgent reaches of heavy metal.'[17] Steve Rosen in *Guitar Player* attempted to pinpoint the technique, saying that the different sounds he achieved are created by hand, guitar and amplifier. He described how Gallagher used the neck of the guitar:

> On its lower reaches Rory's use of finger/pick muffling causes the notes to sound like a synthe-sizer, while notes 'pinged' higher up the neck sound like they're in a tape loop and are coming

out backwards. When asked how he manages to extract such a clean, ringing sound Gallagher hems and haws and finally just chalks it up to experience. 'I've been doing it for years,' he says. 'It depends on the tone, and how much you really want to get them out. You can get a lot of interesting effects from it. Mind you, you wear your nail down to a shred though.'[18]

When Jas Obrecht asked him about recording solos, he answered: 'I try to split the difference between being fairly clever and technical, and still primitive.'[19] Wolf Marshall chose to forensically analyse the guitar solo from the studio version of 'Laundromat': 'Here typical pentatonic blues-rock licks are replaced by pure diatonic scale melodies more often associated with Irish fiddle tunes, folk music and post-modern jazz.'[20] An interview with Gallagher in *Guitar* magazine bears this out: 'One night I might start a solo from an Irish jig position, and another night it could be a pure Buddy Holly thing. Any element of jazz in my playing is more from the theory point of view, a freedom point of view, where the sky's the limit and you can hit notes that aren't necessarily the orthodox. Whereas if you actually start playing very obvious jazz type progressions it soon starts to make certain songs sound over sophisticated, and I like to keep that bluesy sound. At present I'm trying to keep the … Celtic blues might be right. Let's put it this way, I like to leave a lot of open strings hanging on during solos, when I'm up in the seventh or eighth fret, keeping things running below.'[21] In the same interview, Gallagher was expansive when asked about harmonics by the writer, John Dalton:

The classical style I only use once in a blue moon, but the main kind of harmonic stuff I do with a plectrum and a bit of flesh or nail from the first finger. Eventually you become so used to it you can do it with freak ways of hitting the string in different spots. You can get a true harmonic, or you can get a freak one. It really makes the guitar very lively; it really gives you a sense of being in charge of the instrument, instead of having to press a button to get that effect. Obviously some people mightn't find it an important thing, but I think it is because it gives the guitar a kind of an extra register. I mean if you use feedback for pure effect, and bend the string at the same time, you can create exciting things. It's great if you're doing, say, a double section of a solo, and the second part you really want to get an insane sort of leap forward – harmonics come in handy then.

Gallagher was fortunate to live in an era of guitar heroes, when the sounds from the instrument could cast a spell they don't seem to in the 21st century. So where does he rank in relation to the late 1960s white blues explosion, as it's called? According to another music writer, Doug Collette, Rory Gallagher was unique among guitar heroes of his era: 'In marked contrast to his peers of the prior generation – Eric Clapton, Jeff Beck and Jimmy Page – Gallagher eschewed compromise in any form and so engendered a loyalty in his fans that matched his own fiery demeanor onstage.'[22] However, he will always be compared to these other big names. And it may be an uncomfortable fact for some, but in the *Rolling Stone* '100 Greatest Guitarists' list in 2015, Gallagher only makes number 57, with Hendrix at number one, Clapton at two, followed by Jimmy Page. In *Mojo*'s 1995 list, Gallagher is 87th.

Polls and charts aside, Gallagher burns brightly in rock history. He is seen as a star with an endearing lack of conceit of any kind, his music a beacon of sincerity and principle. And from an Irish point of view, if he wasn't *the* greatest, he was *our* greatest. The Edge, for one, gave his judgement: 'There was a lyricism to his playing that was quite his own. No other player really had his particular approach and phrasing. While I don't think he ever thought of it as being Irish, I picked up a lot of the Irish influence in his particular version of the blues.'[23]

There's at least one probable myth in the Gallagher story. It's the often-repeated alleged remark by Jimi Hendrix about him. Hendrix was reputedly asked 'How does it feel to be the world's greatest guitarist?' He is said to have replied: 'I don't know. Ask Rory Gallagher.' Extraordinary as it may seem, the remark has never been authenticated. It has become something of an urban legend. The 'quote', and the frequent repetition of it, also exposes the perils of endorsement. Those who appreciate Gallagher's music know that it doesn't need the imprimatur of anyone else, even a musician and innovator of Hendrix's stature. Rory Gallagher was not quite the ground-breaker Hendrix was, if they must be compared. He had other qualities.[24] There's a practical point, too: why was Rory Gallagher not asked about it during the remainder of his life, in the 25 years between Hendrix's death and his own? Tellingly, Jimi Hendrix's autobiography, *Starting at Zero*, makes no reference to Rory Gallagher.[25]

Gallagher's faith, his Catholicism, has to be part of his legacy. He regularly attended Mass. According to Avril MacRory: 'I think he had a really sincere faith, though he never would proselytise. But he always said "God bless" and he had a way of saying it ... it was utterly Cork, but it was sincere and said in the loveliest and gentlest of ways.' Whether unconsciously or knowingly, Bob Geldof used religious imagery to characterise Rory in 2010: 'Rory always struck me as a priest – with long hair ... [lowers his voice] that sort of quiet Cork thing ... He could have been in a seminary, except that his chalice was the guitar and his prayers were the Blues.'[26]

Gallagher could use a religious reference to make a point. As a panellist on the BBC Radio 1 programme *Round Table* with Kid Jensen in 1979, while discussing punk, which he described as 'a brute force return to a good aggressive beat', he said that there was too much intellectualising about it: 'That's always the trouble with rock 'n' roll: when they try to write the New Testament with it, it loses its point.' His co-panellist, Anne Nightingale, complimented him on his metaphor, saying 'Nicely put, Rory!'

* * *

To anyone looking at Rory Gallagher's life, his relationship with his brother is an interesting one. The family factor made it more complicated than other manager/client relationships. Dónal told a magazine in 2003, 'not only would I be on tour as tour manager, but also I was also agent, booking manager and having to make managerial decisions. It evolved that way. But Rory, being an older brother, also didn't like to be told by a younger brother. Sibling rivalry would come into it.'[27] He talked candidly about their relationship in 2000: 'We all used to have in-depth family conversations and he could sum up a situation in one word. I miss that. I miss the understanding.' But he also missed something more pervasive – how Rory made him feel: 'He was such a strong person that you felt you could defeat the world with him around. You felt as though you were in the front line of life with someone like him.' When it is suggested that Rory might have thought the same about Dónal, the self-deprecating reply could have come from the guitar maestro himself. 'I don't know. Perhaps without me he would have been even bigger. But life is full of luck and coincidence.'[28] For his part, Rory once described his brother as having 'a good head on his shoulders and can't be deceived easily.'[29]

Dónal Gallagher's work in safeguarding his sibling's estate has been both diligent and strongly protective (though he has yet to produce an (anticipated) account of his brother's life, and his role in it). Rory Gallagher's standing in the public mind is, to a significant extent, due to his efforts, though he has had an ideal resource to work with – his brother's talent and likeability. The legacy has a significant business dimension, too, a careful commercial managing by Dónal of the Gallagher name and music.

On a human level, Rory could also be described as a ghost in his brother's life. Dónal once related a curious incident, a throwback to Rory's folk beliefs. For a remixing session in 1996 he had brought in one of the original engineers, who decided to record the mix in a different way from how Rory would have done it. 'Because he had worked with Rory so much, I indulged him. But during the mixing, the mixing desk, which was world-class quality, developed a fault, which had never happened before. The engineers couldn't work out what was wrong with it, even when they examined it afterwards. One of the guys remarked that maybe Rory didn't want the music mixed this way, so we altered the mix to how Rory would have preferred it. After that, the problem went away and didn't occur again.'[30] Was there a ghost in the machinery?

There is no doubt that Gallagher enjoys a very high status in music history, and yet it is worth considering whether his relatively early death is a factor in this. A *Guitar World* retrospective in 2009, referring to the phenomenon of 'posthumous cult adoration', put a critical perspective on the legacy: 'Gallagher was an agile riff meister whose scrappy, energetic style was punctuated by occasional bursts of fluid, six-string poetry. His playing was steeped in bluesy authenticity.' The writer concluded: 'Rory Gallagher possesses in spades the most important qualification for posthumous cult adulation; a sad life story.'[31] Certainly, Gallagher avoided the anguish of becoming an elderly rocker, something Jimmy Page reflected on in 2009. He said that a point will certainly come when 'you're too old to pick the guitar up. And we just try to keep that day far away and out of sight.'[32]

* * *

Gallagher will inevitably be compared to other significant names in Irish rock. Notwithstanding Van Morrison's great talent, moving around inside American music and coming out with something unique, he has always remained aloof as a person. Tony Palmer, the director of the *Irish Tour '74* film summed up in 2012 what Gallagher meant to him: 'Rory had two incredible qualities – he could play like nobody else, and somehow his personality was something the audience responded to in quite a loving and open way. They thought he was on their side. It's one of those indefinable things you immediately sense – if a performer is on your side or in your face – they just knew he was one of them.'[33] And there was Philip Lynott, a supreme showman and a gifted lyricist, but reckless with his life, to the extent of dying from a drug overdose at the age of 36. Graeme Thomson in his Lynott biography quotes the poet Peter Fallon: 'Philip rose and he fell, and somehow that rise and fall was simultaneous.'[34] There were the great highs of songwriting achievement, like 'The Boys Are Back in Town' where machismo becomes art, great shows, chart success and then, by the late 1970s, as Thomson says, 'Lynott's rocker persona had become a caricature, and he was trapped inside.'

Should Gallagher have been 'more pushy', his nephew, Daniel, asked Brian May? The Queen veteran replied: 'If he had, he wouldn't have been Rory Gallagher.' He went on to say that he did not get the recognition he deserved. 'I think he sidestepped the things that could have made him a Springsteen ... or an Aerosmith.'[35] Pat Egan suggests that Gallagher 'underachieved a little bit', and not just because of the singles issue. In comparing Rory to Clapton, Hendrix and Jeff Beck, he says they had 'a more show business feel to them. Or they had better people working for them. So much of it is about opening doors – or getting them opened!'

Gallagher could not get away from one uncompromising aspect of his nature, the 'singles issue'. Even when he was reminded that highly regarded bands like (the early) Fleetwood Mac released records in the shorter format, he was stubborn. He told Shiv Cariappa in their 1991 discussion: 'I would never squander my whole credibility, whatever that is, just for one silly song.' Some Gallagher singles were released, 'disguised' as radio play or DJ singles. 'Philby' was one of these, though its fate would not have endeared the superstitious Gallagher to this form of promotion; just after it was released, Kim Philby was in the news again when Anthony Blunt, an art historian and Surveyor of the Queen's art collection, was revealed as the 'fourth man' of English Soviet agents, in November 1979. In the March 1980 interview, Dave Fanning asked Gallagher about the unfortunate timing, and he replied with a laugh, 'maybe I should have waited a few weeks?'

Gallagher did a lot for his hometown's self-esteem. Louis de Paor was fifteen when he first saw Rory perform in the City Hall in 1976. In his poem 'Rory, Cork City Hall 1976', he captures the wonder of musical appreciation, and Cork pride:

> Did you really not hear
> the tide flooding in behind you,
> the waves of pounding feet
> that rocked the floor of the City Hall
> until it rolled like the deck of a ship,
> that will never fill the emptiness
> you left behind you on stage?[36]

The poem was written more than twenty years after the event, an indication of Gallagher's power for de Paor. One of his memories of the gig was the applause: Gallagher liked to use 'false endings' to songs. The drums would go 'Bam!' and the crowd would start cheering, but Gallagher would drive the band again for another, and another ending. De Paor, in his poem, wondered would Gallagher have actually missed the strength of the initial response. 'By the time he ended the song he'd missed the applause at its peak.' Looking back now, de Paor can extend this thought: 'In the inevitable quieter days of his career, did he know how much we appreciated him, how much we owed him? Did he think we'd forgotten him? Maybe we did, for a while?'

Christy Moore says 'soulfulness' was a great Gallagher quality. 'His legacy is the fact that we are still talking about him.' Norman Damery says of his one-time bandmate: 'His legacy? It's his genuineness.' Martin Carthy compares him to the renowned Irish tenor, Count John McCormack, because of both men's ability to captivate people. 'He was astonishingly inventive. He loved music. Full stop. He loved it to bits and he loved other people who loved it to bits. That's a pretty good legacy.'

For Gallagher, music always came first, onstage and offstage. The star could become the fan again very easily. After his gig in Vancouver in 1974, he slipped into the crowd, as he often did, this time to see Paul Butterfield's show. He was being observed. 'A swell of people gathered round the front of the stage for Butterfield just as they had for Gallagher during his performance. They seemed unaware that the man they had hailed back for a frenzy-inspiring encore an hour ago was now among them and safe within their anonymity.'[37] Dave McHugh sees genius and humility: 'The kind of person he was, meant that he would have considered himself more as a hard-working curate than the high priest he was.'

Like so many great artists, Gallagher had the power to inspire others, to bring moments that changed lives. Dino McGartland from Omagh, County Tyrone, remembers clearly the day he bought *Live in Europe* in his local record shop more than 40 years ago. He became irrevocably enthralled as the vinyl played. 'I like to be thrown across the room – and I was that day.' His passion for Gallagher has not dimmed in all the years. He sees Gallagher as a 'Dylanesque' figure for blues music.

Musical conviction was Gallagher's essence. You can hear it in his shouts of joy on the live recordings, as he spurred himself on. With the guitar in his hands he became a kind of sorcerer. But how can the kernel of his art – his magic – really be described?

One journalist, Philip Nolan, had this simple observation as he ate with the guitarist one evening: 'I'm fascinated by his command of chopsticks until it suddenly dawns on me – those fingers, the self same ones that have given the world a million of the best guitar solos it's ever been treated to, the nimblest, meanest, most exciting, electric fingers Ireland has ever produced.'[38]

Drinking pints with a *Sounds* writer in a Cork pub in 1974, Gallagher combined erudition and mystery in describing where his music came from: 'The goals of my sort of music, they can't be reached by technique, nor by hardship either.' Then he returned to the blues, referring to the music of Waters and Hooker: 'that spiritual thing they get across to me … it's as fresh as a newborn baby, but it's as old as a man of 65, and its pure twentieth century. It's twice as flash, tough as any of your metal rock or street punks.'[39]

His conclusion that day could even be his epitaph: 'The music's beyond that altogether … and there again, it's something you can't explain.'

Chapter 15

ETERNITY BECKONS

'Words like fire, passion, friendliness and openness:
these are all words that apply. He was an open book ...
Rory Gallagher graced music as he graced humanity.
The word is grace.'

— MARTIN CARTHY[1]

'The future ...?', responded a 23-year-old Rory Gallagher to Michael Wale of *The Times* in 1971. 'I want to walk out on to the stage at 40 or 50 and have people watching me, like I go to see Muddy Waters. I've nothing but respect for a musician who stays with it and improves and improves.' But for Gallagher, this was not to be.

By the early 1990s, his physical appearance had changed. His face was bloated. He had slowed down on the stage. Health was an issue. In his book, Jean-Noël

Coghe described Gallagher after a gig in September 1989 in Deinze, Belgium: 'Rory had visibly put on weight and was thought to be suffering from something, but the subject was never brought up in public, out of decency and respect. Nothing in his attitude seemed to have changed – he was still his same old polite, kind self.' Dónal Gallagher has spoken frankly about this period of his brother's life. 'I felt he was giving up. His physical exhaustion had led to mental exhaustion. I think, with hindsight, that the poor man had had a series of nervous breakdowns that were not visible to other people. When I saw how serious the situation had become, I reckoned it was better for him to go out and work, he had been under strain during his time off the road in London, trying to create new music. It had become counter-productive.'[2] Michael Ross wrote about Gallagher's recordings at that period: 'He gets so consumed by them that he frequently turns against them ... He re-mixed endlessly, completely unable to rely on the judgement of others and barely able to rely on his own.'[3] Colin Harper was blunt: 'The abiding impression of Rory in his final years is of a lonely, shy man who had simply lost confidence in what he did.'[4] In a sense, music – what had made him great – was threatening, ironically, to kill him. Dónal Gallagher spoke about this in 1998:

> Rory was performer, producer, manager in a way, and songwriter. The physical exhaustion took its toll, as did the pressure to bring out albums, as did being ignored by the media. He withdrew into

himself. He didn't go to as many gigs or buy as many albums. When he was off the road he didn't know what to do with himself and this made him depressed and disoriented, he didn't have the ability to relax or unwind. Even when he went back to Ireland he was uneasy. He felt people were fickle and mightn't like him any more.[5]

Rory's situation was now challenging. He had in his time tried to crack America; now four new kids on the block, from the north side of Dublin, had that continent eating out of their hands. In 1991, Rory was asked a candid question by Stephen Roche of *Seconds* magazine:

There are a lot of music fans out there who don't know who Rory Gallagher is. How do you feel about that?

GALLAGHER: Well, it's very frustrating, particularly in Ireland. Because of the success of U2, you can easily become forgotten, especially if you don't have hit records for a while. I don't mean to sound envious. Staying away from America for five years hasn't helped, but I never went out of my way to be a pop artist. Like I said, I'm not a record company dream. I'm not selling an image or standing on my head too much. There are certain TV shows I can't do because I refuse to mime. So I have been my own worst enemy.[6]

There's a darker tone in Liam Fay's *Hot Press* interview in July 1992 when Gallagher said he had stopped wearing the trademark denim jacket and check shirts, elaborating with a blunt, religious image: '[They] have become like a stigmata to me. I never treated it as a uniform but that's what it has become over the years, a uniform I just don't want to wear anymore. Lately I wear an ordinary black shirt and a black jacket when I'm on stage. Right now, I feel a lot happier in black.' It was in that same year, 1992, that Christy Moore recalls seeing him for the last time. They were, he says, 'backstage buddies', and this occasion was the Glasgow Fleadh in May: 'I saw him surrounded by fans, signing autographs. I thought he looked real lonesome, unhappy, maybe even lost, but we never got a chance to talk ... I still regret that.'

When he headlined the Temple Bar Blues Festival in Dublin on 15 August 1992, at the old Parliament House building on College Green, it was his last gig in the city. Brian Palm and Mary Stokes met Gallagher in the bar of Blooms Hotel the day before the gig. Gallagher was apprehensive about how he would go down with the audience. 'It was the first time I'd seen evidence of fragility. I wasn't expecting it,' Palm says. 'He was nervous, and we were amazed by that.' The writer John Waters had been sceptical about how the gig might go: 'But on the night Gallagher was, if possible, even better than I remembered. He captivated the huge crowd – half curious bystanders, half now-greying lumberjackshirted hordes – like the angel he was.'[7]

He gave an interview that month to Joe Jackson for *The Irish Times*, in which, Jackson says, Gallagher was anxious to clarify the impression people might have had from the *Hot Press* interview in July. As for his drinking, or his physical and mental health, he had 'nothing to hide', he said. He noted that the Dublin gig was to take place on the eve of the fifteenth anniversary of Elvis Presley's death, 16 August. He talked about early death, excess in rock, firstly in relation to drink and drugs. 'The idea that you can't play the blues unless you're an alcoholic is nonsense and potentially a lethal notion to be selling to young musicians.' At the same time, he believed that there were primeval forces that were needed in music, referring to 'black cat feelings' and their presence in his life. Perhaps the most revealing thing he said was in relation to Robert Johnson's music. While listening to it some years previously, he 'got a strange feeling of maybe connecting with some evil force which made me switch off the music and I haven't played Johnson since. I get that black cat feeling and, blues or no blues, there is a strong post-Celtic pagan element within the Irish, which I don't think we've ever completely shaken off. So, as a superstitious Catholic, I think it's extra dangerous for us to toy with these forces.' He continued: 'You have to step over a certain line, not necessarily to connect with evil, but to take yourself as close to the brink as you can, to give the music that essential edge. It's a dangerous balance you have to try and maintain.'[8]

Gallagher's final London gig, at the Town and Country Club on 29 October that year, did not go as well as the Dublin one had; apparently, brandy combined with his medication caused him to appear to be drunk, leading to a shortened set and annoyance by some of the audience. Dónal Gallagher recalled that night. 'The first few numbers were fantastic – I mean he really lashed on to it. But then suddenly, the concoction of taking a couple of brandies, to wake up before getting on stage, counteracted with his medicine he had taken. And then suddenly you realize that you have a battle on your hands. As close I was to my brother, I wasn't rude enough to look at his medicines. I knew some of the medicines he was taking were for flying. And I thought fair enough if it helped him with flying, travel and stresses. It was from that moment on, I was very concerned.'[9]

This was the first gig with his new band: David Leavey on bass, Richard Newman on drums, Jim Leverton and John Cooke alternating on keyboards, and Mark Feltham on harmonica. He played his last gig in Ireland, an acoustic set with Feltham and Lou Martin, at the Cork Institute of Technology 'ArtsFest', on 18 November 1993, in honour of his deceased uncle Jimmy, who had been principal of the college. The loyalty towards Gallagher in Cork was expressed in a comment made by his old classmate in St Kieran's, Mick 'Tana' O'Brien, when he told the *Evening Echo* in 2005: 'We used to hope that when he'd retire, he'd come home to Ireland and we'd all be playing the blues together in some old pub, just like the old days.'[10] Gallagher had expressed a similar sentiment in his December 1990 interview in the *London-Irish News*:

'You would miss Ireland, there is no doubt about it', he says. 'You miss the people. I never entirely mentally left Ireland. That might be because when you're touring for years and living in hotels in Germany and France or whatever, you have to apply yourself to the road and become gypsy-minded, in a sense. In the long run, I'll go back to Ireland. But I'm trying not to think about retirement yet, I still have a few years left in me', he says with a slight laugh.

In his last years, Gallagher's relationship with the press became fraught on at least one occasion. In December 1992, he advised one writer, Uli Twelker, to 'burn' the article that David Sinclair had written for Q magazine in 1990. Gallagher said he found it 'very offensive'. 'The guy caught me literally the day I finished *Fresh Evidence*, and I really was wrecked. You know, the end of an album, it's like having a baby or something. I must have given a bad impression, and I did my best to be accurate and pleasant and so on, and it didn't come out that way. I shouldn't have done it, but that's life.' The journalist probably perceived vulnerability, but perhaps Gallagher was just being honest and open.

Sinclair, though he praised Gallagher musically, had written in Q: 'He is in poor shape. Rheumy eyes peer from a face that looks as if it has been pumped up like a football. His hair is a virulent shade of dark henna red, but grey roots push up along the crease of a ragged centre parting. What can do this to a man?'

When Twelker reminded him that *Q* gave the album a good review, in spite of the portrayal of him, Gallagher's answer reveals his character – and his problems at this point in his life: 'I get involved in the production and I get very hyper and really work my heart over the damn thing. It's dangerous for your health, you don't realize. You stop eating and then the next thing you know you get into dangerous territory. So it's unfair then when somebody misrepresents you.' He returned then to a recurring theme of his life: 'I'm against planning. You know, that's something Van Morrison says: "Rory, you gotta time-plan, man. You gotta plan out your holiday and your work." But I just can't work that way.' Gallagher was now the living embodiment of one of blues music's abilities – to express isolation and loneliness, according to Philip King. 'He was not so much a lonely man as a lonesome man.' And Bill Graham's 1988 article was succinct: 'He accepts the existence of a nervous, terrier, and obsessional quality within his psyche: "It's fine to have free time. One failure I've always had is that I don't plan free time. I don't take holidays in the sun because so many prospects get delayed. So I might have had free time – but it was more agony than free time. It wasn't sitting on a beach getting healthy."'

In 1993, Rory moved out of his London apartment to live at the Conrad Hotel, Chelsea (now the Chelsea Harbour Hotel), in room 710. Jean-Noël Coghe recalled that when you rang the hotel and asked to be put through to his room you had to give a code name, 'Alain Delon' (one of Gallagher's favourite actors). There's a sense of gloom from Gallagher in an interview in February that year. 'To be truthful, I feel a bit used up after all these years. I've given so much of myself to this business that I really have difficulty getting enthused about anything. Often, I think that I'd be better off dropping everything and going fishing or back to my painting.'[11]

Some friends were always there for him. He played a gig in Ghent in Belgium in spring, 1993. Catherine Mattelaer, Jean-Noël Coghe and Roland Van Campenout came to the show. Mattelaer was married and had a child at that stage. After the show she and Rory met and had a conversation that Coghe in his book says 'seemed like hours' and that he 'sensed the intensity of the discussion'. Mattelaer revealed, according to Coghe's account, that Rory talked to her, 'like he'd never done before, about his innermost feelings and the things that were dearest to his heart. It was almost as if he sensed his days were numbered.' Towards the end of their meeting that night, Rory bought her the entire stock of flowers from a passing seller.

Dónal Gallagher organised touring activity in 1994, including what became a resurgent performance at Lorient, Brittany, in October, but his brother's health deteriorated dramatically in the first two months of 1995. A short tour of Holland in late January was cancelled halfway through when he became ill. In his *Sunday Times* interview in May 1998, Dónal Gallagher said: 'When he started having abdominal pains, which, with hindsight was probably the first sign of his liver trouble – he was prescribed paracetamol, which, where a liver is damaged, can cause more damage. I wish more checks had been made at the time.'

One of Gallagher's last television interviews was for a Dublin production company working for Ulster Television, in early 1994. Brian Reddin was the director and remembers the circumstances. They were working on a series called *Rock 'n' the North*, broadcast later that year, and presented by Terri Hooley. An interview had been arranged with Rory, but when the group arrived in London they got a call from Dónal saying that it was off – Rory just couldn't do it. They had given up hope when at 10 p.m. that night the phone rang and it was Dónal saying he had persuaded his brother to change his mind. But the interview would not be in the studio that had been booked; instead they would have to go to Rory's hotel, right there and then, which they did. 'It was one of the weirdest interview situations I'd ever been in. He appeared paranoid. He was anxious about the interview, anxious about everything. He didn't want to play anything.' But Hooley later recalled that the mood suddenly changed: 'I asked him why did Irish people like the blues so much. That set him off and he talked for it seemed like hours, about Irish traditional music, Cajun, the Blues and how they were all interlinked.'[12] Gallagher picked up a guitar to perform a gentle take on 'That's All Right, Mama', a glimpse of the Gallagher magic coming from the strings. 'It was a real privilege to be there, but it was uncomfortable,' Reddin says. He also remembers that, despite Gallagher's demeanour that night, he had retained a little vanity, making sure he held his head for the camera in a way that didn't reveal the double chin that had become a feature of his appearance. In another interview later that year for the Franco-German TV channel ARTÉ, in the same hotel room, he was forlornly trying to be upbeat, but let his guard down. 'My writing is getting better. My playing is getting better. I'm much more happy today as a musician. I'm not happy as a person, but I'm happy as a musician.'

Gallagher, despite the great years of total confidence on a stage, was apparently at low ebb as he faced gigs in Switzerland and Austria in July 1994, which included his last appearance at the Montreux Jazz Festival. Martin Carthy was asked by a mutual friend to get in touch with him. Carthy, surprised that it had come to this, responded by firstly reminding Rory of his audience: 'I said, "They're not there to shoot you down, you know. They're there because they love you. You're Rory Gallagher!"' He believes that though he was aware of health issues, what he calls 'rust' was also part of the problem. He says he experienced it himself when he had a period without performance. Gallagher had not been performing that frequently and had cancelled a gig in Buxton, England, in April that year for health reasons. The two men talked on the phone after the first of the gigs. It had gone well, Rory reported. 'He seemed almost perplexed that an audience would still want to see him. But audiences don't forget. Especially, they don't forget someone like Rory.'

In January 1995, a Dutch interviewer, Jip Golsteijn, despite describing himself 'more fan than professional', included some stark details from an encounter in the Conrad Hotel: 'A man in a black uniform brings beer and sandwiches. "Breakfast!" Rory says as he uncaps two bottles of Heineken. It is half past four in the afternoon.' Golsteijn continued, not sparing any blushes:

> Rory Gallagher is the type who screams before he has been hit. Every question is possibly a trap question. Although he does not see the forest through the trees, he sees an enemy behind every tree. If he has completely forgotten it, he repeats it over and over again that he is just a simple Irish buffoon who just happens to be able to play and sing the blues very well. But at least as often, he jumps to put my hand in a vice with both his hands, embrace me, surprised, if not touched, to have found a partisan. I don't have to fake it in Rory Gallagher's case. He is the most energetic guitar player I have ever seen or heard.[13]

Around this time, Eric Bell, who had not seen Rory for years, met him by chance one day on Denmark Street in London. Eric was there to buy a present for a family member in one of the street's famous music shops. They went for coffee, but Rory decided on a glass of wine instead. They discussed drink and its effect on people. He says Rory complained of pain in his arms. Bell, who had experience of dependency in his Thin Lizzy days, said it was alcohol related. Gallagher agreed, he says. Eric then went about his shopping but they agreed to rendezvous. He eventually found the great musician in a guitar shop. Rory, he remembers, was holding down an E major chord and pondering the merits of a particular instrument. They walked the short distance to premises on Tottenham Court Road, where his companion chose to have more wine. Then Eric was quite surprised when Rory asked him, at least once, 'Where are we?' They had walked only a short distance. 'He seemed disorientated.' Bell felt this to such an extent that he asked Gallagher to ring him when he got back to his home, then the Conrad Hotel. Bell's phone rang about 8.30 p.m. Rory was safely home.

Dónal Gallagher said in an interview with Dutch magazine *Aardschok* in 2000 that he found it hard to talk about his brother's last months because it was such a painful time. 'Rory wasn't averse to a drink,' he said. 'And that became a bigger and bigger problem. Over the years he had become more and more dependent on medication that he took for all sorts of ailments. They ruined him from inside, poisoned his blood. He retained water and that's how he became heavier. In 1994, it got rapidly worse. He succumbed to more and more physical ailments.' In his tribute in *Hot Press* in June 1995, Gary Moore recalled meeting Rory just months before he died. 'What tells you more than anything about Rory was that he didn't say anything about his problems. He was more interested in my problems. He was such a selfless person. He really did care about other people. But I knew there was something up with him because he sounded so beaten down.'

Rory had insisted on going ahead with a short tour of the Netherlands. Dónal told *Aardschok* in 2000 that it became a drama. 'Already during the first gig it became clear that he was much too sick to give a coherent show. I cancelled the tour, but Rory wanted to continue. It was the only time in thirty years that we had a big fight. I drew back and went home. Rory still did a couple of gigs but eventually was sent home. It's painful that such a dedicated artist had to say good-bye to the stage in this way.' Mark Feltham in *Guitarist* in 1998 recalled a moment from that brief, final tour, an act of kindness when Rory was 'sinking', as he described it. It was on 7 January. 'We were playing at the Paradiso in Amsterdam. I remember him distinctly walking a long way across the road to purposely throw money into a busker's hand – a guy there who had no money sitting in the sidewalk. He would do that often. He was always a man for the underdog.'

Rory Gallagher's last gig was at the Nighttown venue in Rotterdam on 10 January 1995. After his concert in nearby Enschede four days previously, he gave what would be his last interview, with Radio Hengelo, the station in a nearby town, broadcast on 11 January. He was asked about his approach to the commercial side of music and the old Gallagher principle – or hang-up – surfaced, this time of course with pathos:

> I don't mind them [blues musicians] making singles or videos if they want to. I might even do it, who knows, but I haven't done it so far. I don't

like the system that was run from London, New York and Los Angeles for so long. It's quite hard to explain, the Irish attitude is … it's, I don't mean that in a nationalistic way … the point is I think that the musicians that I have got as heroes, I don't care whether they are #1 in the charts or #101 or not in the charts. I think that real music fans know if it's good or if it's not good.[14]

Keith Donald remembers getting a phone call from Rory at that time. 'He said he had to go into hospital the next week. He asked me, "Maybe you'd come over and we could have a jam here?" I shuffled through the diary and had to say, "Rory, I just can't get out of here. But I'll definitely come over when you're out of hospital." And that's one of my huge regrets, nothing should have been more important.' The Dublin writer Dermot Bolger has another recollection from this time. He was chair of an organisation called Musicbase, whose mission was to help young musicians. 'Our receptionist was a really helpful young woman from Finglas and because we were known to be there to help Irish musicians, she began to often get long phone calls from an Irish musician who was ill in hospital in London. It was Rory Gallagher and I think he called the office because he simply wanted someone to talk to.'

In early March 1995, Gallagher was admitted to Cromwell Hospital in London. He was later transferred to King's College Hospital in Denmark Hill, where he underwent a liver transplant. After spending over two months in intensive care, he was recovering and was about to be transferred to a convalescent hospital when he contracted an infection. In 1998, Dónal Gallagher recalled the events in the *Sunday Times* of 17 May: 'He deteriorated rapidly in the end because his immune system was exhausted. They pumped him full of antibiotics but it was no use.' He then reflected: 'With hindsight I would have done some things differently. But I don't blame myself. You can't change someone if they don't want to change. Rory had a stubborn streak. He wasn't going to change for anybody.'

He was in a coma when Dónal, desperate to save his brother, arranged for Mark Feltham to come to the hospital to play at Rory's bedside. Feltham told Dan Muise: 'I played some blues and country stuff for him, to try to … spark him up. I was there for about an hour doing that.' But even the sound of the music he loved so much was powerless to prevent Rory Gallagher's life ebbing away. He died on the morning of 14 June 1995, aged 47.

Rory Gallagher's funeral Mass was celebrated in the Church of the Descent of the Holy Spirit at Dennehy's Cross, on the western outskirts of Cork, on 19 June. The church that day contained many people who could play music, sing, perform and write songs. But the person in the coffin was different – they knew he had done something more. Lou Martin and Mark Feltham played 'A Million Miles Away' after the church overflowed. A walk by the sea not far from this church had inspired that song. The Dubliners' Ronnie Drew read from The

Book of Wisdom (3:1-9). The words are about what
should happen to the souls of the virtuous. The text is
ancient but the incendiary imagery would not have been
lost on many of the mourners:

> When the time comes for His visitation they will
> shine out;
> as sparks run through the stubble, so will they.

Memories of the great days of fiery performances to
ecstatic audiences must have filled the minds of many of
the assembled musicians. Martin Carthy was among the
mourners, his first time attending a Catholic requiem.
He describes 'a sea of grief' as the coffin left the church.
Then Mark Feltham clutched his harmonica to play
'Amazing Grace' as the coffin was lowered in St Oliver's
Cemetery, Ballincollig. Dónal, of course, carried his
brother's coffin on this final journey, with Ronnie Drew,
Phil McDonnell, Gerry McAvoy, Ted McKenna and
Tom O'Driscoll. The Fender Strat, in the care of Tom,
was a silent witness to the day's proceedings. A group of
fans, including Boots Healy, felt honoured when, as rain
began to fall, Dónal Gallagher beckoned them to join
the family and close friends under a canopy that had
been erected at the graveside. Mourners would also have
noticed a striking middle-aged woman among those
who had the privilege of casting earth into the grave. It
was Catherine Mattelaer paying her last respects.

Chris Welch's obituary concluded: 'Gallagher's fans
will remember his saying farewell at the end of those

tumultuous gigs he performed night after night, for some 20 or more years. Dripping with sweat, he would put his thumbs up and offer a breathless cry of: "Thank you very much. I hope you enjoyed it.'"[15] Ronnie Drew offered a simple tribute in *Hot Press*: 'He didn't have this over-confidence that the mediocre have. He had the quiet, unassuming way that the truly great have. And he was one of the greats.'

The question has been posed: Did Rory Gallagher really want to live on? Mark Feltham said in Gerry McAvoy's book: 'I don't think he wanted to reach 50. I don't think he wanted to grow into an old rock musician.' Brendan O'Neill had a similar thought for McAvoy: 'I'm not sure he hadn't concluded his life in his career. Maybe he felt it was time.' Jean-Noël Coghe recalled something that happened some months later. Dónal Gallagher was clearing out his brother's London home and one of the items was a James Dean poster, which Rory was apparently fond of. It depicted a bare-chested Dean, surrounded by death masks. He gave it to Coghe. On the edge of the frame Gallagher had written, '"Immortality is the only true success" – James Dean 1931–1955'. That thought could be taken as an echo of what William Butler Yeats expressed in his poem 'Sailing to Byzantium', where, in his striving to live beyond the physical world, the poet appeals to 'the sages standing in God's holy fire' to 'gather me into the artifice of eternity'. Niall Stokes of *Hot Press* concluded his tribute with a similar invocation. 'The road goes on forever. No one knows that better than Rory Gallagher.

His spirit will guide us on our way, guide us on our way, guide us on our way. On our way.'

And Gallagher would have probably approved of Louis de Paor's resorting to faith in 'Rory – Cork City Hall 1976'. Recalling the great audience chant, 'Ro – ry, Ro – ry', he concludes his poem with a forlorn appeal for another encore: 'Ar gcloiseann tú anois ár nguí', ('do you hear our prayer/cry now?')

On the first page of a book of condolences opened at Musicbase in Dublin, Dermot Bolger also evoked youthful joy:

> There came a time on teenage summer nights
> When a free house had been found,
> And a cheap stereo rigged with strobe lights
> That froze each moment in your mind.
>
> You just knew when the crowd had waned
> And the wasters had long gone
> That soon the clued-in boys who remained
> Would put Rory Gallagher on.[16]

The Irish harpist, Máire Ní Chathasaigh, from County Cork, recalls that Rory had taken a liking to her playing of one of the great airs in the Irish tradition, with its sad, minor-key landscape, 'O'Carolan's Farewell to Music', by the Irish composer, Turlough O'Carolan. She played it at his London memorial service in Brompton Oratory on 8 November, five months after Gallagher's death. The service also involved a first for the Oratory, something

Gallagher would have been proud of, as he regularly went to Mass here; the choir performed a song in the Irish language for the first time in that church's history (up to then it had been Latin or Greek only). It was Seán Ó Riada's great invocation of faith, 'Ag Críost an Síol':

Ag Críost an síol	Christ's is the seed
Ag Críost an fómhar	Christ's is the harvest
I n-iothalainn Dé	Into God's barn
go dtugtar sinn	May we be brought.[17]

It was in 'Shadow Play' that Rory Gallagher sang 'I can't run away / From this Shadow Play'. He may have been asking a fundamental question with the song's drama metaphor: was he, indeed, are we all delicate but helpless figures, needing a light to illuminate and animate us, a light over which we have really no control, and which will eventually, for all of us, go out?

CODA

The Music Library established in 1978 by Cork City Council to support and develop the city's music traditions was renamed the Rory Gallagher Music Library in 2004, to 'acknowledge Gallagher's impact on the international rock scene and to provide inspiration within the library setting for young talent'. Rory Gallagher might have smiled if he had been told that music tradition in Cork was first documented in the sixth-century breviary lessons of a monk, St Finbarr, the city's patron saint.

Monica Gallagher died on 14 August 2005, aged 87, after a heart attack two days previously, outliving her famous son by exactly ten years and two months. In 1999, she had taken the unusual step of having his remains removed to a more elevated site in St Oliver's Cemetery. Despite great interest and pride in Rory's achievements, she avoided the media all her life and there are no published interviews, or even comments by her. She acknowledged her deceased husband by requesting that the air 'Danny Boy' be played at her funeral. John Sheehan of The Dubliners had the honour. Her grave is next to Rory's.

Eric Kitteringham died in May 2013 aged 66, after several years of poor health. At the funeral, his brother

George quoted from the Fairport Convention song, which Eric had loved since 1969: 'Who Knows Where the Time Goes'. 'Irish' Jack Lyons wrote a message on a guitar-string envelope, which so moved the family that they placed it in the coffin.

Bernie Tobin, leader of the Fontana, retired from show business to become a publican, with his own bar and music venue in Fermoy, County Cork, called The Twilight Zone. He died in July 2007. Taste's first manager, Kevin Sanquest, lost a battle with cancer in November the same year, aged 71. The *Irish Examiner* paid tribute to his 'creative, cultural and business legacy'. He had become successful as an artist and theatre director since his rock days, and also well known in the city as a cancer research fundraiser. Jim Conlon, a founder of the Royal Showband and the first owner of Gallagher's Stratocaster, died in New York in December 2018.

Rory's Welsh drummer in the 1970s, Rod de'Ath died in August 2014, aged 64. He had appeared at the memorial service for Rory at Brompton Oratory in 1995, a surprise symbol of life that day, as most Gallagher associates had thought he had passed away. In the 1980s he had suffered brain damage and the loss of an eye in an accident. In 1996 he told *Signals* fanzine: 'I thought it would be macabre going to Rory's funeral when everyone believed I was dead. It would be out of place showing up then when Rory was actually being buried. That's why I decided to wait for a more suitable moment and November 8 [The Brompton Oratory service] was the right moment.' In August 2012, another chapter closed when he and Gerry McAvoy attended the funeral of their great colleague from the Rory Gallagher heyday, Lou Martin. Gallagher's drummer between 1978 and 1981, Ted McKenna, died suddenly in January 2019, aged 68, during a routine hernia operation.

Many in Cork and elsewhere would appreciate John Spillane's hometown-inspired epiphany in his 2016 book, in which he writes that Rory Gallagher is one of his local heroes, one of the distinguished Cork people who have 'gone over to the other Cork, an imagined other world, the Cork you see reflected in the River Lee.'[1]

ACKNOWLEDGEMENTS

Firstly, many individuals in Cork and elsewhere generously assisted me with their recollections and the interviews I conducted with them between 2016 and 2018 are featured in the text.

For good steers as I researched, I'm indebted particularly to Dino McGartland, once described as Rory Gallagher's biggest fan; Declan O'Keeffe; Gill Bond, for her archive sense and scrap book of the early Gallagher years; John Wilson; Colm Keane; Ágnes Kertész; John Foyle. In Ballyshannon, Barry O'Neill and his Rory Gallagher International Tribute Festival, Pat Melly and Anthony Begley; Gordon Floyd and Liz Reeves of the Wilgar Blues Festival in Belfast. Gerry McCartney and Kevin Hasson were of great assistance in tracing Gallagher's Derry background. The books by Gerry McAvoy and Dan Muise I found particularly insightful, as were several articles by Shiv Cariappa. Publications as diverse as *Guitar* and *The Christian Science Monitor* were sources, as were *Hot Press, The Cork Examiner* and *Examiner, The Cork Evening Echo, The Donegal Democrat* and *New Spotlight*. Kieran Murphy of UCC's Cork Folklore Project and its publication, *The Archive,* were also of great help. I'm indebted to the tireless work of many Rory Gallagher fans, particularly those behind the website roryon.com; its founder John Ganjamie,

'Roryfan', and Joachim Matz for his exhaustive 'Rory timeline'; also Milo of shadowplays.com. Several people offered advice and suggestions along the way: Carol Louthe, Trevor Hodgett, Cathal Goan, Kate Kavanagh, Brush Shiels, Joe Duffy, Fintan Vallely, Ed Mulhall, Stina Greaker, Máire Nic Fhinn and Kjell Ekholm. Also of assistance, the Rory Gallagher Library, Cork, The National Library of Ireland and Dublin City Council Library on Pearse Street, Rob Canning of RTÉ Radio Archives, and the Irish Showbands Forum. I also spent a very productive time at the Tyrone Guthrie Centre, Annaghmakerrig. Paddy O'Doherty and Aoife Maher cast their eagle eyes over the text approaching the final hurdle.

For pictures, I'm grateful to the generosity of Gill Bond, Declan O'Keeffe, Oliver and Frances Tobin and Choice Publishing, Roy Esmonde, Patrick Brocklebank, George Kitteringham and his niece Tara Hynes, Steve Smith and the Rory Gallagher Music Library, Cork, Wolfgang Gürster and rock-shot.com, Ben Upham and his website, ben-upham.pixels.com, Frans Verpoorten and popstockphoto.com, Phillip J. Bosel, Joe Cohen, Blair Whyte, Ed Erbeck, Jon 'Slipkid' Hahn and Cameron Life Photo Library. Dermot Bolger kindly gave permission to reproduce his poem, 'In Memory of Rory Gallagher (1948-1995)'; Louis De Paor and the publishers Coiscéim for 'Rory – Cork City Hall 1976'; Jessie Lendennie and Salmon Publishing for Eamonn Wall's, 'Blues for Rory'.

I'm grateful to The Collins Press, who encouraged me to take my time with the project and saved me from myself on occasion.

My principal consultant throughout the project was Dave McHugh, to whom I'm particularly indebted.

My apologies to any individuals or institutions I have omitted in error.

APPENDIX: THE TRIBUTE BANDS

Rory Gallagher has inspired many tribute bands, the names coming from his song and album titles: Laundromat, The Mississippi Sheiks, Brute Force and Ignorance, Moonchild, Deuce, Blueprint, and many others over the years. They have been led by guitarists like Dave McHugh from Dublin (who emphasises Taste material), and Barry Barnes and Sinnerboy from Manchester, and singers like Freddie Koridon from Holland. There are other artists with a strong Gallagher aspect to their repertoire: Pat McManus, Johnny Gallagher and Boxtie, Seamie O'Dowd, Barry McGivern, Jed Thomas and Tony Dowler. Band of Friends, with Gerry McAvoy and Brendan O'Neill (who replaced Ted McKenna after his sudden death in 2019), are former members of Gallagher's band, with either Marcel Scherpenzeel or Davy Knowles featuring as the singer and guitarist, the 'ghost' of Rory. Gallagher would surely be flattered by the youth of some of the ensembles: the members of Fresh Evidence, from Westport, County Mayo, are all about twenty years of age. Next Passing Breeze has Irish and Turkish members. John Wilson toured as John Wilson's Taste for many years, celebrating that band's big songs, until his retirement in January 2018.

Danny Vlaspoel is a member of the Dutch four-piece, Laundromat, who play only Gallagher material. 'I had just picked up the guitar for a half year and my uncle told me, "You want to play guitar? You must see Rory".' He was fifteen in 1984 when his uncle took him to a Dutch blues festival in Tegelen were Gallagher was headlining. 'I remember the way the whole atmosphere began to change all through the changeover from the support act; flags waving, singing and cheering people. Then the lights go out, everybody screamed their lungs out and ... BAM! Rory came running up the stage and stood still just two metres in front of me. When he kicked into "Double Vision" and then "Follow Me", I was "bought and sold" for the rest of my life.' Dino McGartland, from Omagh in County Tyrone, has played his replica Gallagher Strat with several bands. The depth of his devotion surprised even himself when he found himself shedding tears at Rory's funeral in Cork in 1995, the first his wife, Annie, witnessed from him in their 30 years together. 'Both my parents died since then, but despite my love for them, I couldn't cry for them like I could for Rory.'

Every June since 2004, Ballyshannon celebrates its famous son with the Rory Gallagher International Tribute Festival, directed by Barry O'Neill. Tribute bands and fans from far and wide bring the songs alive again. Dave McHugh summarises the spirit of the gathering: 'For a single man who never married, here you can see that Rory Gallagher has a very big, loving family'.

RORY GALLAGHER DISCOGRAPHY

Taste

▓ Albums

Taste – Polydor (1969)
Blister on the Moon / Leaving Blues / Sugar Mama / Hail / Born on the Wrong Side of Time / Dual Carriageway Pain / Same Old Story / Catfish / I'm Moving On
All songs written by Rory Gallagher, except Leaving Blues (Ledbetter), Sugar Mama and Catfish Blues (trad. arr. Gallagher), I'm Moving On (Hank Snow)
Rory Gallagher: lead guitar and vocals
John Wilson: drums
Richard McCracken: bass guitar

On the Boards – Polydor (1970)
What's Going On / Railway and Gun / It's Happened Before, It'll Happen Again / If the Day Was Any Longer / Morning Sun / Eat My Words / On the Boards / If I Don't Sing I'll Cry / See Here / I'll Remember
All songs written by Rory Gallagher
Rory Gallagher: vocals, lead guitar, harmonica and alto sax
John Wilson: drums
Richard McCracken: bass

Live Taste – Polydor (1971)
Sugar Mama (trad. arr. Rory Gallagher) / Gamblin' Blues (Melvin Jackson) / I Feel So Good (Part 1) (Big Bill Broonzy) / I Feel So Good (Part 2) (Broonzy) / Catfish (trad. arr. Rory Gallagher) / Same Old Story (Rory Gallagher)

Live at the Isle of Wight – Polydor (1971)
What's Going On / Sugar Mama / Morning Sun / Sinner Boy / I Feel So Good / Catfish

All songs written by Rory Gallagher except Sugar Mama (trad. arr. Gallagher), I Feel So Good (Big Bill Broonzy) and Catfish (trad. arr. Gallagher).

■ Singles and EPs

Blister on the Moon / Born on the Wrong Side of Time – Major Minor (1968)
Born on the Wrong Side of Time / Same Old Story – Polydor (1969)
What's Going On / Born on the Wrong Side of Time / Blister on the Moon – Polydor (1969)
Wee Wee Baby / You've Got to Play – Polydor (1972) (exclusive to Germany)
What's Going On / Railway and Gun – Polydor (1972)
Blister on the Moon / Sugar Mama / Catfish Blues / On the Boards – Polydor (1982)

■ Compilations

Pop History Vol. XI: Taste – Polydor (1971)
Record 1: Sugar Mama / I'm Moving On / What's Going On / Born on the Wrong Side of Time / Same Old Story / Eat My Words / Gambling Blues / Railway and Gun / If I Don't Sing I'll Cry / Feel So Good – Part 2
Record 2: On The Boards / Hail / See Here / Dual Carriageway Pain / I'll Remember / Blister on the Moon / It's Happened Before, It'll Happen Again / Leaving Blues / Catfish

In the Beginning – Emerald (1974)
Wee Wee Baby / How Many More Years / Take It Easy Baby / You've Got to Pay / Worried Man / Norman Invasion / Pardon Me Mister.
(The album consists of recordings made by Tast Mark 1 in 1967)
(The same collection was released as *Take It Easy Baby* by the Springboard label in the US in 1976)

The Best of Taste – Polydor (1994)
Blister on the Moon / Born on the Wrong Side of Time / Leavin' Blues / Hail / Same Old Story / Catfish / I'm Moving On / Railway and Gun / Eat My Words / On the Boards / It's Happened Before,

It'll Happen Again / If The Day Was Any Longer / I Feel So Good / Sugar Mama / Sinner Boy

I'll Remember (four-CD set) – Polydor (2015)

CD 1: Taste with bonus songs, alternative versions of Blister on the Moon / Leavin' Blues / Hail / Dual Carriageway Pain / Same Old Story / Catfish
CD 2: On the Boards with bonus songs, alternative versions of Railway and Gun / See Here / It's Happened Before, It'll Happen Again / If the Day Was Any Longer / Morning Sun
CD 3: Live recordings from Konserthuset, Stockholm, 1970, The Paris Theatre, London, Woburn Abbey Festival UK (1968)
CD 4: Belfast (early) Sessions, featuring: Wee Wee Baby / How Many More Years / Take It Easy Baby / Pardon Me Mister / You've Got To Play / Norman Invasion / Worried Man / Blister on the Moon / Born on the Wrong Side of Time

'Hail' The Collection – Spectrum (2015)

What's Going On / Blister on the Moon / I'll Remember / On the Boards / Same Old Story (live) / Morning Sun / Born on the Wrong Side of Time / Sugar Mama (live) / Catfish (live) / Eat My Words / Leavin' Blues / Gambling Blues (live) / I Feel So Good (Parts 1 and 2) (live) / Hail (Peel Session) / I'm Moving On

■ Taste Video

Message of Love 1995 – Isle of Wight Festival the Movie –
Sanctuary Midline (1997) (documentary with recordings of Sinner Boy and Gamblin' Blues)

What's Going On: Taste Live At The Isle of Wight – Eagle
Vision (2015)

Rory Gallagher

■ Albums

Rory Gallagher – Polydor (1971)

Laundromat / Just the Smile / I Fall Apart / Wave Myself Goodbye / Hands Up / Sinner Boy / For the Last Time / It's You / I'm Not Surprised / Can't Believe It's True
Rory Gallagher: vocals, guitars, alto sax, mandolin, and harmonica

Gerry McAvoy: bass
Wilgar Campbell: drums
Vincent Crane: piano
All songs written by Rory Gallagher
Remastered November 2011 and rereleased 2012, with bonus songs:
Gypsy Woman (Muddy Waters) / It Takes Time (Otis Rush)

Deuce – Polydor (1971)
Used To Be / I'm Not Awake Yet / Don't Know Where I'm Going /
Maybe I Will / Whole Lot of People / In Your Town / Should've Learnt
My Lesson / There's a Light / Out of My Mind / Crest of a Wave
Rory Gallagher: vocals, guitars, harmonica
Gerry McAvoy: bass
Wilgar Campbell: drums, percussion
All songs written by Rory Gallagher
Reissued 2012

Live In Europe – Polydor (1972)
Messin' With the Kid (London) / Laundromat (Gallagher) / I
Could've Had Religion (trad. arr. Gallagher) / Pistol Slapper Blues
(Fulton Allen) / Going to My Hometown (Gallagher) / In Your Town
(Gallagher) / Bullfrog Blues (trad. arr. Gallagher).
Rory Gallagher: vocals, guitars, mandolin and harmonica
Gerry McAvoy: bass
Wilgar Campbell: drums
Reissued 2012, with bonus songs: What in the World (trad. arr.
Gallagher) and Hoodoo Man (trad. arr. Gallagher).

Blueprint – Polydor (1973)
Walk on Hot Coals / Daughter of the Everglades / Banker's Blues /
Hands Off / Race The Breeze / Seventh Son of a Seventh Son /
Unmilitary Two-Step / If I Had a Reason
Rory Gallagher: vocals, guitars, harmonica, mandolin and saxes
Gerry McAvoy: bass
Lou Martin: keyboards
Rod de'Ath: drums
All songs written by Rory Gallagher, except Banker's Blues (Big Bill
Broonzy)
Rereleased in 2000 with additional songs: Stompin Ground alt.
version 10 (Gallagher) / Treat Her Right (Roy Head)

Tattoo – Polydor (1973)

Tattoo'd Lady / Cradle Rock / 20:20 Vision / They Don't Make Them
Like You Anymore / Livin' Like a Trucker / Sleep on a Clothesline /
Who's That Coming / A Million Miles Away / Admit It
Gerry McAvoy: bass
Lou Martin: keyboards
Rod de'Ath: drums
All songs written by Rory Gallagher
Reissued with bonus songs, Tucson Arizona and Just a Little Bit
(Rosco Gordon)

Irish Tour '74 Polydor (1974)

Cradle Rock / I Wonder Who / Tattoo'd Lady / Too Much Alcohol /
As the Crow Flies / A Million Miles Away / Walk on Hot Coals /
Who's That Coming / Back on My Stompin' Ground (After Hours) /
Maritime
Rory Gallagher: vocals, guitars, and harmonica
Gerry McAvoy: bass
Lou Martin: keyboards
Rod de'Ath: drums
All songs written by Rory Gallagher except Too Much Alcohol (Hutto),
As the Crow Flies (Tony Joe White) and I Wonder Who (Morganfield)
Reissued in 2012, by Capo/Sony, without Maritime
Reissued in 2014 for the 40th anniversary as an eight-disc box set,
including the documentary, *Irish Tour '74*, and previously unreleased
recordings from the same tour, at Cork City Hall, The Carlton
Cinema Dublin, the Ulster Hall Belfast

Against the Grain – Chrysalis (1975)

Let Me In / Cross Me off Your List / Ain't Too Good / Souped-Up
Ford / Bought and Sold / I Take What I Want / Lost at Sea / All
Around Man / Out on the Western Plain / At the Bottom
Rory Gallagher: vocals, guitars, and harmonica
Gerry McAvoy: bass
Lou Martin: keyboards
Rod de'Ath: drums
All songs by Gallagher, except I Take What I Want (Porter Hodges
Hayes), All Around Man (Davenport) and Out on the Western Plain
(Ledbetter) Reissued in 2013 with additional songs Cluny Blues and My
Baby, Sure

Calling Card – Chrysalis (1976)

Do You Read Me / Country Mile / Moonchild / Calling Card / I'll
Admit You're Gone / Secret Agent / Jackknife Beat / Edged in Blue /
Barley and Grape Rag
Rory Gallagher: vocals, guitars and harmonica
Gerry McAvoy: bass
Lou Martin: keyboards
Rod de'Ath: drums
All songs written by Rory Gallagher
Rereleased in 2012 with additional song Where Was I Going To?

Photo-Finish – Chrysalis (1978)

Shin Kicker / Brute Force and Ignorance / Cruise on out / Cloak and
Dagger / Overnight Bag / Shadow Play / The Mississippi Sheiks / The
Last of the Independents / Fuel to the Fire
Rory Gallagher: vocals, guitars, harmonica and mandolin
Gerry McAvoy: bass
Ted McKenna: drums and percussion
All songs written by Rory Gallagher
Reissued in 2012 with additional songs Early Warning and Juke Box
Annie.

Top Priority – Chrysalis (1979)

Follow Me / Philby / Wayward Child / Keychain / At the Depot / Bad
Penny / Just Hit Town / Off the Handle / Public Enemy No. 1
Rory Gallagher: vocals, guitars, harmonica and dulcimer
Gerry McAvoy: bass
Ted McKenna: drums
Reissued in 2012 with additional songs Hell Cat / The Watcher

Stagestruck – Chrysalis (1980)

Shin Kicker / Wayward Child / Brute Force and Ignorance /
Moonchild / Follow Me / Bought and Sold / Last of the Independents /
Shadow Play
Rory Gallagher: vocals, guitars
Gerry McAvoy: bass
Ted McKenna: drums
All songs written by Rory Gallagher
Reissued in 2013 with additional tracks: Hell Cat, Bad Penny and
Keychain

Jinx – Chrysalis (Mercury in US) (1982)

Signals / The Devil Made Me Do It / Double Vision / Easy Come, Easy Go / Big Guns / Jinxed / Bourbon / Ride On, Red, Ride On / Loose Talk

Rory Gallagher: vocals, guitars, and harmonica

Gerry McAvoy: bass

Brendan O'Neill: drums

Bob Andrews: keyboards

Ray Beavis and Dick Parry: saxes

All songs written by Rory Gallagher except, Ride On, Red, Ride On (M. Levy/H. Glover/T. Reid)

Additional tracks on 2012 rerelease, Nothin' But the Devil (Gerry West) / Lonely Mile (Gallagher)

Defender – Capo (1987)

Kickback City / Loanshark Blues / Continental Op / I Ain't No Saint / Failsafe Day / Road to Hell / Doing Time / Smear Campaign / Don't Start Me Talkin' / Seven Days

Rory Gallagher: electric and acoustic guitars, vocals and harmonica

Gerry McAvoy: bass

Brendan O'Neill: drums

Mark Feltham: harmonica on Don't Start Me Talkin'

Lou Martin: piano on Seven Days

Bob Andrews: piano on Don't Start Me Talkin'

John Cooke: other keyboards.

All songs written by Rory Gallagher

Reissued in 2013 with additional songs Seems to Me and No Peace for the Wicked

Fresh Evidence – Capo (1990)

Kid Gloves / The King of Zydeco (To: Clifton Chenier) / Middle Name / Alexis / Empire State Express / Ghost Blues / Heaven's Gate / The Loop / Walkin' Wounded / Slummin' Angel

Rory Gallagher: vocals, electric and acoustic guitars, dulcimer, electric sitar, mandolin

Gerry McAvoy: bass guitar

Brendan O'Neill: drums

Mark Feltham: harmonica

Geraint Watkins: accordion

John Cooke: keyboards
Lou Martin: piano
John Earle: tenor and baritone sax
Ray Beavis: tenor sax
Dick Hanson: trumpet
All songs written by Rory Gallagher except Empire State Express
(Eddie 'Son' House)
Reissued 2013 with additional tracks Never Asked For Nothin' and
Bowed But Not Broken

Having gained control of his back catalogue in 1990, Rory and Dónal
Gallagher engaged Tony Arnold to remix in some cases, and remaster,
the original releases. This was done during the 1990s and after.

■ Singles

Rory Gallagher did not agree to release singles. But there were several
7-inch and 10-inch vinyls pressed for radio play during his career.

Souped Up Ford / I Take What I Want – Chrysalis (1975)
***Shadow Play / Brute Force and Ignorance / Moonchild / Souped-Up
Ford*** – Chrysalis (1978)
Philby / Hell Cat / Country Mile – Chrysalis (1979)
Wayward Child (live) / Keychain – Chrysalis (1980)
Big Guns / The Devil Made Me Do It – Chrysalis (1982)
Wheels Within Wheels / Going to My Hometown – Capo (2003)

■ Posthumous albums
BBC Sessions – BBC (1999)
Live: Calling Card / What in the World / Jackknife Beat / Country
Mile / Got My Mojo Working (Preston Foster) / Garbage Man (Willie
Hammond) / Roberta / Used to Be / I Take What I Want (Porter
Hodges Hayes) / Cruise on out
Studio: Race the Breeze / Hand's Off / Crest of a Wave / Feel so Bad
/ For the Last Time / It Takes Time / Seventh Son of a Seventh Son
/ Daughter of the Everglades / They Don't Make Them Like You
Anymore / Toredown (Thompson) / When My Baby She Left Me
(Williamson)

Let's Go to Work box set – Capo/BMG (2001)
Containing *Live in Europe*, *Irish Tour '74*, *Stagestruck* and *Meeting With the G-Man*.

Wheels Within Wheels – Capo/BMG (2003)
Wheels Within Wheels (Gallagher) / Flight to Paradise (Juan Martin) / As the Crow Flies (Tony Joe White) / Lonesome Highway (Gallagher) / Bratacha Dubha (Gallagher) / She Moved Through the Fair / An Crann Úll (trad. arr. Gallagher and Bert Jansc) / Barley and Grape Rag (Gallagher) / The Cuckoo (trad. arr. Gallagher) / Amazing Grace (trad. arr. Gallagher) / Walkin' Blues (Robert Johnson) / Blue Moon of Kentucky (Bill Monroe) / Deep Elm Blues (trad. arr. Gallagher) / Goin' to My Hometown (Gallagher) / Lonesome Highway Refraining (Gallagher)

Meeting With the G-Man+ – RCA (2003) (enhanced version of the album featured in Let's Go to Work, 2001)
Continental Op / Moonchild / Mean Disposition / The Loop (featuring Resurrection Shuffle and Jailhouse Rock) / Don't Start Me Talking (featuring Revolution) / Ghost Blues / Messin' With The Kid / La Bamba.
Additional material: She Moved Through the Fair / Out on the Western Plain / William of Green / Mercy River / Walkin' Blues / Don't Think Twice, It's Alright

Live at Montreux – Capo/Eagle (2006)
Recordings made in 1975, 1977, 1979 and 1985
Laundromat / Tore Down / I Take What I Want / Bought and Sold / Do You Read Me / Last of the Independents / Off the Handle / Mississippi Sheiks / Out on the Western Plain / Shin Kicker / Philby
All songs by Rory Gallagher except I Take What I Want (Isaac Hayes) and Out on the Western Plain (Ledbetter).

The Beat Club Sessions – Capo (2010) (recordings from 1971)
Laundromat / Hands Up / Sinner Boy / Just the Smile / I Don't Know Where I'm Going / I Could've Had Religion / Used to Be / In Your Town / Should've Learned My Lesson / Crest of a Wave / Toredown / Messin' With the Kid
Also released in 2010 as *Ghost Blues: The Story of Rory Gallagher and the Beat Club Sessions*, with the *Ghost Blues* documentary

Notes From San Francisco – Capo/Sony (2011)
CD 1 (studio): Rue the Day / Persuasion / B Girl / Mississippi Sheiks /
Wheels Within Wheels / Overnight Bag / Cruise on out / Brute Force
and Ignorance / Fuel to the Fire
Bonus tracks: Wheels Within Wheels (alternative version) / Cut a
Dash / Out on the Tiles.
CD 2 (live): Follow Me / Shin Kicker / Off the Handle / Bought and
Sold / I'm Leavin' / Tattoo'd Lady / Do You Read Me / Country Mile /
Calling Card / Shadow Play / Bullfrog Blues / Sea Cruise
All songs written by Rory Gallagher except Bullfrog Blues (trad. arr.
Gallagher), Sea Cruise (Hughie 'Piano' Smith)

Blues – Chess/Universal (2019)
CD, single CD, 2 LP versions
3 CD version:
Disc 1: Don't Start Me Talkin' (Unreleased track from the Jinx album
sessions 1982) / Nothin' But the Devil (Unreleased track from the
Against the Grain album sessions, 1975) / Tore Down (Unreleased track
from the Blueprint album sessions, 1973) /Off the Handle (Unreleased
session Paul Jones Show BBC Radio, 1986) / I Could've Had Religion
(Unreleased WNCR Cleveland radio session from 1972) / As the Crow
Flies (Unreleased track from Tattoo album sessions, 1973) / A Million
Miles Away (Unreleased BBC Radio 1 Session, 1973) / Should've Learnt
My Lesson (Outtake from Deuce album sessions, 1971) / Leaving Town
Blues (Tribute track from Peter Green 'Rattlesnake Guitar', 1994) /
Drop Down Baby (Rory guest guitar on Lonnie Donegan's Puttin' On
The Style album, 1978 / I'm Ready (Guest guitarist on Muddy Waters'
London Sessions album, 1971) / Bullfrog Blues (Unreleased WNCR
Cleveland radio session from 1972)
Disc 2: Who's That Coming (Acoustic outtake from Tattoo album
sessions, 1973) / Should've Learnt My Lesson (Acoustic outtake from
Deuce album sessions, 1971) / Prison Blues (Unreleased track from
Blueprint album sessions, 1973) / Secret Agent (Unreleased acoustic
version from RTE Irish TV, 1976) / Blow Wind Blow (Unreleased
WNCR Cleveland radio session from 1972) / Bankers Blues (Outtake
from the Blueprint album sessions, 1973) / Whole Lot Of People
(Acoustic outtake from Deuce album sessions, 1971) / Loanshark Blues
(Unreleased acoustic version from German TV, 1987) / Pistol Slapper
Blues (Unreleased acoustic version from Irish TV, 1976) / Can't Be

Satisfied (Unreleased Radio FFN session from 1992) / Want Ad Blues
(Unreleased RTE Radio Two Dave Fanning session, 1988) / Walkin'
Blues (Unreleased acoustic version from RTE Irish TV, 1987)
Disc 3: When My Baby She Left Me (Unreleased track from Glasgow
Apollo concert, 1982) / Nothin' But the Devil (Unreleased track from
Glasgow Apollo concert, 1982) / What In The World (Unreleased track
from Glasgow Apollo concert, 1982) / I Wonder Who (Unreleased
live track from late 1980s) / Messin' With the Kid (Unreleased track
from Sheffield City Hall concert, 1977) / Tore Down (Unreleased
track from Newcastle City Hall concert, 1977) / Garbage Man Blues
(Unreleased track from Sheffield City Hall concert, 1977) / All Around
Man (Unreleased track from BBC OGWT Special, 1976) / Born Under
A Bad Sign (Unreleased track from Rockpalast 1991 w/ Jack Bruce) /
You Upset Me (Unreleased guest performance from Albert King album
Live, 1975) / Comin' Home Baby (Unreleased track from 1989 concert
with Chris Barber Band) / Rory Talking Blues (Interview track of Rory
talking about the blues)

The single CD and 2 LP releases are selected from the above.

Check Shirt Wizard – *Live in '77* Universal (2020)
Do You Read Me (Live From The Brighton Dome, 21st January 1977) /
Moonchild (Live From The Brighton Dome, 21st January 1977) /
Bought and Sold (Live From Sheffield City Hall, 17th February 1977) /
Calling Card (Live At The Hammersmith Odeon, 18th January 1977) /
Secret Agent (Live From Sheffield City Hall, 17th February 1977) /
Tattoo'd Lady (Live From The Brighton Dome, 21st January 1977) / A
Million Miles Away (Live At The Hammersmith Odeon, 18th January
1977) / I Take What I Want (Live From Sheffield City Hall, 17th
February 1977) / Walk On Hot Coals (Live At The Hammersmith
Odeon, 18th January 1977) / Out On the Western Plain (Live From
Sheffield City Hall, 17th February 1977) / Barley & Grape Rag (Live
From Sheffield City Hall, 17th February 1977) / Pistol Slapper Blues
(Live From Sheffield City Hall, 17th February 1977) / Too Much
Alcohol (Live At The Hammersmith Odeon, 18th January 1977) / Going
to My Hometown (Live At The Hammersmith Odeon, 18th January
1977) / Edged In Blue (Live At Newcastle City Hall, 18th February
1977) / Jack-Knife Beat (Live At The Hammersmith Odeon, 18th
January 1977) / Souped-Up Ford (Live From The Brighton Dome, 21st
January 1977) / Bullfrog Blues (Live From The Brighton Dome, 21st

January 1977) / Used To Be (Live At Newcastle City Hall, 18th February 1977) / Country Mile (Live At Newcastle City Hall, 18th February 1977)

▓ Compilations

The Story So Far – Polydor (1974)
Laundromat / Cradle Rock / Walk On Hot Coals / Who's That Coming / In Your Town / Hands Off / Too Much Alcohol / Bullfrog Blues

Sinner ... and Saint – Polydor (1975)
The release was a combination of the albums, Rory Gallagher and Deuce.

Rory Gallagher: The Best Years – Polydor (1976)
Tattoo'd Lady / Bankers' Blues / Used to Be / Just the Smile / Going T to My Hometown / Race the Breeze / Sinner Boy / Crest of a Wave / Admit It

Edged In Blue – Capo Records/Strange Music Ltd (1992)
Don't Start Me Talkin' (Sony Boy Williamson) / The Loop / Calling Card / Heaven's Gate / At the Depot / Brute Force and Ignorance / Loanshark Blues / I Could've Had Religion / Ride On, Red, Ride On (Levy, Glover, Reid) / I Wonder Who (Muddy Waters) / Seven Days
All songs by Rory Gallagher, except where stated otherwise

Etched in Blue – Capo/BMG (1998)
Loanshark Blues / Bought and Sold / Bad Penny / Cruise on out / Crest of a Wave / I'm Not Surprised / Unmilitary Two-Step / Alexis / Edged In Blue / They Don't Make Them Like You Anymore / The Devil Made Me Do It / Too Much Alcohol (Hutto) / I Could Have Had Religion / Shin Kicker

Big Guns: The Very Best of Rory Gallagher – Capo (2005)
CD 1: Big Guns / What's Going On / Tattoo'd Lady / Bad Penny / Shadow Play / Kickback City / Bourbon / Sinner Boy / Used to Be / Going to My Hometown / Bullfrog Blues / Messing With the Kid
CD 2: The Loop / Born on the Wrong Side of Time / A Million Miles Away / Calling Card / Out on the Western Plain / Lonesome Highway / Just the Smile / I'm Not Awake Yet / Daughter of the Everglades / I'll Admit You're Gone / King of Zydeco / They Don't Make Them Like You Anymore

Original Album Classics: Rory Gallagher – Capo/Sony (2008), featuring:
Deuce, with bonus song, Persuasion
Calling Card, with bonus song B-Girl version
Top Priority, with bonus tracks, Hell Cat / The Watcher
Jinx, with bonus songs as in 2012 reissue, Lonely Mile and Loose Talk
Fresh Evidence, with bonus songs, Never Asked You for Nothin' /
Bowed But Not Broken.

The Rory Gallagher Collection – Sony Entertainment (2012)
CD 1: Follow Me / Moonchild / Bought and Sold / Laundromat / Bad
Penny / Edged in Blue / Brute Force and Ignorance / I Fall Apart /
Loanshark Blues / Who's That Coming / As the Crow Flies / Barley
and Grape Rag / Lonesome Highway Refraining / Out on the Western
Plain.
CD 2: In Your Town / Philby / Slumming Angel / Continental Op /
Cradle Rock / A Million Miles Away / Wheels Within Wheels / Crest
of a Wave / They Don't Make Them Like You Anymore / Walk On
Hot Coals / Shadow Play / I Could've Had Religion / Tattoo'd Lady /
Bullfrog Blues

Rory Gallagher – All Time Best – RCA (2011)
What's Going On / Big Guns / Tattoo'd Lady / Sinnerboy / Bad Penny /
Calling Card / I'm Not Awake Yet / Out on the Western Plain / A
Million Miles Away / Kickback City / Daughter of the Everglades /
The Loop / Shadow Play / Goin' to My Hometown / Bullfrog Blues

Kickback City box set – Strange Music/Sony (2013)
CD 1: Kickback City / Continental Op / Kid Gloves / Big Guns /
Loanshark Blues / Secret Agent / B Girl / Slumming Angel / Barley
& Grape Rag / Doing Time / In Your Town / Sinner Boy / The Devil
Made Me Do It / Seven Days
CD 2: Continental Op / Tatto'd Lady / I Ain't No Saint / Off the
Handle / The Loop / Messin' With the Kid / Loanshark Blues
Disc 3: The Lie Factory (Short story) read by Aidan Quinn.

G-Men Bootleg Series 3 CD set (live recordings) – Castle
Communications (1992)

Rory Gallagher on Video

Live at Cork Opera House (Ireland and UK) Capo/Sony (1995)

At Rockpalast (German release) Wienerworld (2004)

Guitar Legends Ultimate Anthology ('Used To Be') Ragnarock (2004)

The Complete Rockpalast Collection (3-disc) Wienerworld (2005)

Live at Rockpalast (five concerts 1976–1990) (3-disc) US release (2007)

Shadow Play – The Rockpalast Collection (five concerts 1976–1990), (3-disc) Eagle Rock (2007)

The Definitive Montreux Collection Eagle Rock (2008)

Ghost Blues (biography with concert footage and interviews) Strange Music (2010)

Irish Tour '74 Eagle Rock (2011)

The Old Grey Whistle Test: Vol. 1: ('Hands Off' 1973) BBC/Warner Brothers (2011)

Live in Cork Eagle Rock (2013)

Live at Montreux (two-disc set) Salvo Sound and Vision (2013)

Recorded Guest Appearances by Rory Gallagher

Date	Album title and artist
1965	'Showbands Around the Corner' (single) (Art Supple and the Victors)
1971	*Bring It Back Home* (Mike Vernon)
1972	*The London Muddy Waters Sessions*
1973	*The Session* (Jerry Lee Lewis)
1974	*Drat That Fratle Rat* (Chris Barber) *London Revisited* (Muddy Waters)
1977	*Gaodhal's Vision* (Joe O'Donnell) *Live* (Albert King)
1978	*Tarot Suite* (Mike Batt) *Puttin' On The Style* (Lonnie Donegan)
1983	*Live on Air 1983* (with Albert Collins) rereleased in 2017

1984	*Box of Frogs* (Box of Frogs) (former members of the Yardbirds)
	The Scattering (The Fureys and Davy Arthur)
1985	*Echoes of the Night* (Gary Brooker)
1989	*Out of the Air* (Davy Spillane)
	Words and Music (Phil Coulter)
1990	*Shadow Hunter* (Davy Spillane)
	At Montreux (Jack Bruce)
1991	*Flags and Emblems* (Stiff Little Fingers)
1992	*Thirty Years A-Greying* (The Dubliners)
1993	*The Outstanding* (Chris Barber)
1995	*Rattlesnake Guitar – The Music of Peter Green*
	Pain Killer (Energy Orchard)
	Strangers on the Run (Samuel Eddy)

Released posthumously

2000	*Phoenician Dream* (Roberto Manes)
2000	*The Peter Green Songbook* (Peter Green)
2007	*Kindred Spirits* (Eamonn McCormack)

ENDNOTES

All quotations in this book are from interviews conducted by the author unless otherwise credited in the following notes.

Introduction

1. *Guitar for the Practicing Musician*, August 1991.
2. Interview with Charley Crespo, *Hit Parader*, May 1979.
3. *Donegal Democrat*, 8 June 2000, interview by Michael McHugh.
4. Published in the Dutch daily *Da Telegraaf*, 7 January 1995.
5. From a tribute delivered by Niall Stokes at a commemorative service for Rory Gallagher at Brompton Oratory, London, 8 November 2005.

Chapter 1: Northern Roots

1. San Diego newspaper *The Door*, 14 May 1973, article by Chuck Lowery.
2. McAvoy, Mark, *Cork Rock: From Rory Gallagher to the Sultans of Ping* (Mercier Press, 2009).
3. The Irish Free State was established in December 1922 after the Anglo-Irish Treaty of December 1921. In December 1937, the Free State adopted a new constitution and became known thereafter as Ireland or Éire, until it became the Irish Republic in 1948.
4. Don Bradley also played accordion in the band. His son Mickey would become a member of Derry's famous group, The Undertones.
5. Interview with Spenser Leigh, BBC Radio Merseyside. Regarding the actual playing of traditional music, Gallagher told David Sinclair in *Q* magazine in 1990: 'The strange thing is I can't play jigs or reels or any of that traditional Irish stuff as well as I ought to, whereas I think I have got a good ear for blues, the tonality of it and so on.'
6. Blair told *The Irish Times* in 2000 that he spent many childhood holidays in nearby Rossnowlagh: 'It was there in the seas off the Irish coast that I learned to swim and my father took me to my first pub, a remote little house in the country, for a Guinness, a taste I have never forgotten and which is always a pleasure to repeat.'
7. *The Donegal Annual* 2005, collected by Helen Meehan of the Donegal

History Society from K. McFadden.

8.   *The Erne Hydroelectric Scheme*, Dessie Doyle and Brian Drummond. Lilliput Press, 2014.

9.   *David Letterman Show*, 2014.

10.   The song, recorded in 1990, includes the lines: *'I am down on my knees/At those wireless knobs...'*

11.   *City of Music: Derry's Music Heritage*, Guildhall Press, 2008.

12.   An RTÉ Radio programme, presented by Ken Stewart, 15 September 1976. He was referring to Donegan's version of 'Rock Island Line', released in 1955.

13.   'Crediting Poetry', the Nobel Lecture, published by The Gallery Press 1995. American troops stationed in Northern Ireland in the run-up to D-Day marching near his childhood home was the inspiration for his poem, 'Anahorish 1944'. The farm's slaughterhouse becomes a stark metaphor.

14.   McAvoy, *Cork Rock*.

15.   Interview by Bill Graham, *Hot Press* 18 March 1988. (Bill Graham died aged 44 in 1996. Many Irish musicians attended his funeral. Bono and Edge were among those who carried his coffin, the U2 singer having performed Leonard Cohen's 'Tower Of Song' during the funeral Mass. (Graham had introduced the band to their manager, Paul McGuinness).

16.   McCafferty, Nell, *Nell* (Penguin, 2004).

17.   'Rory Gallagher and the Town He Loved So Well', Des O'Driscoll, *The Irish Examiner*, 12 June 2015. The article was referring mainly to Cork, though the title was a reference to Phil Coulter's song of the same title, about Derry.

18.   *Donegal Democrat*, 8 June 2000.

19.   Interview with Thierry Chatain in *Folk and Rock* April 1982.

Chapter 2: To the Lee Delta

1.   On the documentary film *Irish Tour '74*, Gallagher is heard saying this in voice over.

2.   'My Brother's Keeper' Marc O'Sullivan, *Irish Examiner* 4 June 2011.

3.   The 'Mad Hatter's Box' in *Hot Press*, 5 August 1983.

4.   *British Rock Guitar*: Guitar Player Books, 1977. (Note the book's title. This would not be the only time a writer designated Gallagher as British).

5.   *It Might Get Loud*, a documentary film on the electric guitar,

featuring White, Jimmy Page and The Edge, directed by Davis Guggenheim, Thomas Tull Productions 2009.

6. Oliver, Paul, *The Story of the Blues* (Penguin, 1969).

7. Harper, Wald, *Escaping the Delta: Robert Johnson and the Invention of the Blues* Elijah (Collins, 2004). With regard to this aspect of blues, Big Bill Broonzy, whom Gallagher greatly admired, wrote a song called 'Just a Dream': 'Dreamed I was in the White House / Sitting in the President's chair / I dreamed he's shaking my hand / And he said, "Bill, I'm glad you're here."'

8. Vintageguitar.com, retrieved April 2016.

9. The Mississippi Sheiks played fiddles and banjos as well as guitars. They entertained across the southern United States in the 1930s, playing country blues and popular songs of the day.

10. *International Musician and Recording World*, February 1992.

11. *Ibid.*, April 1975.

12. In an interview with Stefan Grossman in *Guitar Player* magazine, March 1978.

13. Spencer Leigh interview conducted in Liverpool in December 1987 and broadcast on BBC Radio Merseyside.

14. Scott, Mike, *Adventures of a Waterboy* (Lilliput Press, 2012).

15. Interview with Nick Robertshaw, *New Musical Express*, November 1994.

16. *Giles*, RTÉ Television, July 2017.

17. Michael Ross interview, *Sunday Times*, 17 May 1998.

18. Of all the names that Gallagher referenced as influences in his life, Buddy Holly (1936–1959) appears most frequently. According to Philip Norman, Holly, 'threw back the boundaries of rock 'n' roll, gave substance to its shivery shadow, transformed it from a chaotic cul-de-sac, to a highway of infinite possibilities and promise' – Norman, P., *Rave On: The Biography of Buddy Holly* (Simon and Schuster, 2014).

Chapter 3: Enter Fender Guitar No. 64351

1. Marr, J., *Set the Boy Free – The Autobiography* (Dey Street Books, 2016). Marr's father, coincidentally, was, like Gallagher's, an accordion player.

2. Coghe, Jean-Noël, *Rory Gallagher: A Biography* (Mercier Press, 2002).

3. Sheena Crowley, Michael's daughter, who took over the running of

the shop, recalled an aspect of her father's *modus operandi* with a story about one of the buskers, the Dunne brothers, saying to him: "'I really love this banjo in your shop but I can't afford it" and my father says "I'll give you the banjo if you come up to me everyday after you've done your busking and you give me a few bob and after a year you'll have it paid off.'" (*The Archive* 16).

4. This was the store where Jimi Hendrix made several purchases. It closed in 2009.

5. On Merchant's Quay, the builder, Owen O'Callaghan, developed a shopping centre in the 1980s. The building, housing Dunnes Stores, was controversial and remains a dubious architectural addition to the city.

6. *Guitar Player* interview with Gallagher in July 1991. Obrecht was editor of *Guitar Player* and is the author of several books on American blues musicians.

7. Tobin, Oliver, *A Star Was Born in My Brother's Band* (Choice Publishing, 2009).

8. Robertson, Robbie, *Testimony* (William Heinemann, 2016).

9. Springsteen, Bruce, *Born To Run* (Simon and Schuster, 2016).

10. Quoted in an article on the *Guitar World* website by Damien Fanelli, 12 August 2016.

11. *Guitarist*, February 1983.

12. Minhinnett, R. and Young, B., *The Story of the Fender Stratocaster: A Celebration of the World's Greatest Guitar* (Backbeat Books, 1995).

13. Interview by Eamonn Percival in *International Musician* April 1977. A high action is where the strings are set further from the keyboard; this is more challenging for the player, but allows more tonal possibilities, bending strings and greater use of sustain.

14. Interview by Henry Jackson, *Hot Licks*, March 1975.

15. *Ghost Blues*, documentary directed by Ian Thuillier, Strange Music, 2010.

16. *San Diego Union*, July 1976. Crowe is probably the most famous person to have interviewed Rory Gallagher, going on to great fame as a film actor and director.

17. Interviewed for the *Live at the Isle of Wight* DVD, released in 2015.

18. *Fender Signature Presents … The Edge*, 2016, YouTube.

19. Connaughton, Marcus, *Rory Gallagher – His Life and Times* (The Collins Press, 2012).

20. *Q* magazine, July 1990.

21. *Sounds*, 10 December 1988.

22. *Christian Science Monitor,* June 1991.

Chapter 4: A Showband Apprentice

1. *The Irish Press*, 29 December 1978, interview by John Spain.

2. *Sounds*, February 1973, interview by Jerry Gilbert.

3. Dean, Derek, *The Freshmen Unzipped* (Merlin Publishing, 2007).

4. In an interview in the documentary accompanying the *Taste Live at the Isle of Wight* DVD. Geldof made similar remarks in the *Ghost Blues* documentary in 2010.

5. *Rolling Stone,* interview with Mick Rock in 1972.

6. *Metronome*, presented by Ken Stewart, 15 September 1976.

7. *The Irish Times* 12 June 1999. Billy Brown had died on 6 June, aged 56.

8. Tobin, Oliver, *A Star Was Born in My Brother's Band* (Choice Publishing, 2009).

9. RTÉ Radio 2 (now 2fm), 28 March.

10. Bridie (Bridget) Gallagher (1924–2012), who, like Rory Gallagher, came from Donegal, was arguably Ireland's first international pop star. Her big hits – pre-rock 'n' roll – were sentimental ballads such as 'The Boys From the County Armagh' and 'A Mother's Love's a Blessing'. Livingstone, Jim, *Bridie Gallagher: The Girl from Donegal* (The Collins Press, 2015).

11. 'My Brother's Keeper', by Marc O'Sullivan, *Irish Examiner*, 4 June 2011.

12. *Hot Press* 18 March 1988 interview by Bill Graham.

13. Stephen Hunter in *The Archive*, the journal of the UCC Cork Folklore Project. This initiative, by University College Cork, began in 1996 and collects and publishes oral history.

14. Pat Nolan, a member of the band, told Stephen Hunter of the Cork Folklore Project in 1997 that Gallagher was with them for a couple of weeks, Nolan joining as Rory left.

15. Seán Dunphy (1937–2011) was the most famous of the band's lead singers. The Hoedowners had a number one in the Irish charts in 1969 with, 'The Lonely Woods of Upton', a sentimental account of a disastrous ambush during the Irish War of Independence.

16. Oliver Barry is a Cork impresario and businessman, who brought Michael Jackson to play in Pairc Uí Chaoimh in Cork in July 1988.

17. Larry Mullen of U2 recalled a similar experience when he was briefly

a member of the famous Dublin brass ensemble, The Artane Boys Band. He was asked to cut his hair. 'Reluctantly, I cut a few inches off. They told me to cut more. That was it. I left and never went back.' (*U2 By U2*, Harper Collins, 2006).

18. Despite their close association, Tom O'Driscoll has never spoken publicly or contributed to publications regarding Rory Gallagher's career.

19. Interview with Niall Stokes, *Sunday Independent*, 18 January 1976.

20. Dónal Gallagher said in *The Rory Gallagher Story* on BBC Radio 2 in April 2005 that his brother did not want the definite article used, that it should be just 'Impact'.

21. In an interesting sequel suggesting how much music radio had changed, in one of the early years of the Ballyshannon Rory Gallagher Festival, when RTÉ 2fm was visiting the town, there was a reluctance to actually play Gallagher songs, in the belief that they did not suit the station's sound.

22. *Evening Echo*, 27 April 2005, article by Don O'Mahony.

23. An Irish slang expression meaning 'awful'.

24. *Cork Evening Echo*, 27 April 2005, article by Don O'Mahony.

25. RTÉ 2fm, 28 March.

26. A revamped Fontana went in a new direction in 1967, styling themselves as The Freedom Fighters, making an album called *Irish Rebel Songs*. Among the places they played was the Kennedy family home in Hyannis Port, Massachusetts.

Chapter 5: Next Move: Taste

1. *Sounds*, December 1988.

2. Muise, Dan, *Gallagher, Marriott, Derringer and Trower, Their Lives and Music* (Hal Leonard, 2002).

3. In 1968, they had a number one hit with 'Little Arrows'. For many years a roadside sign, in Glanmire, to the north of the city, said: 'Welcome to Cork, Home of the Dixies.'

4. The Sanquests are a distinguished artistic family in Cork, and the only family bearing the surname in Ireland. Their father, Frank (1912–2007), was a famous painter, and all five children followed him in cultural pursuits in the city.

5. Don O'Mahony article, *Cork Evening Echo*, 27 April 2005.

6. The word 'Town' in the title was actually a misprint on the label; the correct title was 'Born on the Wrong Side of Time'.

7.   Interview with Bill Holdship in the July 1984 issue of *Creem*.

8.   'Timeless', Trevor Hodgett, *R2 Rock 'n' Reel*, July/August, 2015. McCoy similarly described the event for Gerry McAvoy's book: Rory, Norman and Eric appeared at his door, after a taxi journey across the country, asking, '"Is it all right if we stay?" How the hell he found me I don't know because I live on a council estate in West Belfast and the taxi came from Cork.'

9.   Members of The Group and another band, Heart and Soul, later formed Chips, with Linda Martin and Anne Ferguson on vocals. Martin later in her career sang the winning song for Ireland at the 1992 Eurovision Song Contest in Malmo, Sweden.

10.   Morrison, Bill, *Big Hand for the Band – Tales from Belfast's Rock 'n' Roll Years* (Motelands Publishing, 2015).

11.   *Ibid*.

12.   *International Musician and Recording World*, February 1982.

13.   Dawe, Gerald, *In Another World: Van Morrison & Belfast* (Irish Academic Press, 2017).

14.   He sang this line, for example, at Cork City Hall in December 1974 and at Rockpalast in Cologne in 1976.

15.   *ZigZag* magazine, December 1971.

16.   Several groups like the E-C-K-O-S, The Sound, The Montelles and the Outer Limits played the venue during Taste's absence, indicating a healthy beat scene in the city.

17.   Bert Jansch, and later Simon and Garfunkel, achieved fame with this instrumental, written by Davy Graham and recorded by him in 1962. It was also known by the spelling, 'Anji'.

18.   TV interview in Houston, Texas, in May 1985.

19.   Harper, Colin, *Seaside Rock* (North Down Heritage Centre, 2003).

20.   February 1968, article by Michael Wolsey.

21.   Blair Whyte recalls that other band members that night were Keef Hartley on drums and Dick Heckstall-Smith on saxophones, both now deceased.

Chapter 6: From Belfast to the World: Taste Mark 2

1.   The band was known for a large part of their career both as Taste and The Taste. They were billed in London (in the Bluesville '68 Club) as late as December 1968 as The Taste.

2.   In the Chrysalis 'press kit' for *Against the Grain* in 1975, Gallagher was clear: 'I changed the line-up, bringing in Richard McCracken

and John Wilson, we did an audition and ended up with a recording contract with Polydor.'

3. McAvoy, Gerry (with Pete Chrisp), *Riding Shotgun – 35 Years on the Road with Rory Gallagher and Nine Below Zero* (SPG Triumph, 2005). McAvoy's book, though an account of his own career, was the first chronicle of Gallagher's life. The *Cork Examiner* reviewer Ian Duffin-White concluded about Gallagher: '*Riding Shotgun* presents a picture of a man who was charming, polite, painfully shy, obsessed with music, passionate about the Blues, driven, often distant, probably lonely, careful with money, and definitely a control freak.'

4. John Spain interview, *The Irish Press*, 29 December 1978.

5. Gallagher confirmed this to Vivian Campbell in an interview in 1991.

6. August 2015.

7. This song had been released on the Major Minor label during the Taste Mark 1 period, erroneously titled, 'Born on the Wrong Side of Town'.

8. Interview by Marc O'Sullivan in *The Examiner*, 4 June 2011.

9. *Blueprint* magazine, August 1995.

10. From the unedited interview by Daniel Gallagher for *What's Going On – Taste Live At The Isle of Wight*, 2015.

11. *Rolling Stone*, 10 May 1970.

12. *Ibid.* Dónal Gallagher recalled for Dan Muise that Rory was flattered by Bang's comments about his sax playing.

13. *Creem*, July 1984.

14. Rush, Stephen, *Free Jazz, Harmolodics and Ornette Coleman* (Routledge, 2016).

15. Interview by Uli Twelker *Good Times* No. 5 March 1992.

16. *Record Collector*, June 1995.

17. *The Rory Gallagher Story*, BBC Radio 2, April 2005.

18. Harper, C. & T. Hodgett, *Irish Folk, Trad and Blues: A Secret History* (Collins Press, 2004).

19. *Rock 'n' Reel*, issue 9 March/April 2009.

20. *Hit Parader*, March 1970.

21. 'King of the Blooze', by Stephen Roche, *Seconds* magazine, issue no.15 in 1991.

22. Interviewed for The Cork Folklore Project's *The Archive*. He remembers Gallagher performing the Jeff Beck hits 'Hi Ho Silver Lining and 'Tallyman', and the Rolling Stones' 'Lady Jane'.

23. Roy Hollingworth, *Melody Maker* 17 October 1970.

24. *Oor* magazine, October 1977 translated for roryon.com by Iris Rasenberg. [*Oor* is the Dutch word for ear]

25. Article by Donal Corvin.

26. The 11–18 December edition, the letter was from Arva, County Cavan.

27. Q Magazine, number 46, interview by David Sinclair, July 1990.

28. From, *What's going On – Taste Live at the Isle of Wight*, Eagle Vision 2015.

29. In his book, *Hooleygan – Music, Mayhem, Good Vibrations*, with Richard Sullivan (Blackstaff Press, 2010) Terri Hooley, the famous Belfast DJ and founder of the Good Vibrations record label, has a particular memory of Eddie Kennedy. Hooley was an anti-Vietnam War activist in 1967 and Kennedy, he says, had him barred from his DJ gig in the Maritime because of his political activities. Kennedy and he happened to be next-door neighbours in east Belfast: 'From that point on, we used to glare at each other over the garden fence!'

30. 'Tangled up in Blues', interview by Liam Fay, *Hot Press* 12 July 1992.

31. Uli Twelker interview, *Good Times*, December 1992.

Chapter 7: It's the Rory Gallagher Band

1. Interview with Mick Rock in *Rolling Stone*, May 1972.

2. Interview by Swedish journalist Mats Karlsson at Clancy's Pub, Cork, in September 1995.

3. Interview conducted by the author at the Rory Gallagher International Tribute Festival.

4. Sleeve notes for the rereleased CD in 2012.

5. *Zig Zag* magazine, issue 24, 1971.

6. *Ibid.*

7. *Hot Press*, June 1995.

8. Alan Di Pern, writing in the December 2009 issue.

9. For the English TV presenter Andy Kershaw, the Fuller song has a particular resonance; when, as a student, he heard Gallagher's version, he got curious about the blues. His journey began in his local record shop. He could not have foreseen, he says, that in his later career he would be in North Carolina interviewing Fuller's elderly widow.

10. As evidence of the song's resonance, it was included in *On the Banks: Cork City in Poems and Songs*, edited by Alannah Hopkin (The Collins Press, 2016).

11. John Hamblett in February 1977.
12. *Trans-Oceanic Trouser Press (TOTP)*, April/May 1976.
13. Dylan, Bob, *Chronicles* (Simon & Schuster, 2004).
14. *New Musical Express* November, article by Brian Harrigan.
15. Howard Fielding in *Sounds*, December 1972.
16. Fame said on *The Rory Gallagher Story*, BBC Radio 2 in 2005, that his overall impression of Gallagher was, 'when he played hard it could be spine tingling. But he could be very sensitive as well.'
17. Liam Fay, 'Tangled Up in Blues', *Hot Press*, 12 July 1992.
18. *Ibid.*
19. RTÉ 2fm 1984.
20. This song is unique in being the only Gallagher recording with someone else playing guitar. Lou Martin, playing rhythm, had the honour.
21. Gallagher, Rory & Lizabeth Kramer (illustrator), *The Legend of the Seventh Son* (CreateSpace Independent Publishing Platform, 2015). Dónal Gallagher's sleeve notes say the song was partly inspired by the fact that blues music is rich with lyrics concerning supernatural powers.
22. Tom DuPree, writing in *Rolling Stone*, August 1973.
23. 'Soft Spoken Guitar Warrior from County Cork' by Tom Dupree, *Zoo World*, December 1973.
24. Prendergast, Mark J., *The Isle of Noises* (O'Brien Press 1987 and St Martin's Press 1990). The megastar Ed Sheeran gave a great endorsement for 'A Million Miles Away' in *Rolling Stone* of 8 May 2015, naming it as one of nine songs that had a profound impact on him and the first song he learned on guitar.

Chapter 8: The Therapy of Touring

1. Interview with Harry Doherty, *Melody Maker*, November 1975.
2. Shadowplays.com.
3. *New Musical Express*, 8 January 1974.
4. *New Musical Express*, 27 May 1974.
5. 'Guitarist Gracious Despite His Upsets' *Roanake Times*, 12 November 1976.
6. Harry Doherty reporting in California, November 1975.
7. Wall, Eamonn, *The Crosses* (Salmon Publishing, 2000).
8. *Sounds*, 13 May 1972, in an interview with Jerry Gilbert.
9. 19 June 1971.

10. *The Times*, 22 March 1973.

11. *The Irish Press*, 29 December 1978.

12. Interview on the website, AXS.com. In his book *Blues Odyssey* (Dorling Kindersley, 2001), Wyman says Gallagher was a 'brilliant guitarist' who 'never deserted the Blues', and states that he merely 'jammed with the band for a couple of nights in January 1975'.

13. *Ghost Blues – the Story of Rory Gallagher*, directed by Ian Thuillier, Strange Music, 2010.

14. Kirwan, Larry, *A History of Irish Music* (Black Forty-Seven, Inc., 2015). Kirwan was a member of the New York based Celtic-punk band, Black 47.

15. *Record Review*, April 1980, interview by David M. Gotz.

16. *The Sunday Times*, 30 September 2012.

17. Kirwan, *op. cit.*

18. Recounted for Dino McGartland in *Stagestruck* in 2001.

19. *The Rory Gallagher Story*, BBC Radio 2. Ó hÉanaí was, coincidentally, the source of The Dubliners 1967 hit 'Seven Drunken Nights'.

20. The *Radharc* team made the programme. 'Radharc' means 'view' in Irish. It was a pioneering documentary unit set up by the Catholic Church, though independent editorially.

21. Roy Hollingworth (1949–2002), 'MM Man Reports From Rock-Starved Belfast'. Hollingworth's *Telegraph* obituary said: 'Like many writers of that era, he saw his task as one of spreading enthusiasm for music that caught his imagination, and did it with flair.'

22. Eric Bell recalls that the shop was the place to hang out in Belfast. He was there one day in 1966 with friends when Van Morrison approached him and asked him to come to his parents' home in Hyndford Street later that day, and to bring his guitar. His friends couldn't believe it. "Fuck, that's *Van Morrison!*" one said.

23. Interview broadcast on YLE (Finland's national public broadcaster).

24. *London-Irish News*, December 1990, article by Kenneth Kelleher.

25. *Creem*, July 1984, interview by Bill Holdship.

Chapter 9: A Gentle Gaffer

1. Quoted in a BBC obituary, December 2016. He was referring to ageing rockers like Status Quo and the Rolling Stones who, despite 'aches and pains', do not want to stop touring.

2. Springsteen, B. *Born To Run* (Simon & Schuster, 2016).

3. Interview by Neil Jeffries, August 1983 issue of *Kerrang* magazine.

4. From the full interview by Shiv Cariappa, edited for an article in *Christian Science Monitor* in 2003. Some years later it was given by Cariappa to the roryon.com website.

5. *Guitar for the Practicing Musician*, August 1991.

6. Ibbenburen, Germany, radio interview on 18 August 1984, retrieved from YouTube.

7. Jim Washburn, in the *LA Times* 7 March 1991.

8. Interviewed by the author at Ballyshannon Gallagher Tribute Festival in June 2015.

9. Interview with J.P. Sabour and X. Bonnet, *Guitar World*, February 1993.

10. *Guitar for the Practicing Musician*, August 1991.

11. *Starlight* magazine, June 1978. The interviewer, 'Famous Shamus' was Shay Healy, a songwriter and performer himself, probably best known for writing Ireland's 1980 Eurovision Song Contest winner, 'What's Another Year'. Gallagher told David Fricke in *Circus* magazine in 1979: 'a lot of producers don't understand the blues thing. You say you want to try a Slim Harpo sound and they say, "Who's he?" Then you have to explain it to them. You're teaching them.'

12. Radio Hengelo, Netherlands, 11 January 1995.

13. Interview published in *Stagestruck*, issue No. 5, 1998.

Chapter 10: The Chrysalis Years

1. *Metal Hammer* magazine, July 1987.

2. March 1976 issue.

3. *Circus*, March 1976.

4. *15 January 1976*. Joe Cocker had a habit of twitching his hands by his side as he sang.

5. Mazer told *Shadowplays* in 2011: 'They sent me the tapes and I did a new mix. I was not impressed with that album. I mixed it as an American rock album. Rory did not like that either. Somebody else mixed it in London.' This was Chris Kemsey, who had worked with the Rolling Stones.

6. *Metronome*, a radio programme presented by Ken Stewart, 15 September 1976.

7. *Ibid.*

8. Crowley, Roz, *Macroom Mountain Dew – Memories of Ireland's First Rock Festival* (Onstream, 2016).

9. Larry Lyons, who wrote for the *Cork Examiner* in the 1970s.

10. Interview at Ballyshannon June 2016.

11. *Wheels Within His Master's Wheels: An Interview with Elliot Mazer*, by 'Milo' in *Shadowplays.com*, 2011. A significant detail of the abandoned recordings, the original running order, was also different on the 2011 release, and chosen by Daniel Gallagher, Rory's nephew.

12. *Ghost Blues*, the documentary directed by Ian Thuilier (Strange Music, 2010).

13. The great Belgian-born guitarist (1910–1953) lost the use of two of his left-hand fingers in a fire in 1928.

14. RTÉ 2fm, *The Rock Show*, 2 April 1980.

15. *Ibid.*

16. Simon & Schuster, 2003.

17. *Beat Instrumental*, March 1979. (*Beat Instrumental* was a monthly magazine that ceased publication in 1980).

18. *New Musical Express*, 6 October 1979, reviewing a gig at The Venue.

19. Robert Haagsma, *Aardschok* magazine, July 2000. Haagsma formed the view that Dónal 'has mixed feelings about these [late 1970s] records'.

20. Interview by Mark Stevens in December 1978, published in *Triad* magazine, February 1979.

Chapter 11: The 1980s: Uncertainty and Resurgence

1. *Seconds* magazine, 1991.

2. *New Musical Express*, review in October 1979 by Pete Archer.

3. AllMusic.com. Hal Horowitz was reviewing the reissued CD in 2012.

4. *Christian Science Monitor*, June 1991.

5. *All About Jazz*, August 2012.

6. *Creem*, July 1984.

7. O'Neill, another Belfast native in Gallagher's band, recalled for Shiv Cariappa how he first got interested in drums: 'I used to watch marching bands … and Scottish bagpipe bands, and I found the drums exciting in that situation, and it really drew me to them.'

8. Springsteen, *op. cit.*

9. Cline, Sally, *Dashiell Hammett: Man of Mystery* (Arcade Publishing, 2014).

10. *The Sunday Times*, interview by Michael Ross 17 May 1998.

11. Dylan, *op. cit.*

12. Kershaw, Andy, *No Off Switch: An Autobiography* (Serpent's Tail, 2011).

13. An interview with Colm McGinty in the *Evening Herald* 31 July.

14. *Sounds*, December 1988.

15. Hal Horowitz in *AllMusic*.

16. 'Mad Hatter's Box' in *Hot Press*, 5 August 1983.

17. *The Late Late Show* on RTÉ, 12 December 1988.

18. Springsteen, *op. cit.*

19. McAvoy, *op. cit.*

20. *R2/Rock 'n' Reel* from July/August 2015.

21. It was the inaugural gig of this long-running TV event organised by the German network, WDR. Gallagher, Little Feat and Roger McGuinn's Thunderbirds played at the Grugahalle in Essen.

22. From a thread on The Loop (roryon.com) in 2004 begun by Dino McGartland.

23. Prasad, Anil, *Music Without Borders* (published on the web, January 1991).

24. *Jas Obrect Music Archive*, 1991.

25. *Evening Herald*, 18 February1987.

26. Beki Brindle was living in Ireland at the time. She later found some fame in her native United States as a blues guitarist.

27. 18 March 1988.

28. Paul Simon refers to Chenier on his *Graceland* album as 'King of the Bayou'.

29. 2 May 1990. The reviewer, Carol Clerk, concluded: 'Perhaps the most important achievement of *Fresh Evidence* is in re-establishing Rory as something more than an electric guitar virtuoso. Here is the proof that the man is a master, someone with a supreme feel for the instrument and the song, whatever its mood.'

30. Q magazine, July 1990.

31. *Ibid.*

32. Gallagher made the same point about Van Morrison in his last radio interview, in January 1995 in the Netherlands, wishing his friend would record 'an R&B album'.

33. Gallagher rarely referred to Clapton, suggesting an undeclared rivalry on his part. Clapton's 2007 autobiography, however, makes no references to either Gallagher or Taste.

Chapter 12: The Other Rory Gallagher

1. Joe Jackson interview, *The Irish Times*, 14 August 1992.

2. Mark Stevens in the LA-based magazine, *Triad*.

3.   17 May 1998, with additional reporting by Mick Heaney.

4.   30 September 2012, interview by Garth Cartwright.

5.   *U2 By U2*.

6.   An outtake from the *Against the Grain* sessions is an instrumental titled, 'Cluny Blues'.

7.   Muise's book, *Gallagher, Marriott, Derringer and Trower* does not give the source of this and other quotes from Gallagher himself. They appear to come from interviews Rudi Gerlach did with him (Rory addresses 'Rudi' in several places), which Gerlach then gave to Dan Muise.

8.   *Trans-Oceanic Trouser Press*, April/May 1976.

9.   *New Music Express*, 3 January 1976. Pete Erskine interview.

10. A television programme based on Gallagher's Savoy in Limerick gig that year.

11. Interview with Michael Galvin in *Deuce Quarterly*, February 1989.

12. *The Sunday Tribune*, 16 August 1992.

13. *The Rock Show*, RTÉ 2fm, 16 February.

14. Geiringer, Karl, *Brahms, His Life and Work* (Da Capo (3rd ed.), 1981).

15. Keith Altham, *NME*, 13 October 1973.

16. *The Big Questions*, BBC TV, 25 January 2009. McKenna, introduced as someone with experience of the rock 'n' roll lifestyle and working with stars who died young, had been asked why people are more interested in Keith Richards than Cliff Richard.

17. Interview conducted for the release of *Wheels Within Wheels* in 2003 and published on roryon.com.

Chapter 13: 'This Shadow Play ...'

1.   The sleeve notes for the reissue of *Top Priority* in 2012.

2.   Interview with Spenser Leigh at a soundcheck in Liverpool on 9 October 1987, BBC Radio Mersyside.

3.   Shiv Cariappa *The Christian Science Monitor*. After Philby's death in 1988, his wife, Rufina Pukhova, revealed her husband's alcohol and depression problems, at least partly due to his disillusion with Soviet Communism.

4.   *The Fuze*, online rock journal, 2003.

5.   Quoted in Chris Welch's obituary of Gallagher in The *Independent* 15 June 1995.

6.   *Beat Instrumental*, March 1979.

7.   January 2000.

8.   De Paor also recalls that Gallagher told him he would have liked to do some of the interview in Irish, knowing Louis's background and that he used Irish in his broadcasts, but apologised, saying he would have needed some notice to prepare himself.

9.   December 2015, during the launch in Dublin of *The Isle of Wight* DVD.

10. *Rock* magazine, June 1977.

11. In an interview for *The Sunday Times*, 4 March 2018, Annie Lennox of Eurythmics spoke about songwriting and sadness and suggested she would not write songs again. When her muse left, so did sadness, she explained. 'I don't know that I had to be unhappy to write, but I often was unhappy and the feelings were predominantly painful, sad and melancholic.' She added, 'There is beauty in that, without question.'

12. According to Dónal Gallagher's 2012 sleeve notes, '[Rory's] sadness is shown in this soulful blues ballad.'

13. Interview in March 2003 and published on roryon.com.

14. *Hot Press* (Volume 12, Issue 4), 18 March 1988.

15. Wesley Callihan's lecture, to students at the New Saint Andrew's College in Moscow, Idaho, in 2013, was titled: 'The Connections Between the Pinkerton Detective Agency, the Silver Valley of North Idaho, Dashiell Hammett (Author of *The Maltese Falcon* and the *Thin Man* Detective Novels), Clint Eastwood's Spaghetti Westerns, and Rock Guitarist Rory Gallagher.'

16. *Hot Press*, 29 December 1988, interview with Ronan O'Reilly.

17. Wilson, Andrew, *Beautiful Shadow: A Life of Patricia Highsmith* (Bloomsbury, 2010).

18. *Hot Press*, 18 March 1988.

19. *Dashiell Hammett: Man of Mystery*, Arcade Publishing 2014.

20. Liam Fay, *Hot Press*, 12 July 1992. Recalling the interview in 1995, Fay described Rory as 'a superb anecdotist, with a great eye for telling detail and a bone-dry wit'.

21. Trevor Hodgett, *R2 Rock 'n' Reel*, July/August 2015.

22. Pat Stack in *Socialist Review*, Issue 188, July/August 1995.

23. 'Music Without Borders' (self-published on the web).

24. Marcus Connaughton recalls Gallagher telling him in 1992 that one reason he liked to come home was to 'sharpen up' his Cork accent.

25. *Guitar*, April 1992.

Chapter 14: The Rory Gallagher Legacy

1. *Sunday Press*, 2 February 1988, interview with Molly McAnally Burke. The comment has an echo in classical music: Robert Schumann once described Chopin's music as 'cannons hidden among flowers'.

2. An interview with Chris Heim in the *Chicago Tribune* in 1991.

3. *International Musician and Recording World*, February 1982.

4. Eddie 'Son' House (1902–1988) is regarded as a significant influence on Robert Johnson (1911–1938).

5. From an interview with Jas Obrecht, *Guitar Player*, June 1991.

6. *Guitar Player*, March 1978.

7. 'Rory Gallagher – Outside the Establishment', by Anil Prasad, 1991, from *Music Without Borders*, on the website innerviews.org.

8. *Guitar Player* March 1978. He also took issue with Paul Oliver's compilation, *The Story of the Blues* for not including Muddy Waters.

9. Sleeve notes from the remastered CD in 2012.

10. *The Irish Times*, interview by Joe Jackson, 14 August 1992.

11. *Ibid.*

12. Interview for WDR (German TV), Cologne, 10 June 1976 (available on YouTube).

13. Talking to Dave Fanning, on RTÉ 2fm, 16 February 1988.

14. *Hot Press*, 18 March 1988.

15. Bloomfield (1943–1981). In his introduction to his biography *Mike Bloomfield: The Rise and Fall of an American Guitar Hero* (Chicago Review Press, 2016), Ed Ward says: 'Before Bloomfield, there was no glory in being a guitarist; after he appeared, mastering electric lead guitar became the test of manhood.'

16. *Guitar Player*, June 1991.

17. 'Won't See His Like Again', Stephen Hunter, *The Archive*, January 2000.

18. July 1974 issue.

19. *Guitar Player* June 1991.

20. Vintageguitar.com

21. Interview by John Dalton, *Guitar* magazine September 1978.

22. Reviewing the reissue of *Live in Cork*, *All About Jazz*, August 2012.

23. *What's Going On – Taste Live at the Isle of Wight*, Eagle Vision, 2015.

24. Bob Geldof chose to relate the two musicians this way in 2015: 'Hendrix was the great innovator. He did field hollers for the space age. But Rory absolutely injected some Irish thing into it.'

25. Gallagher told Pat Egan in *New Spotlight* in October 1970 that Taste was in Stockholm when they heard the news of Hendrix's death on 18 September and were shocked. 'He was not my own personal favourite as a guitarist, but I had great respect for him.'

26. *Ghost Blues*, directed by Ian Thuilier, Strange Music, 2010. Dónal Gallagher made a similar reference in an interview in *Guitar World* in 2009: 'For him, music was like a vocation in the priesthood.'

27. *The Fuze* (online magazine), 2003.

28. *Evening Echo*, 13 June 2000. Interview by Mark McClelland.

29. Interview with Bert van de Kamp in the Dutch music paper *Oor*, March 1976.

30. *Cork Evening Echo*, 13 June 2000.

31. 'Against the Grain' by Alan Di Pern, *Guitar World*, December 2009.

32. *It Might Get Loud*, 2009.

33. Interview by Gavin Martin in Classic Rock's *The Blues Magazine*, November 2012.

34. From *Cowboy Song*, Graeme Thompson's biography of Phil Lynott, published by Constable in 2016.

35. From the unedited interview by Daniel Gallagher for *What's Going On – Taste Live At The Isle of Wight*, 2015.

36. De Paor, Louis, *Corcach agus Dánta Eile*, Coiscéim, 1999. The Cork singer and songwriter, John Spillane later put the poem's words to music in 'A Song for Rory Gallagher'.

37. Tom Harrison in *Beetle* magazine, October 1974.

38. *Evening Herald* 30 December 1983.

39. *Sounds*, 14 December 1974, interviewed by Mike Flood Page.

Chapter 15: Eternity Beckons

1. From a tribute included in the leaflet for Gallagher's memorial Mass, 18 November 1995, at Brompton Oratory, London.

2. Michael Ross in *The Sunday Times* in 17 May 1998.

3. *The Sunday Tribune*, 16 August 1992.

4. *Mojo*, October 1998.

5. *The Sunday Times*, 17 May 1998.

6. *Seconds*, Issue 15.

7. Recalled in *The Irish Times*, 17 June 1995.

8. 'Black Cat Blues', *The Irish Times*, 14 August 1992. At the masterclass Rory gave in the Guinness Hop Store on Sunday that weekend, the actual anniversary of Presley's death, he performed Elvis's 'Baby I Don't Care'.

9. Interview with Shiv Cariappa at the time of the release of *Wheels Within Wheels*, 2003, published on roryon.com.

10. *Evening Echo*, 27 April 2005.

11. *Guitar World*. From an article that originally appeared in French, written by J.P. Sabour and X. Bonnet and translated by Len Trimmer for roryon.com.

12. *Irish News*, 13 June 1998, article by Tony Bailie.

13. Published in the Dutch daily *Da Telegraaf*, 7 January 1995.

14. Gallagher's last recording was also that month, on a track for a friend, Eamonn McCormack, called 'Falsely Accused', released in 2007.

15. *The Independent* on 15 June 1995. 'Gallagher offered a passionate dedication in his playing, born of a desire to give audiences maximum music and minimum fuss.'

16. 'In Memory of Rory Gallagher 1948–1995'.

17. Father Michael Sheehan from Waterford wrote the words as a poem in 1916. Seán Ó Riada set them to music as the offertory hymn in his setting of the Mass, 'Ceól an Aifrinn', in 1968.

Coda

1. Spillane, John. *Will We Be Brilliant or What?* (2016, The Collins Press). The other people were Patrick Galvin, Frank O'Connor, Seán Ó Faoláin and Seán Ó Riada.

INDEX